SAP BusinessObjects Dashboards 4.0 Cookbook

Over 90 simple and incredibly effective recipes for transforming your business data into exciting dashboards with SAP BusinessObjects Dashboards 4.0 Xcelsius

Xavier Hacking

David Lai

BIRMINGHAM - MUMBAI

SAP BusinessObjects Dashboards 4.0 Cookbook

First published: May 2011

Production Reference: 1180511

Published by Packt Publishing Ltd.
32 Lincoln Road
Olton
Birmingham, B27 6PA, UK.

ISBN 978-1-849681-78-0

www.packtpub.com

Cover Image by David Guettirrez (bilbaorocker@yahoo.co.uk)

Credits

Authors

Xavier Hacking

David Lai

Reviewers

Charles Davies

Joshua Fletcher

Nargisse Skalante

Acquisition Editor

Stephanie Moss

Development Editor

Kartikey Pandey

Technical Editor

Pooja Pande Malik

Project Coordinator

Leena Purkait

Proofreader

Aaron Nash

Indexer

Rekha Nair

Production Coordinator

Shantanu Zagade

Cover Work

Shantanu Zagade

Foreword

The original (and key) innovation of Dashboard Design was to bring together the flexibility, power and ubiquity of Excel with the visualization of Flash. This meant that a whole new group of people (basically anyone who understood Excel formulas) could produce sophisticated Flash animations. Over the years, this has led to an incredible array of Dashboard Design models being produced, many of which, I suspect, go well beyond what the creators of Dashboard Design intended (or even dreamed of). Indeed there is one model (you can find it at `http://www.antivia.com/confoundingmodel/`) which has been doing the rounds for a number of years that, so rumor has it, left even the original Dashboard Design development team scratching their heads as to how it was constructed.

As with any tool that has the flexibility and power to be stretched in this way, it is hard for the core product documentation to comprehensively cover everything users need to know to be successful, and it is books such as this one that fill the gap and allow knowledge that has been distilled through the hands of many individuals to be passed on to the community in general.

I am a particular fan of the recipe format; it allows you to dip in and out of the material for learning in short bursts and also allows you to quickly and easily answer specific questions. In addition, the overall structure provides a smooth flow through all the areas of the product providing a comprehensive review of its capabilities.

In this book, Xavier and David have found something for everyone. For those who are just starting out with Dashboard Design, there are recipes that give advice and guidance to help you start on a solid foundation. For those who are more experienced with Dashboard Design, there are advanced recipes covering inter-dashboard communication and connectivity to external systems. For everyone, there will be something in these pages which is new and will help you take your Dashboard Design knowledge to the next level.

My favorite recipes are in the third-party chapter, not just because I work for one of the vendors featured, but because they advertise the possibilities opened up by the Dashboard Design SDK. Although the initial innovation of Dashboard Design was bringing together the Excel and Flash visualizations, the introduction of the SDK paved the way for a second wave of innovations from third parties, which further widened the bounds of what was possible with this amazing product.

Whatever plans you have for Dashboard Design, I wish you luck; keep pushing the boundaries and share your experiences with the rest of us in the community.

Donald MacCormick
April, 2011
Chief Product and Marketing Officer

Antivia
Web: www.antivia.com
Twitter: @antivia
London.

About the Authors

Xavier Hacking is a SAP BI consultant from Eindhoven, The Netherlands. He has a Masters' degree in Industrial Engineering and Management Science from the Eindhoven University of Technology. He has worked with a range of products from the SAP Business Intelligence portfolio, including SAP BW and SAP Crystal Dashboard Design (Xcelsius). His goal is to deliver business intelligence solutions that enable people to do their work in a better and more productive way.

In 2009, he started his blog HackingSAP.com (http://www.hackingsap.com/), which covers news, tips, guides, and other resources on SAP Crystal Dashboard Design and other SAP and non-SAP Business Intelligence tools. You can also follow Xavier on Twitter (http://www.twitter.com/xjhacking).

Acknowledgement

Firstly, I want to thank the people of the Dashboard Design community on Twitter, SDN, the LinkedIn groups, and the blogs for the interesting discussions on creating dashboards with Dashboard Design and sharing their views and knowledge. I love to see this community growing every day and I encourage everybody who works with Dashboard Design to join us.

Next, I want to thank co-author David Lai for the fine teamwork during this project and the nice discussions we had on the contents of the book.

A big thanks goes out to the entire PacktPub team that supported and guided us through the writing process.

Finally, I'd like to acknowledge Norbert Maijoor for inspiring me to start writing/blogging on business intelligence.

David Lai is an SAP BusinessObjects consultant and specializes in data visualization and data warehousing. He graduated with a degree in Computer Engineering from the University of Toronto. He has a passion for providing organizations with smart Business Intelligence solutions that encompass Best Practices and Techniques. In addition, he is an active contributor to the community by providing his knowledge in best practices and solutions.

He started David Lai's Business Intelligence blog (`http://www.davidlai101.com/blog`) in 2008 where he provides tips, tricks, and the best practices for Dashboard Design and BusinessObjects-related material. He is a Bronze level contributor on the SAP community network, has presented at SAP InsideTrack, and provides Business Objects training to students.

Aside from work, David enjoys physical activities such as weight training, basketball, volleyball, and skiing. He also has a strong passion for Latin dance.

David Lai is the owner of Xinfinity Solutions where he provides consulting services as an SAP Business Objects consultant. He has done work for a long list of satisfied clients in various industries.

Acknowledgement

Writing this book has been a long journey and would not have been possible without the guidance, inspiration, and mentorship provided by many others along the way. From here, I'd like to show appreciation to all those who have assisted me along the path.

First, of all I would like to thank the Dashboard Design developers for their efforts in bringing us new features and fixes with every new version of Dashboard Design.

I would like to thank everyone in the Dashboard Design community for their contributions in SDN, LinkedIn, and blogs. Without the community, we wouldn't have anywhere to look for help when coming across a problem. In addition, thoughts and ideas are taken into account by the development team to create a better product in the long run. A big thanks goes to Kalyan Verma for giving me the opportunity to contribute on his blog http://myxcelsius.com and really getting me kick started with community participation (Excellent Job on getting myxcelsius.com to where it is today!). Another big thanks to Mico Yuk of Everything Xcelsius for her past advice and really getting the community involved with Xcelsius.

I'd like to thank Xavier Hacking for co-authoring the book. Without Xavier's teamwork, knowledge, and expertise, this book would not have been a success. I would also like to commend his great work on his blog @ http://www.hackingsap.com.

A big thanks to the Packt Publishing team (Stephanie Moss, Leena Purkait, Reshma Sundaresan) for providing all the necessary guidance in our writing process. Without the Packt Publishing team, this book would not have been possible.

Finally, I'd like to acknowledge Ryan Goodman for inspiring me to participate in blogging and assisting the community on Business Intelligence best practices and solutions.

About the Reviewers

Charles Davies started his career in accountancy gaining qualifications as a Chartered Management Accountant, but always sat between the Accountancy and IT departments when building systems and reports.

From programming old SuperCalc spreadsheets for product costing purposes, to building statistical packages in MS Excel, to designing, building, and programming SAP Business Objects solutions to meet various reporting needs, Charles has always been challenging the reporting needs of businesses to ensure the reporting and dashboarding solutions meet those needs.

Charles has worked for large corporations in various industry sectors and is currently Director and Consultant of his own company Reportex Ltd., which provides SAP BusinessObjects and Dashboard Design solutions to clients in the United Kingdom and Europe.

Joshua Fletcher has worked with Business Intelligence applications for over 10 years, focusing primarily on the SAP BusinessObjects toolset. He started with Crystal Reports v8 at the beginning of his career, and is now fully certified in SAP BusinessObjects, as a Certified Professional in Enterprise XI 3.x, Data Integrator XI 3.x, Web Intelligence XI 3.x and Crystal Reports 2008, as well as working with the entire suite of SAP BusinessObjects, including many Xcelsius projects. He also has extensive experience in business analysis, dashboard design, data governance, business intelligence strategy and solution architecture, as well as a passion for data warehouse and ETL design and development. Joshua is currently employed as the SAP BusinessObjects Team Lead for CSG, a leading Australian SAP BusinessObjects Solutions Provider. When not working, he loves spending as much time as possible with his wife and son, keeping active at the gym, and playing squash.

Nargisse Skalante is a SAP BusinessObjects consultant in a multi-business group in Dubai, UAE. She combines a Masters' Degree in Information Technology and more than nine years of IT experience, including business intelligence. Throughout her career, Nargisse has had exposure to various business and functional domains namely finance, retail, and real estate. Nargisse has an extensive practice in producing innovative Xcelsius dashboards with WebIntelligence drill down reports. She also has a wide experience in integrating BusinessObjects with SAP.

www.PacktPub.com

Support files, eBooks, discount offers and more

You might want to visit www.PacktPub.com for support files and downloads related to your book.

Did you know that Packt offers eBook versions of every book published, with PDF and ePub files available? You can upgrade to the eBook version at www.PacktPub.com and, as a print book customer, you are entitled to a discount on the eBook copy. Get in touch with us at service@packtpub.com for more details.

At www.PacktPub.com, you can also read a collection of free technical articles, sign up for a range of free newsletters, and receive exclusive discounts and offers on Packt books and eBooks.

http://PacktLib.PacktPub.com

Do you need instant solutions to your IT questions? PacktLib is Packt's online digital book library. Here, you can access, read, and search across Packt's entire library of books.

Why subscribe?

- ▶ Fully searchable across every book published by Packt
- ▶ Copy and paste, print, and bookmark content
- ▶ On demand and accessible via web browser

Free access for Packt account holders

If you have an account with Packt at www.PacktPub.com, you can use this to access PacktLib today and view nine entirely free books. Simply use your login credentials for immediate access.

Instant updates on new Packt books

Get notified! Find out when new books are published by following @PacktEnterprise on Twitter, or the *Packt Enterprise* Facebook page.

Table of Contents

Preface

What is SAP Business Objects Dashboards (formerly Xcelsius)?

SAP BusinessObjects Dashboards (formerly Xcelsius) is a desktop dashboard and visualization solution that is a core part of SAP BusinessObjects BI 4.0. Once a user creates a dashboard model, it can be deployed in Flash format to Web portals, SAP environments, the SAP BusinessObjects BI platform, and desktop applications such as PowerPoint, Word, or PDF.

For Dashboard designers/developers, SAP BusinessObjects Dashboards allows for rapid development of data visualizations through a flexible and easy to use graphical user interface.

Using Xcelsius, we can accomplish the following:

- Create interactive dashboards that have a *wow* factor, unlike other dashboard tool competitors
- Connect dashboards to 12 different types of data connections
- Integration and interoperability with the existing SAP BusinessObjects BI Content
- We can embed our dashboards into a variety of different formats to allow for convenient sharing between users
- Ability to create custom add-on components using the Dashboard Design SDK

Xcelsius, in its original conception, was a way to build visualizations and dashboards using Excel data. Over the past several years, SAP Business Objects has enhanced Xcelsius into a full-featured enterprise ready dashboard solution that works with any data source. As SAP continued on its mission to make Xcelsius a dashboard product to serve all its customers (beyond being just a personal productivity tool), the name Xcelsius was no longer meaningful or relevant. The BI market and SAP customers were also demanding an enterprise dashboard solution for the types of projects they were using Xcelsius for; that is dashboards for thousands of users. By changing the name Xcelsius to SAP BusinessObjects Dashboards, SAP is showing its commitment to delivering a solution that serves the needs of all BI customers as well as aligning the name to the product's growing capabilities and roadmap.

The SAP BusinessObjects Dashboards portfolio consists of several different packages (see the edition comparison on next page). In this book we use Dashboard Design to refer to the tooling itself.

What this book covers

Chapter 1, Staying in Control: In this chapter, you will find best practices on using the SAP BusinessObjects Dashboards spreadsheet, the data model, and connections with the components on the canvas.

Chapter 2, Data Visualization: This chapter presents users with recipes on how to use different components such as charts, tables, and graphs to visualize data on the dashboard.

Chapter 3, From a Static to an Interactive Dashboard: This chapter shows users how to add interactivity to their dashboards by adding selectors, maps, buttons, drilldowns, and so on.

Chapter 4, Dynamic Visibility: This chapter shows users how to make components visible/ invisible and provides scenarios where dynamic visibility becomes useful.

Chapter 5, Using Alerts: This chapter contains examples of different ways of showing alerts on a dashboard.

Chapter 6, Advanced Components: This chapter provides recipes on SAP BusinessObjects Dashboards more advanced components.

Chapter 7, Dashboard Look and Feel: In this chapter, learn how to tweak the visuals and user experience of the dashboard by customizing the look of components.

Chapter 8, Dashboard Connectivity: This chapter talks about the various options to connect a dashboard to external data sources.

Chapter 9, Exporting and Publishing: This chapter contains recipes on how to export SAP BusinessObjects Dashboards into different environments.

Chapter 10, Top Third-Party Add-ons: This chapter contains a tutorial section on some of the most useful third-party add-ons for SAP BusinessObjects Dashboards.

Appendix A, Real World Dashboard Case Studies: This appendix demonstrates how to implement various techniques covered in the book by creating two applications-a calculator that displays monthly payments of mortgage and Sales Profit Dashboard that displays the sales or profit of each state on the map.

Appendix B, Additional Resources—Supported Excel Functions and System/Software Requirements: This appendix lists some helpful online resources for further reference and some useful Microsoft Excel functions supported by SAP BusinessObjects Dashboards.

What you need for this book

The following image provides a comparison of the different dashboard design packages offered by SAP. You will need to install one of the dashboard design packages in order to use this book.

Dashboard Design edition comparison   SAP

	SAP Crystal Presentation Design	SAP Crystal Dashboard Design Personal	SAP Crystal Dashboard Design Starter package		SAP BusinessObjects Dashboards
			SAP Crystal Dashboard Design Departmental	Dashboard Viewing option	
Basic data presentation components	☑	☑	☑		☑
Export to Adobe PDF and PPT	☑	☑	☑		☑
Dashboard creation components and export to Web and Adobe Flash, AIR		☑	☑		☑
Live, refreshable data connections – including SAP BusinessOne	0	2	Unlimited		Unlimited
Connectivity to Adobe LiveCycle Data Services			☑		☑
IBM WebSphere, MSFT SharePoint and Reporting Services integration			☑		☑
Crystal Reports Server connectivity and platform integration			☑		☑
Viewing rights for dashboards connected to live data sources		☑		☑	☑
Deploy dashboards to more than 100 named users					☑
Deploy SAP BusinessObjects Edge and SAP BusinessObjects BI Platform					☑
Access SAP ERP and SAP BW data					☑

Note: The majority of recipes from Chapters 1 to 8 can be accomplished with all of the dashboard design packages. Only for the recipes that require connecting to an SAP environment or using SAP related data sources in Chapters 9 and 10, do you need SAP BusinessObjects Dashboards.

Who this book is for

If you are a developer with a good command and knowledge of creating dashboards, but are not yet an advanced SAP BusinessObjects Dashboards user, then this is the perfect book for you. You should have a good working knowledge of Microsoft Excel, as well as knowledge of basic dashboard practices, though experience of SAP BusinessObjects Dashboards as a specific dashboard tool is not essential.

This book provides an interactive hands-on approach to SAP BusinessObjects Dashboards education by allowing you to work with components, learn best practices, and practice trouble shooting techniques.

Conventions

In this book, you will find a number of styles of text that distinguish between different kinds of information. Here are some examples of these styles, and an explanation of their meaning.

Code words in text are shown as follows: "You must be able to view hidden files and folders in the `C:\Documents and Settings\ your_user_id` folder."

A block of code is set as follows:

```
final String BO_CMS_NAME = ""server"";
final String BO_AUTH_TYPE = ""secEnterprise"";
```

New terms and **important words** are shown in bold. Words that you see on the screen, in menus or dialog boxes for example, appear in the text like this: "In the **Scale** section, select the **Auto** radio button."

 Warnings or important notes appear in a box like this.

 Tips and tricks appear like this.

Reader feedback

Feedback from our readers is always welcome. Let us know what you think about this book—what you liked or may have disliked. Reader feedback is important for us to develop titles that you really get the most out of.

To send us general feedback, simply send an e-mail to feedback@packtpub.com, and mention the book title via the subject of your message.

If there is a book that you need and would like to see us publish, please send us a note in the **SUGGEST A TITLE** form on www.packtpub.com or e-mail suggest@packtpub.com.

If there is a topic that you have expertise in and you are interested in either writing or contributing to a book, see our author guide on www.packtpub.com/authors.

Customer support

Now that you are the proud owner of a Packt book, we have a number of things to help you to get the most from your purchase.

Downloading the example files for this book

You can download the example files for all Packt books you have purchased from your account at http://www.PacktPub.com. If you purchased this book elsewhere, you can visit http://www.PacktPub.com/support and register to have the files e-mailed directly to you.

Downloading the color images of this book

We also provide you a PDF file that has color images of the screenshots used in this book. The color images will help you better understand the changes in the output. You can download this file from https: https://www. packtpub.com/sites/default/files/1780EN_images.pdf.

Errata

Although we have taken every care to ensure the accuracy of our content, mistakes do happen. If you find a mistake in one of our books—maybe a mistake in the text or the code—we would be grateful if you would report this to us. By doing so, you can save other readers from frustration and help us improve subsequent versions of this book. If you find any errata, please report them by visiting http://www.packtpub.com/support, selecting your book, clicking on the **errata submission form** link, and entering the details of your errata. Once your errata are verified, your submission will be accepted and the errata will be uploaded on our website, or added to any list of existing errata, under the Errata section of that title. Any existing errata can be viewed by selecting your title from http://www.packtpub.com/support.

Piracy

Piracy of copyright material on the Internet is an ongoing problem across all media. At Packt, we take the protection of our copyright and licenses very seriously. If you come across any illegal copies of our works, in any form, on the Internet, please provide us with the location address or website name immediately so that we can pursue a remedy.

Please contact us at copyright@packtpub.com with a link to the suspected pirated material.

We appreciate your help in protecting our authors, and our ability to bring you valuable content.

Questions

You can contact us at questions@packtpub.com if you are having a problem with any aspect of the book, and we will do our best to address it.

1
Staying in Control

In this chapter, we will cover:

- ► Making the spreadsheet more readable with colors
- ► Making the spreadsheet more readable with comments
- ► Making the spreadsheet more readable with borders
- ► Using Named Ranges
- ► Selecting all worksheet cells with one click
- ► Copying the format of one cell to another cell or range
- ► Debugging the spreadsheet
- ► Navigating between worksheets
- ► Grouping canvas components

Introduction

During the development of a typical **Dashboard Design** dashboard, the number of components on the canvas increases steadily and the exact type of used components may change over time. Also, several interactions between components are added and maybe one or more connections with external data sources are created. All those canvas components are bound to the Excel data model that has been defined in the spreadsheet area.

To prevent us from getting lost in an unmanageable chaos of components, interactions, bindings, and several different Excel functionalities, a structured approach should be followed right from the start of the dashboard development. Also, we should use the advantages Excel gives us to build an optimal data model that is easy to read and maintain.

Making the spreadsheet more readable with colors

To make clear what the exact purpose of a cell is we need a set of guidelines to follow.

Getting ready

You need a basic Dashboard Design dashboard containing a few components in the canvas with some bindings to the data model in the spreadsheet.

How to do it...

1. Go to your data model in the spreadsheet.
2. Select the cell(s) you want to color.
3. Click on the **Fill Color** button and select the desired color. You can find this button in the **Font** section of the **Home** tab.
4. Color the cells that have dynamic visibility values in orange.

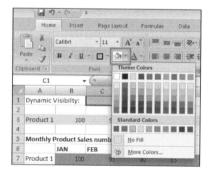

5. Color the cells with input values from canvas components yellow. In the following screenshot, row A3:N3 is used as the destination range for a drill down from a chart.
6. Color the cells that will be filled with data from an external data source in blue.
7. Color the cells with Excel formulas in green.

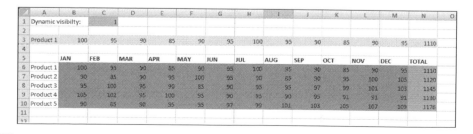

	A	B	C	D	E	F	G	H	I	J	K	L	M	N	O
1	Dynamic visibilty:		1												
2															
3	Product 1	100	95	90	85	90	95	100	95	90	85	90	95	1110	
4															
5		JAN	FEB	MAR	APR	MAY	JUN	JUL	AUG	SEP	OCT	NOV	DEC	TOTAL	
6	Product 1	100	95	90	85	90	95	100	95	90	85	90	95	1110	
7	Product 2	90	85	90	95	100	95	90	85	90	95	100	105	1120	
8	Product 3	95	100	95	90	85	90	95	95	97	99	101	103	1145	
9	Product 4	105	102	95	100	95	90	95	90	95	91	91	91	1130	
10	Product 5	90	85	90	95	95	97	99	101	103	105	107	109	1176	
11															

How it works...

A cell in an Excel spreadsheet can have several different roles. It can contain a fixed value, it may show the result of a (complex) formula, and it can be used by formulas in other cells. Within Dashboard Design, an additional role can be recognized—the **insertion** role. In this type of cell, an interaction from an Dashboard Design component results in a certain value being inserted into this cell.

There's more...

To make the data model readable, not only for yourself but also for others, it is helpful to create a **legend** in your spreadsheet that explains what each color represents. Any color scheme can be used, but it is important that you stick to the chosen scheme and use it consistently throughout the development of your dashboards.

Make sure that you add another worksheet to your spreadsheet to place this legend in. You can also use this overall summary worksheet to include the information such as project name, description, uses, version (history), and so on.

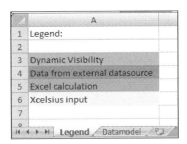

Making the spreadsheet more readable with comments

Sometimes cells need additional information to explain how they are used. Of course you can write this text as a label in another spreadsheet cell, but a better solution is to use comments.

Getting ready

You can use the same basic dashboard as for the previous recipe.

How to do it...

1. Right-click the cell to which you want to add the extra information.

2. Choose **Insert Comment**.

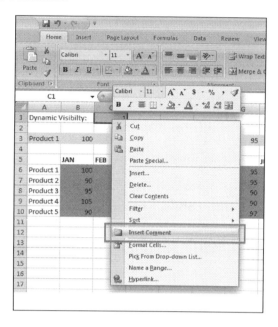

3. Add your text. A small red rectangle will appear in the right upper corner of the cell.

4. Now hover your mouse over the cell and the comment you just entered will appear.

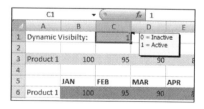

How it works...

Comments are related to one spreadsheet cell only and are only shown if you hover the mouse over this cell. This is a great way to document information that you do not need to see all the time, which keeps your data model clean.

A good case to use this is when you are building a dashboard with multiple layers in combination with dynamic visibility. You might use numbers to identify each layer and use a cell to contain the number of the active layer. You can use a comment to describe the meaning of these cell values.

A little remark about the usage of comments is that they do increase the size of the Dashboard Design file a bit.

Making the spreadsheet more readable using borders

To separate cells from each other and create different areas within a spreadsheet, you can use cell borders.

Getting ready

You can use the same basic dashboard as for the previous examples.

How to do it...

1. Select the cell(s) you want to add a border to and right-click.

2. Now select **Format cells...**.

3. Go to the **Border** tab.

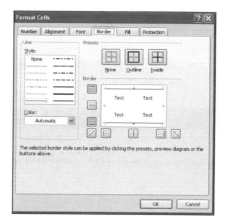

4. Select the desired style of the border line.
5. Select on which side(s) of the cell(s) the border should appear.
6. Click on **OK**.

There's more...

Toolbar border button

Instead of right-clicking the cells and using the **Format Cells** option you can also use the **Border** button on the toolbar to adjust the border styles for a cell or a group of cells. You can find this **Border** button in the **Font** section of the **Home** tab. If you select the cell(s) and click on this button, a list of options will be shown, which you can choose from.

Use multiple worksheets

You can use borders to split data within a spreadsheet. But if your Dashboard Design dashboard contains data from a lot of different (functional) areas, it is recommended that you split your spreadsheet in several sheets. This will help you to keep your dashboard maintainable.

A good strategy to split up the spreadsheet is to divide your data in different areas that correspond to certain areas, layers, or tabs that you created on the dashboard canvas. You can also use separate sheets for each external data connection. Give each worksheet a meaningful name.

Place your logic wisely

Another general guideline is to place as many cells with logic and Dashboard Design interactivity functionality at the top left of the spreadsheet. This place is easy to reach without a lot of annoying scrolling and searching. Even more importantly, your data set may grow (vertically and/or horizontally) over time. This can especially be a risk when you are using an external data connection, and you don't want your logic to be overwritten.

Using named ranges

With **named ranges**, it is possible to define a worksheet cell or a range of cells with a logical name.

How to do it...

1. Select a range of cells (for example B1:B12).
2. Put a description (for example **Total_Sales**) for this range in the **Name Box** in the upper left-hand side of the worksheet.

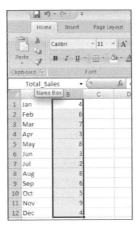

3. Now this named range can be used in formulas in other worksheet cells. Type the formula **=SUM(Total_Sales)** in cell B13.

	A	B	C	D	E
		B13		fx	=SUM(Total_Sales)
1	Jan	4			
2	Feb	6			
3	Mar	7			
4	Apr	3			
5	May	8			
6	Jun	3			
7	Jul	2			
8	Aug	8			
9	Sep	6			
10	Oct	5			
11	Nov	9			
12	Dec	4			
13		65			
14					

How it works...

Using named ranges makes your formulas more readable, especially when you are working with multiple worksheets and using formulas that refer to cells on other worksheets.

There is more...

Defined named ranges

By clicking on the little triangle in the **Name Box**, it will show a list of all your defined named ranges in all your worksheets.

Name Manager

If you use a lot of named ranges, the **Name Manager** can be a helpful tool to manage your named ranges. Here, you can also edit and delete the existing named ranges. You can find the **Name Manager** under the **Formulas** tab or by using the shortcut *Ctrl-F3*.

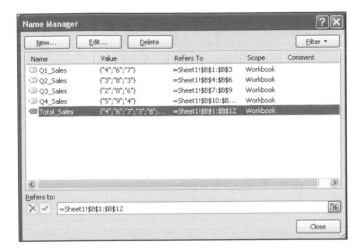

Selecting all worksheet cells with one click

With a click of the mouse button, we can select everything on a worksheet.

How to do it...

If you want to select an entire worksheet without having to drag your mouse to select everything, you can just click on the half triangle on the top left corner of the worksheet.

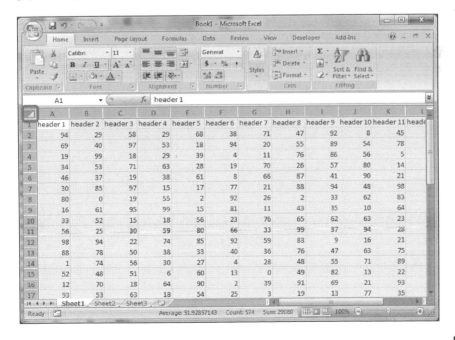

How it works...

Clicking on the half triangle button will allow you to select the entire worksheet with just one click. Here are some reasons why we would want to select an entire worksheet:

- ▶ With an entire worksheet selected, you can easily apply formatting or change attributes to all cells.

- ▶ You can copy the selection from one workbook and paste it onto a worksheet from another workbook. A common use would be copying data elements from an external spreadsheet and pasting it onto the internal Dashboard Design spreadsheet.

- ▶ You can easily perform row height or column width formatting that will apply to all rows or columns in that spreadsheet.

There's more...

Another way of selecting everything on a worksheet is using the *Ctrl+A* shortcut.

Copying the formatting of one cell to another cell or range

This recipe shows you how to copy the formatting of one cell to another cell or range. For example, we can copy a yellow background and Calibri font from cell A1 to cell A2.

How to do it...

1. Click on the source cell that you want to copy the formatting from.
2. Click on the Format Painter icon which you can find on the **Clipboard** section of the **Home** tab.

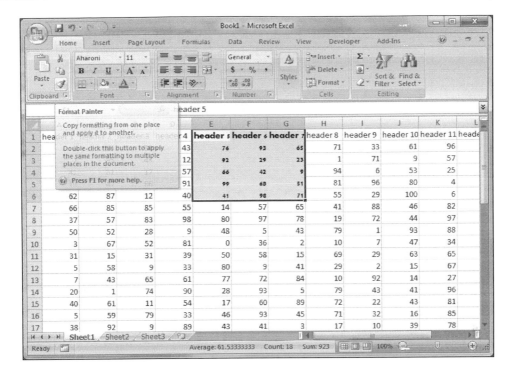

3. Click on the cell or range that you want to copy the source cell's formatting to.

How it works...

The **Format Painter** works by taking the source cell that you have selected and applying the formatting to the cell(s) that you paint to.

This is very useful because we can copy cell formats without having to perform a **copy** and **paste special** every time.

For Dashboard Design developers, it happens very often where we have to copy colored cells that represent different types of logic such as dynamic visibility cells, insertion cells, and so on.

There's more...

An alternative to accomplishing the same task is to copy a cell and then click **Paste Special...** and choose to **Paste Formats** only.

Debugging your spreadsheets

It is common that Dashboard Design developers may accidently put in the incorrect formula when developing logic on their spreadsheets. Using the *Ctrl +* ` hotkey will make things much easier.

How to do it...

1. Select the worksheet you want to see formulas for.

2. Hit the *Ctrl* key and ` (grave accent) key together.

3. You will see the value in the cell change to the formula.

How it works...

The hotkey *Ctrl+* ` works by showing the underlying formula of a cell. This is extremely useful if you are comparing formulas from multiple cells, the reason being that the developer does not have to flip between formulas in order to see what they are doing wrong when comparing multiple cells. Developers can quickly analyze their worksheet and find the cause of their problem quickly.

The following screenshot shows the results of two Excel formulas in cells A1 and A2:

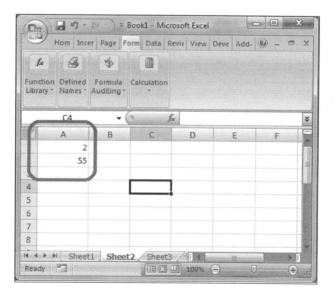

After using the *Ctrl+* ` hotkey, the formulas of both cells are displayed as you can see in the next screenshot:

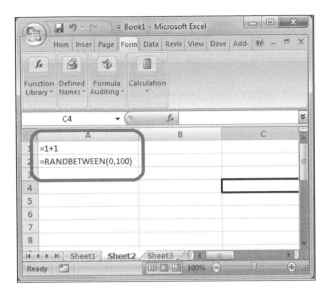

There's more...

An alternative way to accomplish the same task is to go to the **Formulas** tab and then click on **Show Formulas**. Refer to the following screenshot:

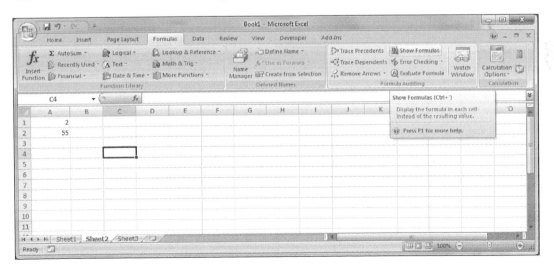

Navigation between worksheets

It is often the case that when we are developing Dashboard Design dashboards, we run out of room for our worksheet tabs. We then have to scroll through each tab in order to get to the one that we want; this is kind of a pain. To access tabs that are not visible, we are used to pressing the arrow keys to move to the desired tab.

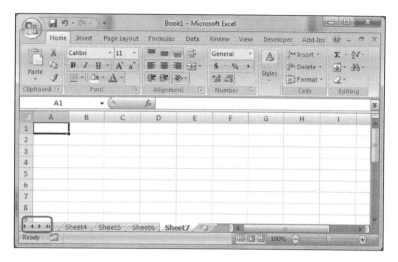

How to do it...

1. To have all tabs displayed in one menu, right-click on the tab at bottom, left-hand side navigation area. You will then see the list of tabs that you can choose from.

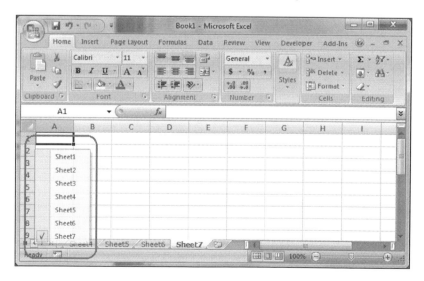

2. You can also use *Ctrl + PageUp,* which will move to the previous sheet in your workbook.

3. *Ctrl + PageDown* will activate the next sheet in the workbook.

How it works...

The methods explained work by allowing developers to move between worksheets more quickly. Being able to quickly right-click and show a menu of all available tabs is faster than scrolling through each tab in order to reach tabs that are not visible. In addition, the ability to use a hotkey to cycle through each tab brings some time savings benefits for those who are comfortable with using the keyboard to perform all their actions.

Grouping the canvas components

Canvas components can be grouped with one or more other components.

Getting ready

Drag several components to the canvas.

How to do it...

1. Select the components that you want to group by either selecting them by dragging the mouse over the components, or clicking the components one-by-one while holding the *Ctrl* button on your keyboard.

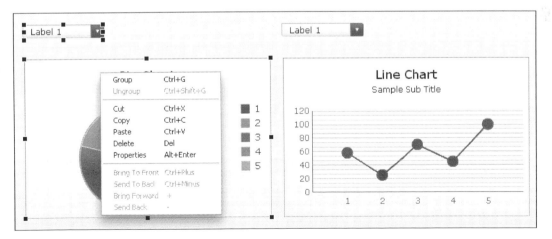

2. Right-click anywhere on the canvas and select **Group** from the context menu. You can also use the shortcut *Ctrl + G* to group these components. As you can see, the components are now a group with a common border (**Dynamic Visibility** and **Entry Effect**):

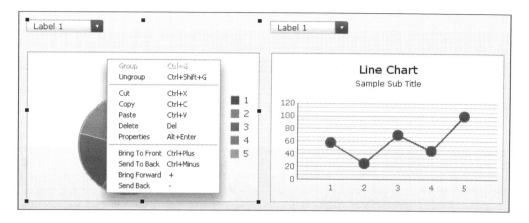

And some shared preferences (**Dynamic Visibility** and **Entry Effect**):

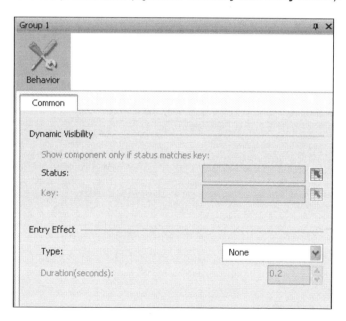

3. If you create a lot of groups of components, we advise that you name these groups to prevent you from getting lost and confused during the dashboard development. First go to the **Object Browser**.

4. Select the group you want to rename.

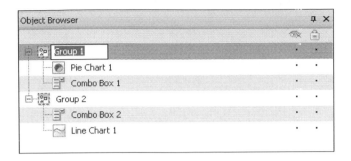

5. Double-click the group or right-click and select **Rename** from the context menu.

6. Type in the new name for this group.

How it works...

When your dashboard gets more complex, not only will the data model in the spreadsheet grow, the number of components used on the canvas will also increase. Using groups to differentiate the canvas components from each other is a great way to stay in control of your dashboard.

There's more...

Besides browsing through your (grouped) components, the **Object Browser** has two additional options which come in very handy during the development of a complex dashboard.

Hiding components

Firstly, you can hide components and/or groups of components, which will make your life easier if you are using a lot of overlaying components. By checking **Hide** for some components, you won't be bothered by these components and you can work with the components that are unhidden.

 There is one thing you should keep in mind: If you hide a component that is part of a group and the group itself is unhidden, the complete group will still be movable and its properties will be changeable.

Locking components

Secondly, the **Object Browser** gives us the possibility to lock one or more components and/or groups of components. Doing this makes it impossible to select these components so it won't be possible to move, change, or do anything else with it.

Hiding or locking components is easy. In the **Object Browser** you will see two symbols with two columns of dots beneath them. The first column is the 'hide' column; the second one defines which components are locked. To hide or lock a component, you just have to click on the correct dot in the row of the component. The dot will be replaced with a checkmark. In the following screenshot, you can see that the **Budget** group is hidden while the **Actual** group is locked:

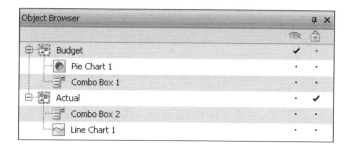

2

Data Visualization

In this chapter, we will cover:

- ▶ Adding a line chart to your dashboard
- ▶ Using the bullet chart
- ▶ Using sparklines
- ▶ Using the combination chart
- ▶ Using the pie chart
- ▶ Using the XY chart
- ▶ Using the bubble chart
- ▶ Using the radar chart
- ▶ Using the OHLC chart and the candlestick chart
- ▶ Sorting series
- ▶ Zooming in on charts
- ▶ Scaling the y-axis
- ▶ Using the tree map
- ▶ Showing a trend without a chart
- ▶ Displaying raw data
- ▶ Illustrating single values

Introduction

Data visualization may be the most important topic when we are talking about dashboard creation. It enables us to view data, compare values, and make analysis in a clear and effective way. A dashboard is the ideal platform to present these visualizations.

Data can be presented in a graphical way, for example with lines, bars, colored areas, gauges, or just with a simple red/green indicator. But on the other hand, in some cases, it may be more effective to use a simple list of values instead of these graphs. This totally depends on the purpose of the dashboard.

Dashboard Design provides a great toolkit with lots of visualization components. This chapter will discuss these components and show you how to use them.

Adding a line chart to your dashboard

A line chart is very useful to visualize data that changes over time. It consists of a set of data points that are connected by a line. The horizontal x-axis typically shows the categories in which the data is divided. The vertical y-axis shows us the values.

This recipe shows how to add a line chart to a dashboard and how to link it to the data in the spreadsheet. Also, we will discuss the components that are similar to the line chart component—**Bar chart, column chart, area chart,** and **stacked charts**.

Getting ready

Open a new Dashboard Design file and enter the data into the spreadsheet, as shown in the following screenshot:

	A	B	C	D	E	F	
1							
2							
3							
4		Q1	Q2	Q3	Q4		
5	Apple	500	750	600	350		
6	Banana	1000	650	850	750		
7	Cherry	400	500	600	300		
8							

How to do it...

1. Drag a **Line Chart** component from the **Components** browser into the canvas.

 You can also click on the **Line Chart** component in the **Components** browser, move your cursor to the canvas area (the arrow will now change into a cross), and click again. You can use whatever method you prefer.

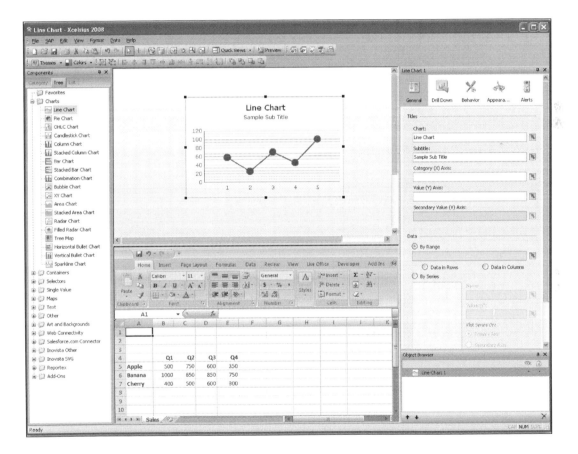

2. Select the **Line Chart** component you just added to the canvas by clicking on it. Now the component is surrounded by eight blocks that enable you to adjust the size of the component.

3. The properties pane for this component is also visible now. By default, the **General** tab is selected. In the **Data** section we can bind the data we entered earlier in the spreadsheet to this component. Click on the button on the right-hand side of the **By Range** field.

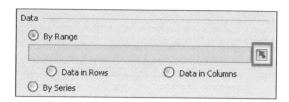

4. In the spreadsheet, select the range from A4 to E7 and click on **OK**. The data is now bound to the component.

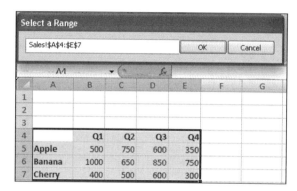

5. The **Data** section of the properties pane now looks like the following screenshot. The chart will already show the data series we just bound.

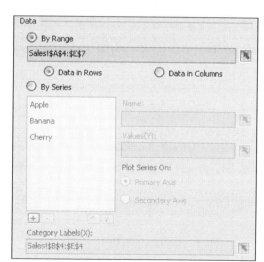

6. In the same way, we can add titles to this chart. Select spreadsheet cell A1 and enter **Sales data**; also, enter **2011** in cell A2.

7. Bind the **Chart** field in the properties pane with spreadsheet cell A1 and bind the **Subtitle** field with cell A2.

You can also enter a value in these title fields directly.

8. In the **Category (Y) Axis** field, enter **Tonne**.

9. Your setup should now look like the following screenshot. Click on the **Preview** button to try the dashboard.

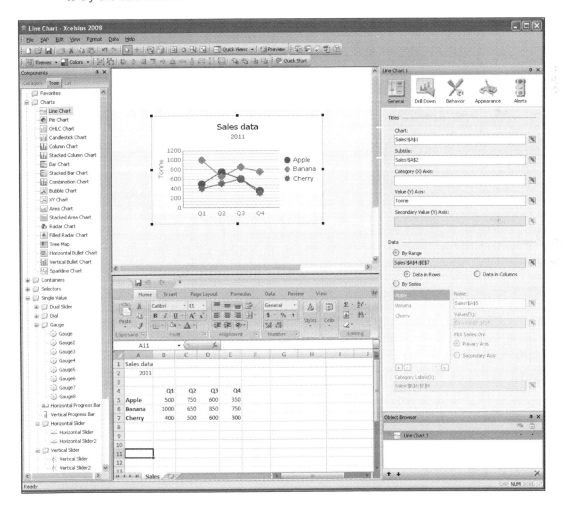

How it works...

This recipe showed how to connect the data in one or more spreadsheet cells to the **Line Chart** component through several options in its properties pane. This is how we bind data and you will be using this a lot during the development of dashboards with Dashboard Design.

There's more...

Manually binding data

In this recipe, we used a pretty straightforward data set with the category labels in the first row (Q1, Q2, Q3, and Q4) and the series names in the first column (Apple, Banana, Cherry). Dashboard Design is able to understand this data set and bind this information automatically. This may not always be the case, and therefore not always lead to the visualization you had in mind.

To change the direction of the visualization of the spreadsheet data in the chart, you can select the **Data in Columns** option in the **Data** section of the properties pane. This will switch the series and the labels.

By clicking on **By Series** in the **Data** section of the properties pane, it is possible to manually adjust all binding settings for the name and values of each series. Additionally, you can select the axis a series should be plotted on (primary or secondary). You can change the series order by using the two arrow buttons and add or remove series by using the **+** and **-** buttons. Also, you can manually bind the category labels to a range of cells.

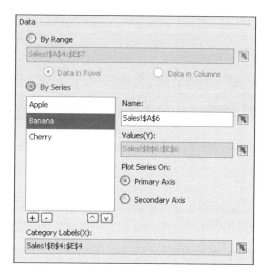

Hide/show series

Series in a chart can be hidden or shown by the user when using the dashboard.

1. Go to the **Appearance** tab and select the sub-tab **Layout**.
2. Make sure that **Enable Legend** is selected.
3. Select **Enable Hide/Show Chart Series at Run-Time**.
4. Set **Interaction** to **Check Box**.

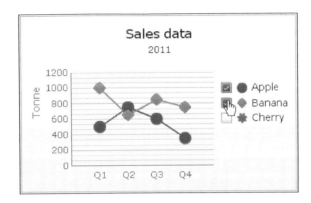

Other charts: bar chart and column chart

The bar chart and column chart components can be configured in exactly the same way as a line chart component. A bar chart presents values in horizontal bars while the column chart uses vertical bars. These types of charts are typically not used to present data over a long time period, but to show data from different categories that need to be compared.

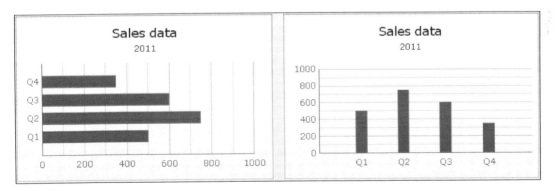

Other charts: area chart

The area chart component is a line chart with a filled area beneath the line. Other differences between these types of charts are that for the area chart the first value (Q1) is plotted on the far left-hand side and the last value (Q4) on the far right-hand side of chart. An area chart is used to visualize the cumulated total value over a period of time. This component can be configured in the same way as the line chart component.

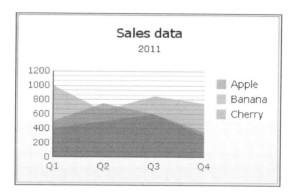

Other charts: stacked charts

The bar chart, column chart, and area chart component all have a **stacked** version—stacked bar chart, stacked column chart, and stacked area chart. These stacked chart components show the values for the series on top of each other in the same column. You can use the stacked charts if the dashboard user needs to be able to compare totals.

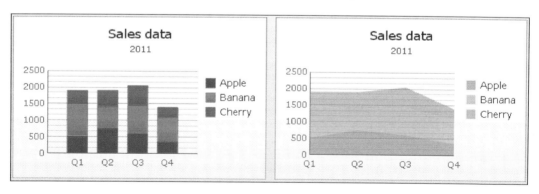

Using the bullet chart

The **bullet chart** is in fact a bar or column chart with a lot of extra options. Besides visualizing a data point like how the bar and column charts do, the bullet chart is able to show a **target** and two or more qualitative **ranges**. These ranges can indicate whether a value can be considered as bad, satisfactory, good, and so on.

This recipe will show you how to configure a bullet chart. Dashboard Design has two bullet chart components—a horizontal and a vertical version. Both components have exactly the same configuration options and work in the same manner. This recipe will use the horizontal bullet chart.

Getting ready

Open a new Dashboard Design file and enter the data into the spreadsheet, as shown in the following screenshot:

	A	B	C	D	E
1	Sales data				
2	2011				
3					
4		2011	Target	Satisfactory	Good
5	Apple	2200	2000	1800	2400
6	Banana	3250	3500	3000	3600
7	Cherry	1800	1500	1400	1700

How to do it...

1. Drag a **Horizontal Bullet Chart** component into the canvas.

2. Bind the **By Range** field to the spreadsheet range from A4 to E7.

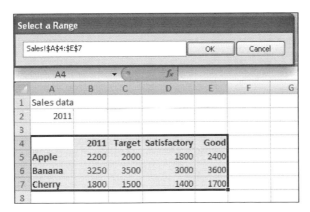

3. Also bind the **Chart** field in the **Titles** section to spreadsheet cell A1 and bind the **Subtitle** field to cell A2. Your setup should now look like the following screenshot:

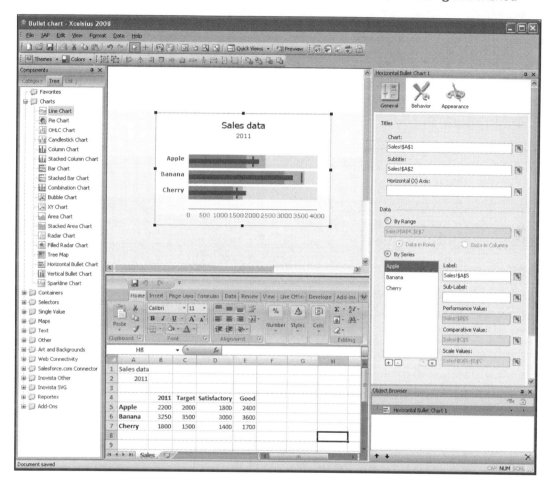

4. Hit the **Preview** button and hover on the different sections of the bars. The dashboard now shows the detailed information we just bound.

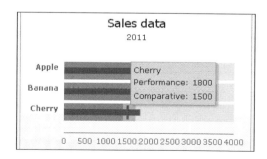

How it works...

As already stated at the beginning of this recipe, the bullet chart components can show a result value, a target, and qualitative ranges. Furthermore, each series can have its own label and sub label. Let's have a look at exactly how these variables are configured in the previous recipe.

First, select **By Series** in the **Data** section of the properties pane for the **Horizontal Bullet Chart** component; then, select the **Apple** series. You can now see the detailed bindings Dashboard Design made for this series.

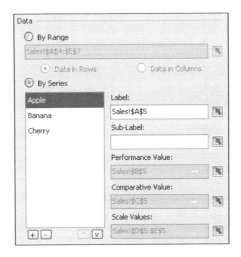

The **Label** field is bound to spreadsheet cell A5 (Apple). We did not edit the **Sub-Label** field so this remains empty, but you can bind it to a cell with a certain value or enter a value in this field directly. The result value, cell B5 (2200), is bound to the **Performance Value** field, which is presented in the chart by a small horizontal bar. Next the target value of cell C5 (2000) is bound to the **Comparative Value field**. This value is visualized by a vertical dash. There are two cells that are bound as **Scale Values**: D5 (1800) and E5 (2400). Using two values means that the chart will show three areas—0 - 1800, 1800 - 2400, and 2400 - max. You can use as many values as you need. These areas are shown in the chart as three colored blocks in the background. If you don't use scale values, there won't be a colored block in the chart.

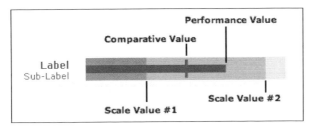

There is more...

The bullet chart in the recipe uses the same x-axis for all three series. It is also possible to configure separate x-axes.

1. Select the **Bullet Chart** component and go to the **Behavior** tab. Select the **Scale** sub-tab.

2. Select **Configure scale by series**. Now you can edit the scaling settings for each series separately.

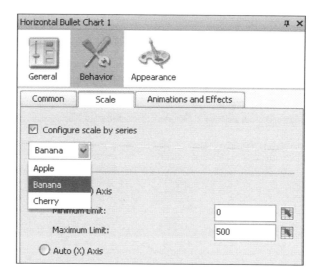

3. Go to the **Appearance** tab and select the **Text** sub-tab.

4. Here, you can select which **Horizontal Axis Labels** should be shown.

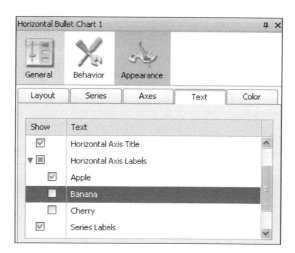

Using sparklines

Sparklines are typically small graphics, showing a horizontal line connecting several data points without labeling the values on its axes. The purpose of the sparkline is to show the movement of a trend over a certain period. Since its details are not available, the context of a sparkline must be clear to the dashboard user to interpret its meaning properly. This recipe will show you how to configure a sparkline.

Getting ready

Open a new Dashboard Design file and enter the data into the spreadsheet, as shown in the following screenshot:

	A	B	C	D	E	F	G	H	I	J	K	L	M
1	Sales data												
2	2011												
3													
4		Jan	Feb	Mar	Apr	May	Jun	Jul	Aug	Sep	Oct	Nov	Dec
5	Apple	800	750	600	500	450	550	650	800	1000	1200	1100	900

How to do it...

1. Drag a **Sparkline Chart** component into the canvas.
2. Bind the **By Range** field to the spreadsheet range from A4 to M5.
3. Bind the **Chart** field to cell A1 and bind the **Subtitle** field to cell A2.
4. Go to the **Behavior** tab of the properties pane of the **Sparkline Chart** component. In the **Normal Range Area** section, select **Normal Range Area**.
5. Enter the value **600** in the **Normal Range Low** field and enter **1000** in the **Normal Range High** field.

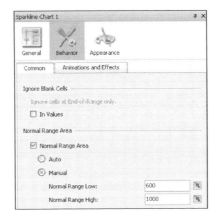

6. Go to the **Appearance** tab and select the **Text** sub-tab.

7. Select **Show** for the **Start Value**.

8. Set the **Position** for this **Start Value** text to **Left**.

9. Select **Show** for the **End Value**.

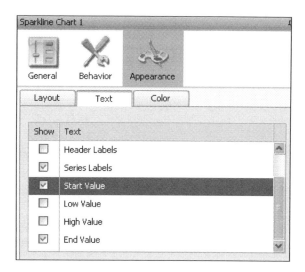

10. Now go to the **Color** tab and select all **Markers**.

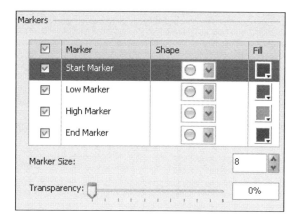

11. Your dashboard should look like the following screenshot:

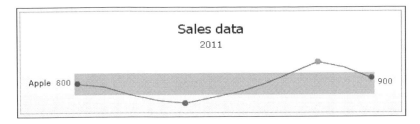

How it works...

The configuration of the **General** tab within the properties pane of a sparkline chart component looks like the configuration of a line chart component. But, a sparkline chart component has fewer options here: No axis and no category labels can be defined.

With the **Normal Range Area** in the **Behavior** tab, is it possible to illustrate that the values of this series should be between what boundaries. Also, the start, end, the highest, and the lowest values of the presented series can be emphasized.

There's more...

Header labels

Header labels can label two parts of the sparkline chart component: The series name(s) and the sparkline(s). To activate these labels follow the given steps:

1. Bind the **Header Labels** field in the **General** tab to two spreadsheet cells.

2. Enter the value for the series name(s) header in the first cell, and enter the sparkline(s) header value in the second cell.

3. Now go to the **Appearance** tab and select the **Text** sub-tab.

4. Select **Header Labels**. The labels will now appear in the component.

Show low and high values

Besides the start and end values of a sparkline you can also show the lowest and highest values. In the **Text** sub-tab of the **Appearance** tab, you can select them to be visible.

Using the combination chart

With the combination chart you are able to use both columns and lines to visualize data in one single chart.

Getting ready

Open a new Dashboard Design file and enter the data into the spreadsheet as shown in the following screenshot:

	A	B	C	D	E
1	Marketing				
2		2011			
3					
4		Q1	Q2	Q3	Q4
5	Marketing budget	100000	70000	150000	150000
6	Market share	5%	4%	8%	12%

Use the **Percent Style** option to convert the market share values into percentages. You can find this option in the **Number** section of the **Home** tab of the toolbar.

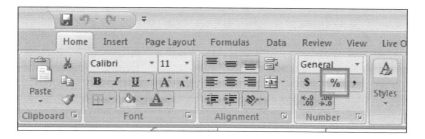

How to do it...

1. Drag a **Combination Chart** component to the canvas.

2. Bind the **Chart** field to cell A1 and the **Subtitle** field to cell B2.

3. Bind the **By Range** field to the spreadsheet range from A4 to E6.

4. Select **By Series** and select the **Market Share** series. Select the option to **Plot Series On: Secondary Axis**.

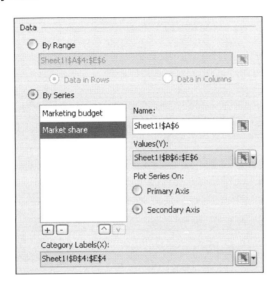

How it works...

After binding the data to the component, we had to adjust the **Market Share** series to plot its data on the secondary axis. After doing this, a second y-axis appeared on the right-hand side of the chart, labeled with percentages.

There is more...

In the **Series** sub-tab within the **Appearance** tab of the properties pane, you can determine how each series should look—either a column or a line. Here, you can also set the series **colors** and **Marker Shape**, **Size**, and **Transparency**.

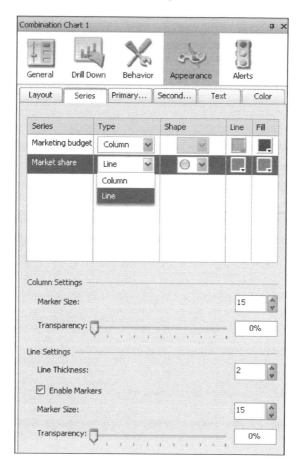

Using the pie chart

The **pie chart** is circular chart divided in one or more slices. Each slice represents the proportion of a value to the total of all values. Pie charts can be used to show the impact of a value in contrast to other values or the grand total. However, it may be hard to compare the size of slices within a pie chart when there are more than three slices, or across other pie charts. Therefore, if you need to compare data, we recommend using the bar chart instead.

Getting ready

Open a new Dashboard Design file and enter the data into the spreadsheet, as shown in the following screenshot:

How to do it...

1. Drag a **Pie Chart** component onto the canvas.

2. Bind the **Values** field to spreadsheet cells B5 through B7.

3. Bind the **Labels** field to cells A5 through A7.

4. Bind the **Chart** field to cell A1 and the **Subtitle** field to cell B2.

5. **Preview** the dashboard.

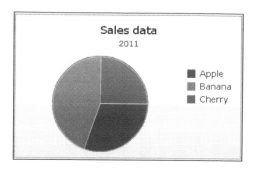

How it works...

We bound the fields from the **General** tab to the data in the spreadsheet making this chart to show the three labels and the according portions of the total in a pie. Obviously, the pie chart component cannot use multiple series of data like the line chart component and other chart components.

Using the XY chart

An **XY chart**, or **scatterplot**, can display values that consist of two variables. The chart shows a set of points that, for each point, refer to a combination of a value on the X-axis and a value on the Y-axis.

Getting ready

Open a new Dashboard Design file and enter the data into the spreadsheet, as shown in the following screenshot:

	A	B	C
1	House price vs. Weeks until sale		
2			
3			
4		House price	Weeks until sale
5	Cat 1	100000	4
6	Cat 2	200000	20
7	Cat 3	300000	32
8	Cat 4	400000	18
9	Cat 5	500000	22

How to do it...

1. Drag a **XY Chart** component into the canvas.

2. Bind the data **By Range** to spreadsheet cells B5 until C9.

3. Bind the **Chart** field to cell A1 and delete the subtitle.

4. Bind the **Value (X) Axis** field to cell B4 and the **Value (Y) Axis** field to cell C4. Now it is clear what the implication is of each axis.

5. Go to the **Behavior** tab and select the sub-tab **Scale**. Now select **Fixed Label Size**.

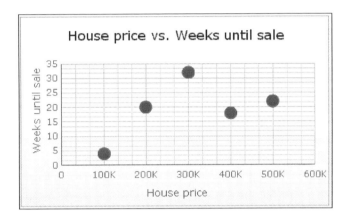

How it works...

In this example, we created a dashboard that compares the price of a house (variable 1) with the number of weeks until it is sold (variable 2). It shows us that cheap houses are sold very quickly, the houses priced between cheap and expensive (midclass) take a very long time to sell, while the expensive houses are somewhat in between.

Using the bubble chart

A **bubble chart** can display values that consist of three variables. The only difference with the XY chart is that the size of the points in the bubble charts is adjustable. Next to the value on the X and Y-axes this is the third variable that can be illustrated with this chart.

Getting ready

You can reuse the dashboard from the *Using the XY chart* recipe and add the values in the D-column as shown in the following screenshot:

	A	B	C	D
1	House price vs. Weeks until sale vs. # houses for sale			
2				
3				
4		House price	Weeks until sale	# houses for sale
5	Cat 1	100000	4	560
6	Cat 2	200000	20	680
7	Cat 3	300000	32	1130
8	Cat 4	400000	18	120
9	Cat 5	500000	22	70

How to do it...

1. Drag a **Bubble Chart** component into the canvas.
2. Bind the data **By Range** to spreadsheet cells B5 through D9.
3. Bind the **Chart** field to cell A1 and delete the subtitle.
4. Bind the **Value (X) Axis** field to cell B4 and the **Value (Y) Axis** field to cell C4.
5. Go to the **Behavior** tab and select the sub-tab **Scale**. Now select **Fixed Label Size**.

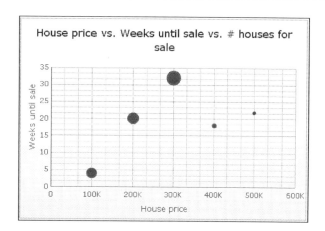

How it works...

In addition to the analysis we made in the *Using the XY chart* recipe, we can now also see that the number of houses for sale in the midclass market is very high, while the availability in the expensive market is very low.

Using the radar chart

The **radar chart** is able to represent more than two variables in a single chart. Therefore, this chart has multiple axes that all start in the same point. The radar chart can be used to make comparisons between series, based on their score on a set of variables.

Getting ready

Open a new Dashboard Design file and enter the data into the spreadsheet as shown in the following screenshot:

	A	B	C	D	E	F
1						
2						
3						
4		Price	Availability	Performance	Quality	Usability
5	Product 1	5	3	4	2	1
6	Product 2	2	4	2	2	5
7						

How to do it...

1. Drag a **Radar Chart** component to the canvas.

2. Enter a name and subtitle for the chart.

3. Bind the cell range A4 to F6 to the **By Range** field.

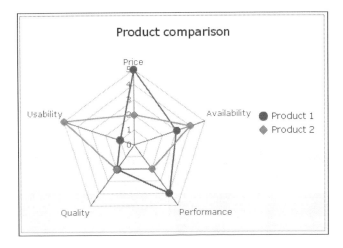

How it works...

Our dataset has two series and five categories. The chart has an axis for each category and on these axes the accompanying values are plotted for each series. The values of a series are connected with a line.

There is more...

The filled radar chart component does the same job as the radar chart component and has the same configuration options. The only difference is that the area between the connected value points is filled with a color in the filled radar chart component.

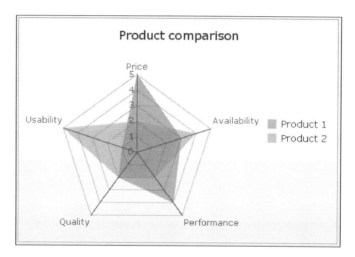

Using the OHLC chart and candlestick chart

The **OHLC chart** and **candlestick chart** are both designed to show the movement of a stock price over time. OHLC stands for Open, High, Low, and Close. These four stock price values are illustrated for each time unit.

Both components work in exactly the same way, so you can use both the OHLC chart component and the candlestick chart component for this recipe. The only difference between them is the graphical visualization.

Getting ready

For this recipe, we need some historical stock data. Open your browser and go to
`http://www.nasdaq.com/` and look for historical quotes on the SAP AG stock.

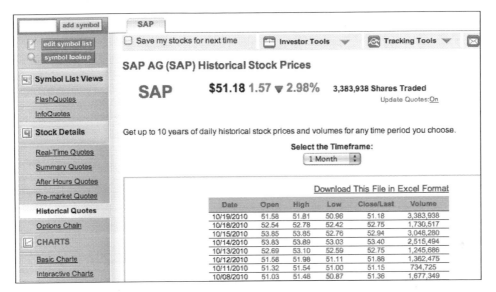

Select a timeframe of one month and copy-paste the quotes to the spreadsheet of a new
Dashboard Design file.

How to do it...

1. First we need to prepare the data in the spreadsheet. It is now sorted from new
   to old quotes. As the **OHLC Chart** component does not enable sorting (see the
   recipe *Sorting series* later in this chapter) we have to sort the data ourselves in
   the spreadsheet. First, select all the cells you just pasted into the spreadsheet.

2. Sort this selection by using the **Sort & Filter** function in the **Editing** section of the **Home** tab of the spreadsheet toolbar and choose the **Sort Oldest to Newest** option.

3. Add an **OHLC Chart** component to the canvas.

4. Enter a chart title and subtitle, or bind these fields to cells in the spreadsheet.

5. Bind the data **By Range** to the range of cells that include all values in the **Open**, **High**, **Low**, and **Close** columns.

6. Select **By Series** and enter SAP in the **Series Name** field.

7. In the dataset we copied from the NASDAQ website and pasted to the spreadsheet, the dates are in the first column. Bind the **Category Labels** field to the cells in the **Date** column.

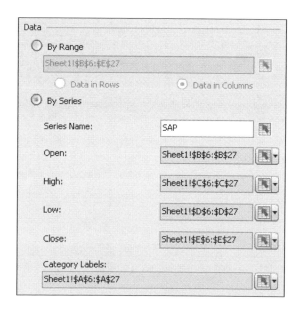

The OHLC chart we just created works as follows: The vertical lines show the price range (from the highest to the lowest value) of a stock for each day. The little mark on the left of these vertical lines indicates the opening price. The little mark on the right indicates the closing price. In addition to this, a set of a line with marks has a dark color if the closing price is lower than the opening price and a light color if the closing price is higher than the opening price.

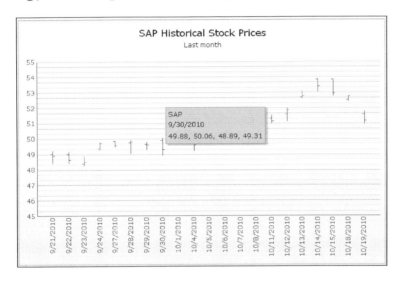

The candlestick chart shows exactly the same data as the OHLC chart. In the candlestick chart a rectangle is used to illustrate the opening and closing prices. If this rectangle is transparent, the closing price is higher than the opening price and if it's filled the closing price is lower.

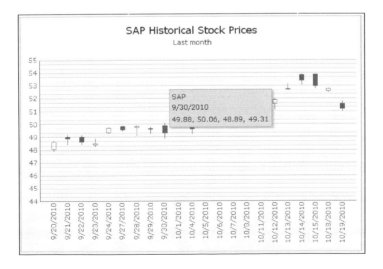

Sorting series

A chart does not always look like what you had in mind. In some cases, you may want to see data sorted from high to low values, while in other situations, you want to see the categories to be displayed in a more logical order. For example, in the following bar chart, the quarters are sorted from last (Q4) to first (Q1). To change this, you can of course adjust the data model in the spreadsheet, like we did in the *Using the OHLC chart and Candlestick chart* recipe. An easier and better way is to use the **Sorting** settings for the bar chart component.

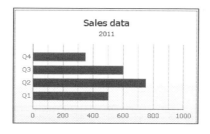

 Sorting is available in the following components: line chart, pie chart, column chart, stacked column chart, bar chart, stacker bar chart, combination chart, area chart, stacked area chart, radar chart, and the filled radar chart.

Getting ready

You can reuse any of the dashboards you created earlier, as long as they contain one of the components listed above.

How to do it...

1. Select the component, go to the **Behavior** tab, and select the sub-tab **Common**.
2. Select **Enable Sorting**.
3. Select **By Category Labels**.
4. Select **Reverse Order**.

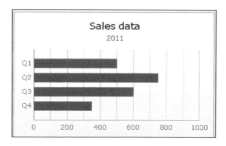

How it works...

As you can see in the previous screenshot, the order of the quarters has changed. In Dashboard Design, the first category is by default the lowest category on its axis. With the reverse order setting, this can be changed.

There is more...

Besides sorting on category labels, it is also possible to sort by data. If you have more than one series, you have to choose one of these series to base the sorting order on.

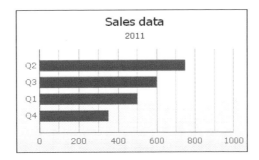

The following chart shows the data shown in an ascending order:

Zooming in on charts

If you are visualizing a data set with a large number of values on the x-axis, the chart might be a bit hard to use. To see a section of such a chart in more detail, we can use the **range slider** to zoom in on the data.

The range slider option is available in the following chart components: line chart, OHLC chart, candlestick chart, column chart, bar chart, stacked column chart, stacked bar chart, combination chart, area chart, and the stacked area chart.

Getting ready

You can reuse any of the dashboards you already made, which include one of the components mentioned above. In this recipe we will use the dashboard created in the *Adding a Line chart to your dashboard* recipe.

How to do it...

1. Select the chart, go to the **Behavior** tab and select the **Common** sub-tab.
2. Select **Enable Range Slider**.
3. At **Beginning Range Value** select **Category Label** and enter value Q1.
4. At **End Range Value** also select **Category Label** and enter value Q3.
5. Bind the **Range Labels** field to cells B4 until E4.

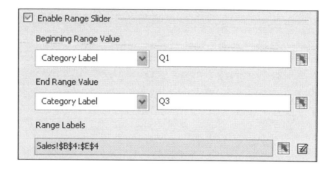

6. Go to the **Appearance** tab and select the **Text** sub-tab. Select **Range Labels** and set the text size to 8.
7. Run the dashboard by hitting the **Preview** button and try the functionality of the range slider.

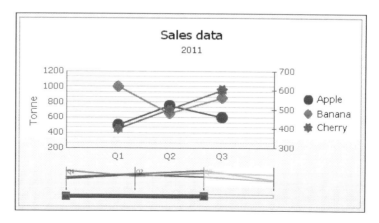

How it works...

The range slider option makes it possible to select a section of the chart by sliding the beginning and end values of this range. In this recipe, we used the category labels to define the initial range values. You can also choose to use the **Position** field and enter the position of the desired value in its series. Q1 would be position 1 and Q3 would be position 3.

Scaling the y-axis

After binding a chart to a data set in the spreadsheet, Dashboard Design makes up a scale on the y-axis by default, based on the lowest and the highest values in the visualized data set. The problem with this auto scaling is that it creates a y-axis that doesn't start with 0, which may cause a bad interpretation of the data.

In the following image, the same results are presented in two bar charts. The chart on the left-hand side gives the indication that **Product B** has performed a lot better than **Product A**; the bar is more than two times as big! This is of course wrong, as the y-axis starts with $470,000. The chart on the right-hand side shows a version that is way more useful for analysis:

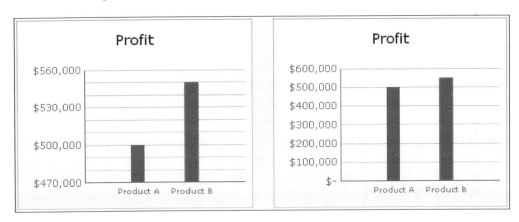

Getting ready

You can reuse any of the dashboards you already made with chart components. In this recipe, we will use the dashboard created in the *Adding a Line chart to your dashboard* recipe.

How to do it...

1. Select the chart, go to the **Behavior** tab and select the **Scale** sub-tab. If your chart has a secondary axis, there will be two sub-tabs—**Primary Scale** and **Secondary Scale**.

2. Select **Manual (Y) Axis**.

3. Enter 0 as **Minimum Limit** and 1000 as **Maximum Limit**.

4. Select **Fixed Label Size**.

5. Set the **Size of Divisions** to 200 and **Minor Divisions** to 1.

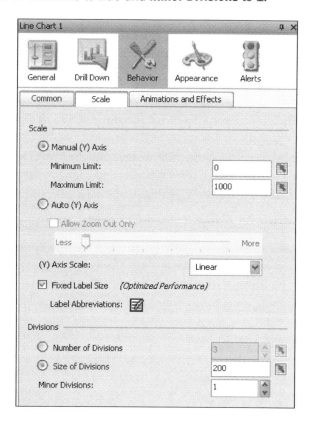

How it works...

The y-axis of the chart will now have a fixed minimum and maximum limit. Remember that this also means that values bigger than 1000 won't be displayed correctly with these settings. They will be placed on the maximum value (1000) of this chart.

The **Fixed Label Size** option keeps the labels on the y-axis readable. 1000 will be 1K, 1,000,000 is 1M, and so on.

There is more...

Variable maximum limits

To make sure that values in the data set never pass the maximum limit, we can use a variable maximum limit.

1. Go to the spreadsheet and enter the following formula in cell D1: **=MAX(B5:E7)**. This will result in the maximum value of the range B5 through E7.

2. Bind the **Maximum Limit** to cell D1. The y-axis will now display the exact maximum value that resulted from the formula.

3. To make this value a more rounded number we have to adjust the formula. Change the formula to: **=ROUND((MAX(B5:E7)),-3)**. The **-3** indicates that the value will be rounded to the nearest thousand. So if the maximum value is 1978, the maximum limit on the y-axis will be 2000. -1 rounds to the nearest tens, -2 to the nearest hundred and so on.

Allow Zoom Out Only

If you do want to use an automatic axis, Dashboard Design offers the **Allow Zoom Out Only** option. This option is only useful if a data set that is presented in a chart is variable (for example by switching with a selector; see *Chapter 3*). By selecting this option, the y-axis will only scale to larger values when a data set is presented that has higher values. If the values are smaller, the scale will not change. With the slider, you can set the sensitivity of the growth factor.

Using the tree map

▶ The **tree map** visualizes values by dividing an area into a set of rectangles. The following image shows an example of a tree map:

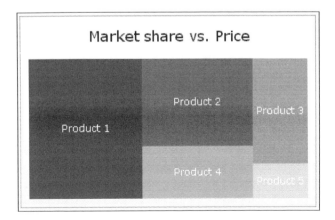

As you can see, two variables are used in this chart—one variable expressed by the relative size of each rectangular and another one illustrated by the color intensity. Instead of using the tree map, you can also choose the XY chart to display two variables in one chart.

Getting ready

For this recipe, we can re-use the file we created in the *Using the XY chart* recipe.

How to do it...

1. Drag a **Tree Map** component to the canvas.
2. Enter a name for the chart.
3. Bind the cell range A4 to C9 to the **By Range** field.
4. Select **Data in Columns**.
5. Select **By Series** and bind the **Name** field to cell A1.

6. Go to the **Appearance** tab and select the **Series** sub-tab.
7. Select a very dark color as **High Color** and a very light color as **Low Color**.

8. **Preview** the dashboard to check the result.

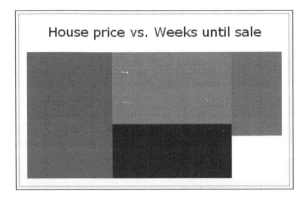

How it works...

The tree map arranges the rectangles from big to small. The Cat 5 data (most expensive houses) is presented on the far left-hand side, while the Cat 1 (cheapest houses) is illustrated by the block on the lower right-hand side. This rectangle also has the lightest color, indicating the lowest **Weeks until sale** value. In the recipe, we changed the colors to a more extreme range so that the differences between the rectangles are clearer.

Showing a trend without a chart

Showing a trend with a line chart is very useful if you want to show data over more than two periods. In some cases, all this historical information is unnecessary and you only want to display the direction of the trend—up, down, or no change. The **trend icon** component delivers this functionality. This recipe will show you how to use it.

Getting ready

Open a new Dashboard Design file and enter the data into the spreadsheet as shown in the following screenshot:

	A	B
1	Value A	1000
2	Value B	250
3		

How to do it...

1. Drag a **Trend Icon** component into the canvas.

2. Enter the following formula in spreadsheet cell B3: **=B2-B1**.

3. Now bind the **Data** field of the **Trend Icon** component to cell B3. The **Trend Icon** component will now turn red and show a downward arrow.

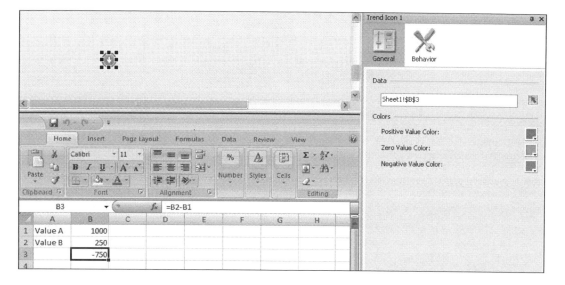

How it works

The trend icon component can only be bound to a single cell. If this cell has a positive value, the component will be shown in positive state (arrow up). If the value is negative, the component will turn into its negative state (arrow down). If the value is zero, a neutral state is shown (flat line icon).

We used the formula to calculate whether the change in trend is positive, negative, or neutral.

Displaying raw data

If you want to display numbers and text, and not by a chart, but just in a table, you can use the spreadsheet table component.

Getting ready

Open a new Dashboard Design file and enter the data into the spreadsheet, as shown in the following screenshot:

	A	B	C	D	E
1					
2					
3					
4		Q1	Q2	Q3	Q4
5	Apple	500	750	600	350
6	Banana	1000	650	850	750
7	Cherry	400	500	600	300

How to do it...

1. In the spreadsheet, select cells A4 through E4.

2. Add a **Bottom Border** by using the **Borders** menu of the **Font** section of the **Home** tab in the spreadsheet.

3. Select cells A4 through A7 and add a **Right Border**.

4. Drag a **Spreadsheet Table** component into the canvas.

5. Bind the **Display Data** field with the spreadsheet range from A4 to E7.

6. Go to the **Behavior** tab and deselect **Row** in the **Row Selectability** section.

7. Go to the **Appearance** tab and deselect **Show Gridlines** in the **Layout** sub-tab.

8. The dashboard should now look like the following screenshot:

	Q1	Q2	Q3	Q4
Apple	500	750	600	350
Banana	1000	650	850	750
Cherry	400	500	600	300

How it works...

The spreadsheet table component shows a range of cells exactly as they are formatted in the spreadsheet. You can add borders, colors, change fonts, alignments, and so on. If you make any changes to the formatting, you have to re-bind the cells again to the component to make the new formatting visible.

The data insertions options, as well as the selectability options, are not used in this recipe, but will be explained in *Chapter 3*.

Illustrating single values

Dashboard Design offers three component types to display single values—**gauges**, **progress bars**, and **value component**. A gauge and progress bar show data on a scale, while the value component only shows a value in numbers. The gauge is the only component of these three types that has the possibility to show more than one value. There are eight different gauge versions available, and a horizontal and vertical version of the progress bar. All these components are ideally used in combination with Alerts. Alerts will be discussed in *Chapter 5*.

This recipe will show you how to set up a gauge. The other two component types work in the same way.

Getting ready

No preparation is needed, just open a new Dashboard Design file.

How to do it...

1. Add a **Gauge component** to the canvas.

2. Enter **75** in spreadsheet cell A1 and bind this cell to the **By Range** field.

3. Select **By Indicators** and rename **Indicator 1** to **Result**.

4. Add a second indicator by clicking on the plus button.

5. Rename this indicator to **Target**, enter **Value 90**, and select **Type** as **Outside Marker**.

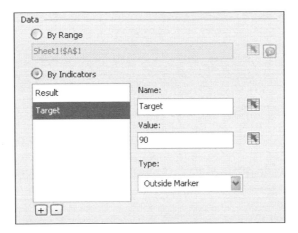

6. Go to the **Appearance** tab and select the **Text** sub-tab. Select **Show Limits** and set size to **8**.

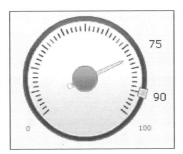

How it works...

As you can see, binding single values works in the same way as binding data series for charts. The gauge component can show more than one indicator and has the option to enter fixed values.

There is more...

Scaling

Single value components can be manually scaled or auto-scaled. There are four options for auto-scaling:

- ▶ Value-based: The limits cover a range around the value

- ▶ Zero-based: The higher limit is equal to the bound value, while the lower limit is zero

- ▶ Zero-centered: The limits cover a range that includes the value and its negative/positive with zero in the middle

- ▶ Alert-based: The limits are based on the selected alert method (see *Chapter 5* for more on using alerts)

3
From a Static to an Interactive Dashboard

In this chapter, we will cover:

- ▶ Drilling down from a chart
- ▶ Selecting your data from a list
- ▶ Using the filter selector component for hierarchies
- ▶ Alternative hierarchy selection method
- ▶ Using filtered rows
- ▶ Using maps to select data of an area or country
- ▶ Adding a MacOSX looking dock to your dashboard
- ▶ Resetting your data (reset button)
- ▶ Making selections from a custom image (push button and image component)
- ▶ Inputting data values
- ▶ Using the play selector/play control
- ▶ Opening up a Web intelligence report using dashboard parameters
- ▶ Selecting calendar dates
- ▶ Using sliders to create a what-if scenario

Introduction

An important strength that Dashboard Design has is the amount of control a developer can provide the user with. This leads to totally customized dashboards, which gives users the interactivity to help guide them to make the right business decisions. It is important that developers know what type of interactive tools are available so that they can utilize the power of these tools.

With the right interactivity, users are able to retrieve information more quickly and efficiently. This chapter will provide developers with recipes on interactivity, which will improve the dashboard user experience.

Drilling down from a chart

Being able to drilldown from higher level data to more granular detail is a very important feature in Dashboard Design. We want to be able to retrieve high level and granular level data easily without hunting for it. Using drilldowns, users can easily navigate through the different levels of data.

Getting ready

Insert two charts onto the canvas (Parent = Column Chart; Child = Line Chart). Data from the child chart is driven from the parent chart.

 Please refer to the example source file Drilling down from a `chart.xlf` on how to set up and bind the data appropriately to the charts.

How to do it...

1. In our example, the parent chart contains Regional Sales information. The child chart contains a drilldown of a monthly trend.

2. Turn on drilldown capability from the parent chart by clicking on the **Drill Down** icon and click on the **Enable Drill Down** check box.

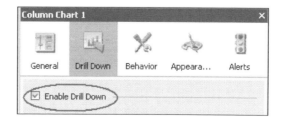

3. Select the **Insertion Type** that you will use for the drilldown bars. In our case, we will drill down based on type **Row** and bind to the line chart data on cells D6:I9. Then select the destination of the drilldown value. We have selected cells D3:I3 in our case.

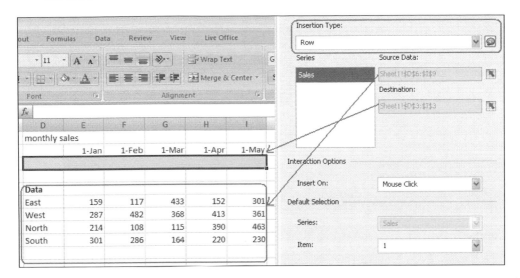

4. The destination cells D3:I3 control the chart data for our monthly trend data set as shown in the following image:

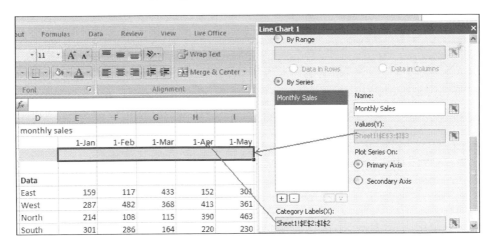

5. Preview the finished example and verify that the drilldown works by clicking on each bar of the **Regional Sales chart**.

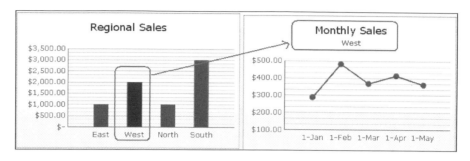

How it works...

In our example, we saw how to drill down from a set of regional sales to a monthly trend for a selected region. In the drilldown properties screen, the source rows D6:I9 from step 3 are linked to each bar. When a user clicks on the bar, it will select the appropriate row from D6:I9 and transfer it to the destination at D3:I3 where the child chart binds its data to.

There's more...

In our example, we had all the data available to us on the spreadsheet. We can also accomplish drill down capability on a query by sending in the drilldown parameter when clicking on a bar and then retrieving the appropriate child data.

Selecting your data from a list

Filtering data into a smaller dataset is a very important feature to implement when building dashboards. The reason being that people want to have a large amount of data available to them, but not to have to see all of it at once, otherwise it will become too overwhelming to the user and will require them to hunt for data, which is not the purpose of a dashboard.

In our example, we will be selecting from a list of regions that will populate a gauge value appropriately.

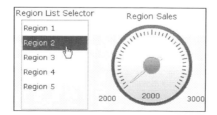

Getting ready

Have your data list set ready. In our example, we will show a simple list of five elements with corresponding values:

How to do it...

1. Select a **List Box** selector from the **Selectors** section of the **Components** window and drag it onto the canvas.

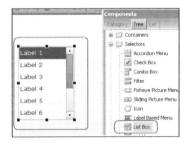

2. In the general section of the **List Box** selector, bind the labels to A2:A6, source data to B2:B6, and destination to D2 as shown on the image below. Select **Row** as the **Insertion Type**. The destination cell D2 will be the cell where the gauge is bound to.

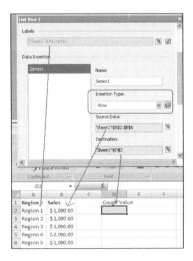

3. Drag a **Gauge** onto the canvas from the **Single Value | Gauge** section of the **Components** window. Bind the gauge data to cell D2.

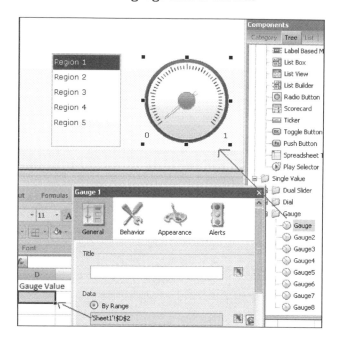

4. Preview and test your result.

How it works...

Selecting from a list of data using an Dashboard Design selector is quite easy, as you have seen in the earlier example. Basically, you'll need to have a set of labels to identify the list items you are selecting from. You will then need your source data that relates back to the list of items being selected from. In our example, we used a row one cell wide as the selected item type. If we wanted to, we could even choose a row that's 100 cells wide. Just try not go to go over a width of 512 cells, otherwise you may start running into performance issues. Finally, the destination in our example is one row as that is what we have selected as our Insertion Type.

There's more...

We just showed how to use the List Box selector. However, we could have used other selector components to accomplish the same task such as a combo box drop down, list view, label-based menu, spreadsheet table selector, and so on. It is important to choose the selectors that best fit your dashboard, visually.

In addition, for the Insertion Type. Dashboard Design allows us to use a large amount of Insert Types, whether it be by filtered rows, by row, by column, by label, by position number, and so on.

See also

For more detailed information on using the Filtered Row, which is an advanced Insertion Type, please refer to the *Using filtered row* recipe.

Using the Filter Selector component for hierarchies

Dashboard Design provides an easy to use selector component for hierarchical data. For example we may have a hierarchy that consists of a **Region | Sales District | Sales Office**. As shown in the following image, we can easily create this with the Dashboard Design Filter selector component tool:

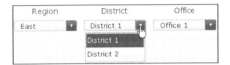

Getting ready

It is important to set up the data, as shown next, so that the filter component can consume it properly. Every row has to have the Region, Sales District, and Sales Office as well as the metric value(s) that you want populated on your destination. I've highlighted the destination portion in yellow and the filter related stuff in blue. Information on how everything works can be found in the *How it works* section.

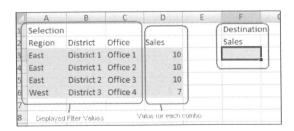

How to do it...

1. Add a **Filter selector** component onto the canvas and on the properties set the **Number of Filters** on the bottom to **3** as our hierarchy has three levels:

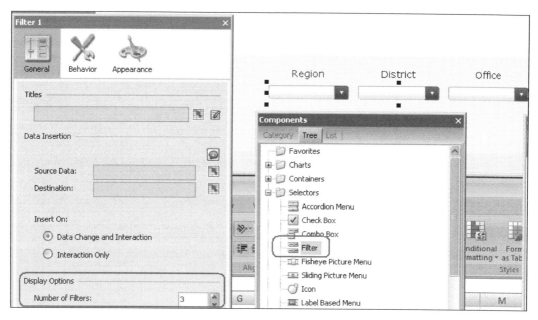

2. Bind the source data to the area in blue A3:D6 from the data set up in the *Getting ready* section.

3. Bind the destination to the cell F3 highlighted in yellow.

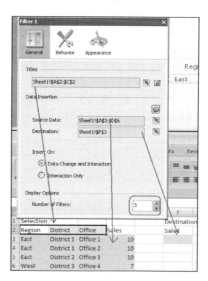

4. Insert a **Label Text** object onto the canvas and bind it to destination cell F3. Preview and make sure the filter component works

How it works...

The filter selector component works by grouping values in each column of the source data. In our example we selected three filters, so the first three columns of the source data will consist of the three hierarchies. The main parent is the Region, and then we branch down to the District, and finally, the Office.

Now that we are familiar with the blue portion from the image in the *Getting ready* section in this recipe, *Using the Filter Selector component for hierarchies,* we'll explain what the yellow portion is. The yellow destination can be of arbitrary width and will consist of metrics or values associated with the particular hierarchy combination chosen. For example, if we select **East | District | Office 1**, it will retrieve the values corresponding to that combination row.

Note that the destination width is the same width as the second part of the source data, which in our case is one column.

There's more...

The dropdown filter selection component isn't the only way to select from a hierarchical approach. We can also try a more advanced method found in the next recipe, *Alternative hierarchy selection method,* that will show the hierarchies in a set of list boxes. This may be the preferred approach if a user wants to see more than one value at a time. In addition, the recipe *Presenting Microcharts in a Tree Grid* shows users how a third-party component can accomplish a hierarchy selection using the familiar windows tree explorer.

Alternative hierarchy selection method

When navigating through a hierarchy selection, it is often that a user wants to see a list of available parents or children instead of only being able to see one at a time when looking at drop-down filters. Here is an alternative using the more complex listbox breadcrumb type approach for three levels:

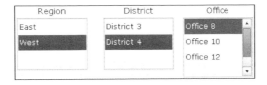

Getting ready

Set up the data as shown next. The blue section contains the initial full hierarchical data. The yellow section contains each breadcrumb trail whose source is one column less than the parent. More about how everything works will be explained in the *How it Works* section.

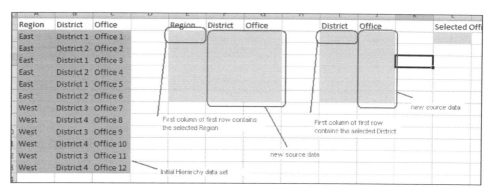

How to do it...

1. Insert three **List Box** selectors onto the canvas. On the first **List Box** selector, set the **Labels** to the **Region**, Column A, in blue.

2. Select **Filtered Rows** as the **Insertion Type** and set the **Source Data** to columns A to C. Set the **Destination** to columns E to G. Notice that we select all three source columns because the first row of the first column of the destination contains the selected region.

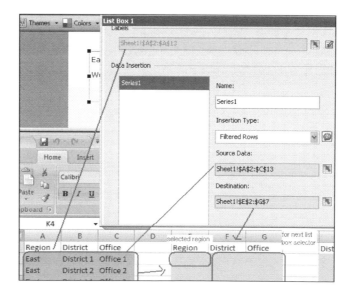

3. Do the same with the next list box, except we will select the labels and filtered rows from the new area columns E to G.

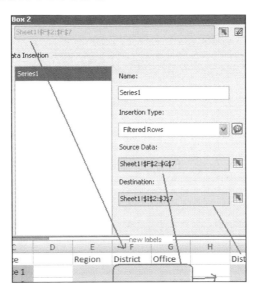

4. Finally, the last child **List Box** will be getting its **Labels** from column J. We can either use **Label** or **Row** as the **Insertion Type** as we are only down to one selection column.

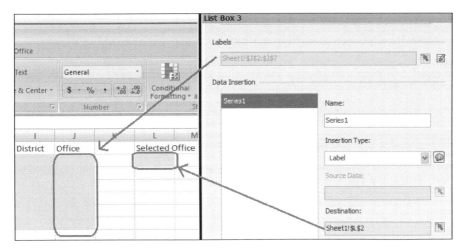

How it works...

In this example, each list box is a hierarchical level. In order to transfer all the appropriate values from one parent to the next data source, we must use the filtered rows method to grab all of the parent's children, until the last child where we can use label or row for the Insertion Type.

See also

For more detailed information on using Filtered Rows, read the *Using Filtered Rows* recipe.

Using Filtered Rows

Filtered Rows was one of the greatest additions to Xcelsius 2008 (*now SAP BusinessObjects Dashboards 4.0*) from Xcelsius 4.5. If we look at the following figure, we have a set of **Sales** metrics that are grouped by **Region** and **Office**:

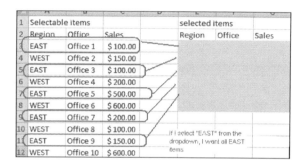

Let's say I wanted to be able to select a region and show a sales comparison chart between the different sales offices of that region. Before the advent of Filtered Rows, we would have to perform complex **VLOOKUPs** or have the result come back through a query every time a region is selected, which is very time consuming.

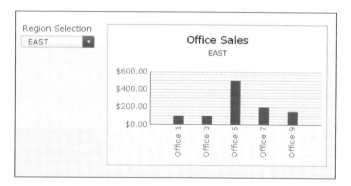

How to do it...

1. We will use a **Combo Box** selector to choose the desired region.

2. In the **Combo Box** selector properties, bind the **Labels** to the **Region** column circled in red.

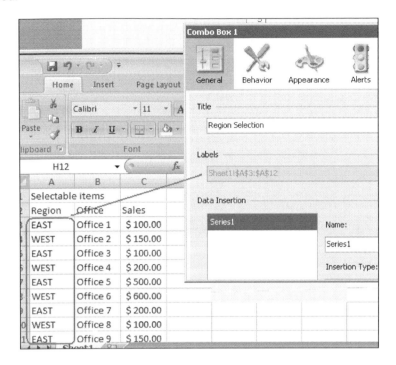

3. Select **Filtered Rows** as the **Insertion Type**. Bind **Source Data** to the area circled in red. The **Destination** will contain the chart values as well as the selected region.

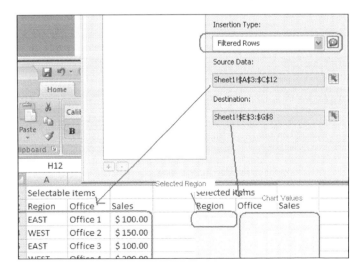

4. Bind the chart values to the **Destination section** from step 3.

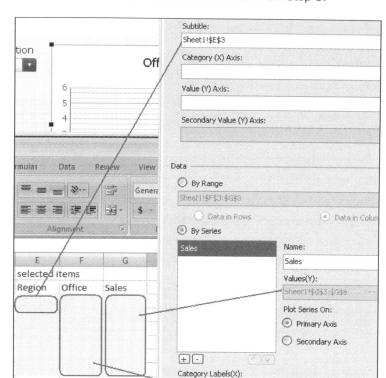

How it works...

The Filtered Rows Insertion Type allows users to select groupings of data easily without having to do complex VLOOKUP logic or a database querying; this allows for performance gains and ease of future maintenance.

Using maps to select data of an area or country

Maps are commonly used in dashboards to visually identify areas or regions. Using maps on a dashboard allows us to visually identify using a picture instead of a table/chart and see, for example, which regions are doing poorly versus which regions are doing well. As you can see looking at the map of Canada, users are able to visually distinguish between each province.

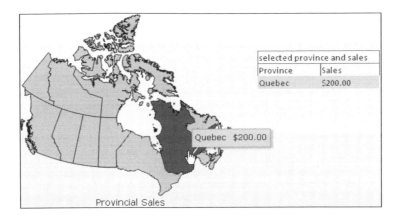

How to do it...

1. Select a map component from the **Maps** section. In our example, we will use Canada.

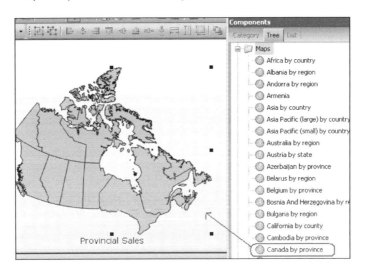

2. In the map properties, you will need to bind the region keys appropriately, as shown in the following spreadsheet:

Tip for finding the map regions

A full list of the region keys for each map included in Dashboard Design can be found in the `MapRegions.xls` spreadsheet in the `<install path>\Xcelsius\assets\samples\User Guide Samples\` directory.

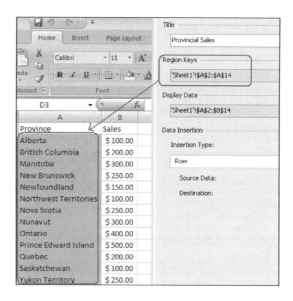

3. Next, bind the **Display data** which will be the key/value pair. The key comes from the key that you used in step 2 and the value can be any value associated to that key.

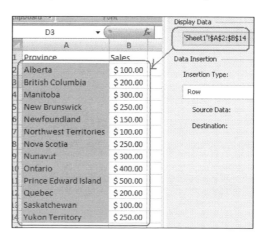

4. We will now need to bind the source data. Make sure that the first column of the source data contains the matching key value from step 2.

5. The **Destination** will be bound to the row highlighted in yellow, as shown in the following screenshot:

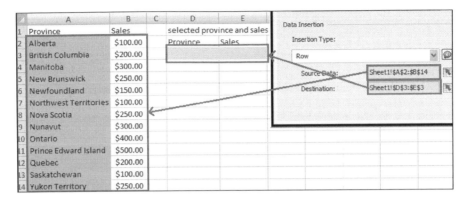

6. Now bind a spreadsheet table **Display Data** to the destination area in yellow. This will change according to the province you click on during runtime.

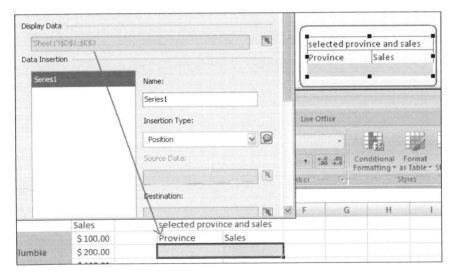

How it works...

The map component works by using a key/value pair that is assigned to each map section. It is important that the order of items bound to the **Region** section is in alphabetical order. Otherwise the wrong keys will be bound. For example, looking at the following image, Yukon and Nova Scotia are in the wrong alphabetical order, thus the key/value pair will be incorrect:

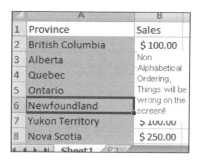

The display data section in step 3 is used to show what will be displayed when a user hovers the mouse over a region. There are two columns that can be shown (key/value). The key must match a key from what was bound to the Region data, otherwise it will not show up.

Finally, we have our **Source Data**, and again we must have a matching key at the first column in order to match the correct row.

There's more...

To make the visualization even better for a map component, it is common to use alert coloring to show how the provinces are doing. To accomplish this, please read the recipe *Displaying alerts on a map*.

Adding a MacOSX loading dock to your dashboard

It is well known that Macs have a great user interface and one of the great things they have in particular is the program loading dock. We can emulate this in Dashboard Design using the **Fisheye Picture Menu**. But why would someone want to use the loading dock? Well, you can use the loading to switch between dashboards on the main dashboard. You can use it to open up another dashboard, or you can use it as a selector to change your charts or data. In this recipe, we are going to emulate the swapping between dashboards.

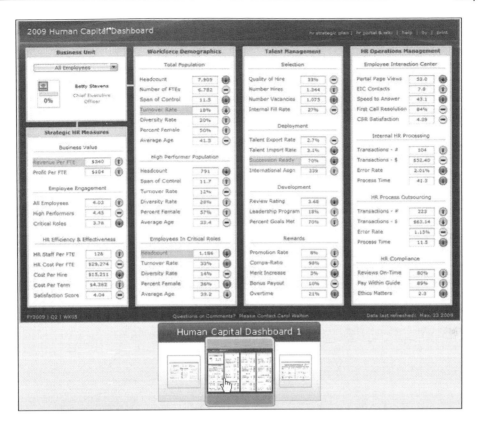

How to do it...

1. Select the **Fisheye Picture Menu** selector.

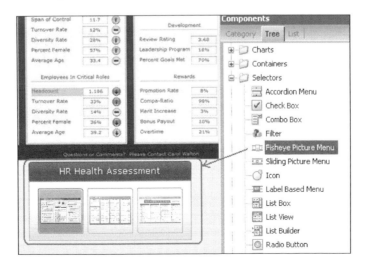

2. We'll need to link an image of each dashboard to the **Fisheye Picture Menu**. To do this, press the **Import** button on the **Images | Embedded** section of the fisheye menu properties. In our example, we are using three dashboards, so click on the **Click to Add Images** button to load each of the three dashboard images.

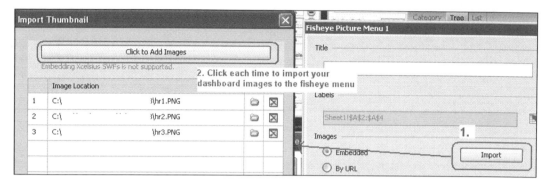

3. Bind the **Labels** to the spreadsheet, as shown, so that the user knows the name of the dashboard when they hover the mouse over any of the icons.

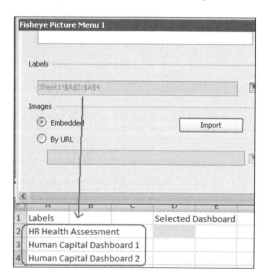

4. Bind the **Source Data** and **Destination**. In this case, we are just using the **Position** for the source. The destination will be bound to cell D2.

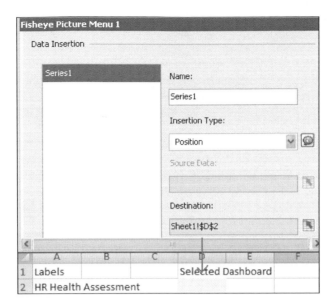

5. Set the dynamic visibility of each dashboard to the corresponding position of the **Fisheye Picture Menu** selector. For example the **HR Health Assessment** dashboard has position 1, so in the dashboard properties, the dynamic visibility should be set to **1** for cell D2.

How it works...

The **Fisheye Picture Menu** is a very simple component that emulates the MacOSX loading dock by allowing users to scroll through icons that will zoom in as you mouse over them. As outlined in step 2, we can see that we have to bind the images that are similar to program icons. Those icons are linked to the source data in step 4.

There's more...

There is another component called the *Sliding Picture* menu that acts the same way and is set up the same way as the Fisheye Picture Menu, except that you don't get the 'zoom mouse-over' feature.

Resetting your data (reset button)

It is common that a user may want to go back to their default or starting point view. Let's say I have five selectors and modified all five of them. To get back to the starting point would be a pain. Thus, having a one-click approach to go back to the default can be useful.

How to do it...

- Select the **Reset Button** from the **Other Components** section and drag it onto the canvas.

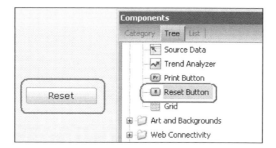

How it works...

When you first load the dashboard, the state of the first load is remembered. So when you click on the **Reset** button, it will go back to the original state.

Making selections from a custom image (push button and image component)

As shown in the recipe _Adding a MacOSX looking dock to your dashboard_, we can use a Fisheye selector menu to emulate a program dock-type style when selecting items. However, there may be cases where we may want images in different locations that we can click on to perform different actions.

In this recipe, we will go through an example on how to use a push button combined with an image component to create a clickable image that can perform actions when clicked on.

How to do it...

1. Drag an **Image Component** from the **Arts and Backgrounds** section of the **Components** window onto the canvas.

2. Open up the image properties window and click on the **Import** button. Select the image from your computer that you want to show.

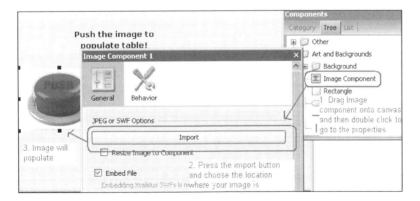

3. Drag a **Push Button** object from the **Selectors** section of the **Components** window and put it on top of the image. Then resize the **Push Button** so that it is the same size as the image. To make the button the same size as the image, use the sizing icons on the toolbar circled in red. Make sure you click on the image first and then the push button in order for the push button to match the sizing properties of the image and not the other way around.

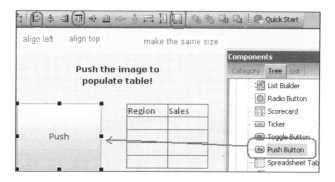

4. On the **Push Button** properties, first bind the **Source Data** and **Destination** data to the appropriate cells. In our example, we want to transfer the table data from the yellow section to the destination section highlighted in black. Also, in the **Label** section, don't forget to delete all text.

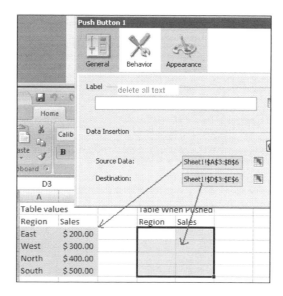

5. Go to the **Appearance** tab of the push button and set the **Transparency** to **100%** and uncheck the **Show Button Background** checkbox.

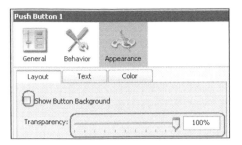

6. Drag a **Spreadsheet Table** component onto the canvas and bind it to the destination cells D2:E6 of the push button.

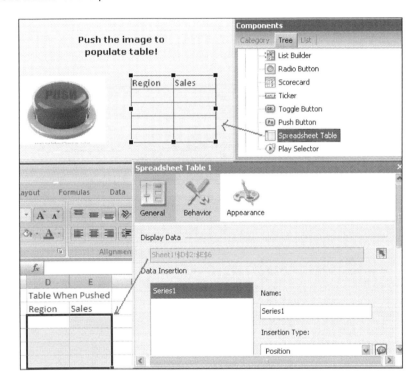

7. Preview and make sure that when you click on the image, the details of the image show up on the table.

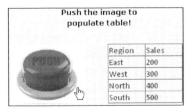

How it works...

In this recipe, we overlay a push button on top of an image component. By default, an image component can't perform any actions, however with an invisible push button on top, it will seem as though we can click on the image to perform an action.

See Also

For more information on formatting objects in terms of sizing and alignment setting appearance of objects, please read *Chapter, 7 Dashboard Look and Feel.*

Inputting data values

The ability to input values into a dashboard is a very useful feature. An example of a useful situation is when a user wants to enter an exact value through a large range of numbers onto a 'what-if' scenario instead of having to scroll. Another good example could be a search box to find a value on a selector that has over 100 items. This way, you don't need to hunt for your value and just type it in.

In this recipe, we will create an input text box to control a what-if scenario.

Getting ready

Create a chart with its values bound to cells that will be controlled by the input text box value. An example of a sales forecast chart and its cells that are controlled by the what-if scenario is shown as follows:

D6				f_x	=IF(ISNUMBER(D3),IF(AND(D3>=-20,D3<=20),D3,"INVALID"			
A	B	C	D	E	F	G	H	I
Region	Sales		What-if input		Region	Sales		
EAST	$ 100.00		0		EAST	$ 100.00		
WEST	$ 80.00				WEST	$ 80.00		
NORTH	$ 120.00		valid value		NORTH	$ 120.00		
SOUTH	$ 90.00		0		SOUTH	$ 90.00		

You may refer to the source file Inputting data `values.xlf` to retrieve the pre-populated data from the earlier image, if you don't want to manually type everything in yourself.

How to do it...

1. Drag an **Input Text** object from the **Text** section of the **Components** window onto the canvas.

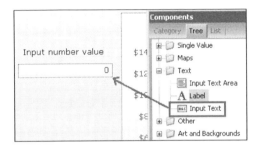

2. On the properties window of the **Input Text** component, bind the **Link to Cell** and **Destination** to the yellow cell D3 from the _Getting ready_ section.

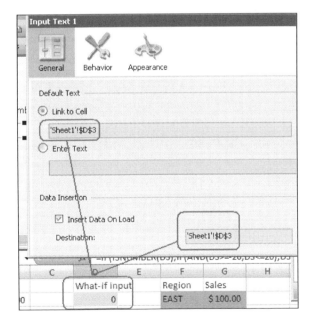

3. Go to the **Behavior** icon of the input text properties and make sure **Treat All Input As Text** is unchecked.

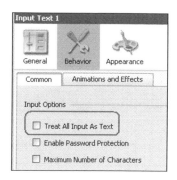

4. The blue cell D6 from the *Getting ready* section that's labeled as **valid value** will check to make sure the input text entered by the user is valid. To do this, we use the formula **=IF(ISNUMBER(D3),IF(AND(D3>=-20,D3<=20),D3,"INVALID"),"INVALID")**.

The formula checks to make sure that the cell contains a number and is between -20 and 20.

Now every cell in the chart-binding destination will depend on D6. The binding destination cells will not add the D6 value if D6 is "INVALID". In addition, a pop up will show up saying "Input is invalid" if D6 is "INVALID".

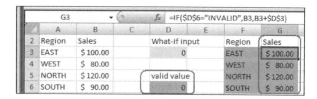

Create the pop up by dragging a label text component onto the canvas with **Input is invalid** as its text. Next, go to the behavior tab and for dynamic visibility, bind it to **D6** and set the **Key** as **INVALID**.

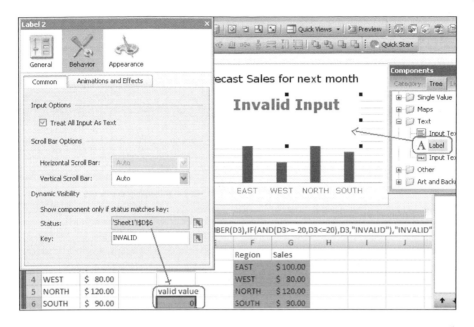

How it works...

In this example, we use an input value text box to control the forecast bars on the chart. If we type 20, it will add 20 to each value in the forecast. If we type -20, it will subtract 20 from each value in the forecast.

We also add a check in step 4 that determines whether the value entered is valid or not. Hence, the reason for using the Excel formulas. If a value is invalid, we want to output an error to the user so that they are aware that they entered an invalid value.

		f_x	=IF(ISNUMBER(D3),IF(AND(D3>=-20,D3<=20),D3,"INVALID"),"INVALID")					
	D	E	F	G	H	I	J	
Non-numeric is invalid			Forecast Chart					
	What-if input		Region	Sales				
	aa		EAST	$ 100.00				
			WEST	$ 80.00				
	valid value		NORTH	$ 120.00				
	INVALID		SOUTH	$ 90.00				

See also

For more information on Dynamic visibility, please read the *Chapter 5, Dynamic visibility.*

Using Play Selector/Play Control

The Play Selector component can be used when you want to change chart values or components on a dashboard without having the user do anything. Some common uses where we need an automatic change of components are listed as follows:

▶ A company dashboard presented on a large LCD monitor in a company common room. This dashboard will refresh or switch views every 20-30 seconds.

▶ A dashboard at a technical support office that shows information on calls coming in and how they are being handled. This dashboard changes views every 20-30 seconds.

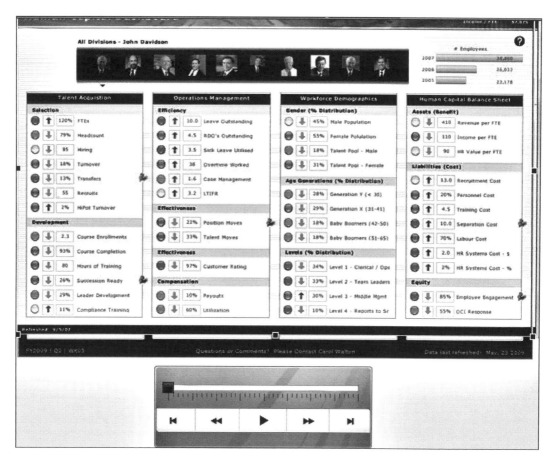

In this recipe, we will create a play selector that changes the image every 20 seconds. We can pretend that the images are different dashboards.

Getting ready

Have a set of three images ready on the canvas and overlay them on top of each other.

 There are three dashboard images that you may use for this example. They are `hr1.png`, `hr2.png`, and `hr3.png`, and can be found in the `images` folder.

How to do it...

1. Drag a **Play Selector** component from the **Selector** section of the **Components** window onto the canvas.

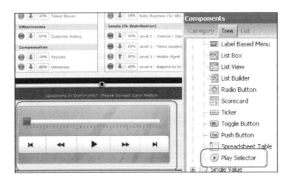

2. In the **Play Selector** properties, select **Row** as the **Insertion Type** and bind the **Source Data** to the dynamic visibility rows that are set up in Column A of the spreadsheet. Bind the **Destination** to the yellow-colored cell C2, which will control the image shown:

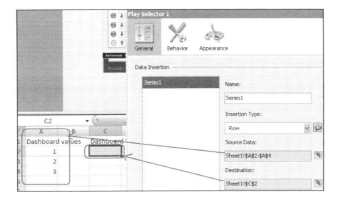

3. Go to the **Behavior** icon of the **Play Selector** properties and check the **Auto Play** checkbox. Change the **Play Time** value to **20** seconds.

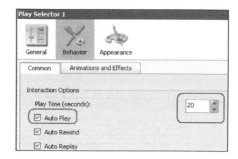

4. Go to the **Appearance** icon of the **Play Selector** properties and set the **Transparency** to **100%**. Also, uncheck all the available checkboxes.

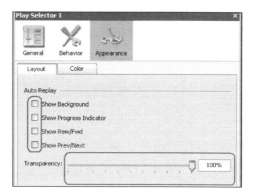

5. On each of the image components, set the **Dynamic Visibility** status binding on the **Behavior** icon to the yellow colored destination cell C2 from step 2. The key values will be **1**, **2**, or **3** depending on what order you want your images to play at. In the following image, I've shown the dynamic visibility example for the first dashboard:

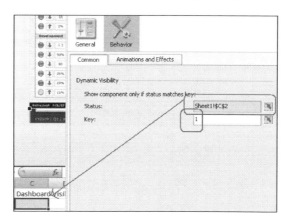

How it works...

In this example, we use a play selector to control which image is being shown. Each iteration of the play selector control is linked to one of the rows that we set up in the source data in step 2. In step 4, we set the transparency of the play selector to 100% because we want to hide the play selector but still have it active. Finally, in step 5, we configure the dynamic visibilities of the images appropriately so the correct one will show up as the play selector runs.

See also

To learn how to use dynamic visibility, please read *Chapter 5, Dynamic Visibility*.

Opening up a Web Intelligence report using dashboard parameters

It is important to distinguish the difference between a dashboard and a report. A dashboard should be a one page visualization of the most important data a user needs to see. A report contains details that are usually to the lowest granularity, thus should remain at the SAP BusinessObjects Web Intelligence (WEBI) report level. It is a common dashboard requirement to drill down from a chart or scorecard to view individual detail items. Instead of showing the detailed items on the dashboard, we can pop up a WEBI report using parameters passed from the dashboard. In this example, we will pop up a WEBI report using one input parameter from the Dashboard Design dashboard.

Getting ready

A WEBI report with a prompt must be set up first. In our example, the WEBI report will ask for a Region parameter.

 You can use the source file Opening up a Web Intelligence report using dashboard `parameters.xlf` as a reference to help guide you through the OpenDoc URL construction part of the recipe.

How to do it...

1. Drag a **Combo Box** selector onto the canvas and bind the label values to the list of **Regions** on the Excel spreadsheet, as shown in the next screenshot. Set **Label** as the **Insertion Type** and bind the **Destination** to the cell highlighted in yellow, which will be the input parameter passed to the OpenDoc call.

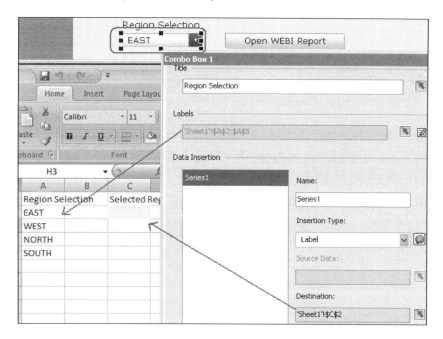

2. Log into BI Launch Pad (formerly Infoview) and go to the location of where the Web Intelligence report is located. Right-click and select **Properties**.

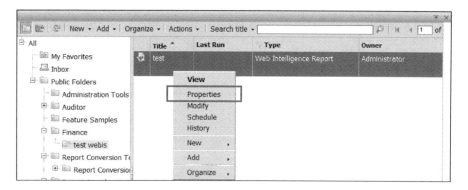

3. Copy the **CUID**.

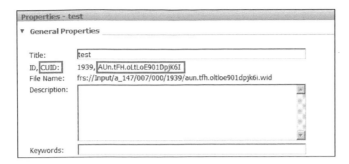

4. On cell B14, shown as follows, an OpenDoc URL is constructed. Paste the **CUID** from step 3 into cell B23 highlighted in gray. Cell C23 equals the **Selected Region** cell C2 from step 1.

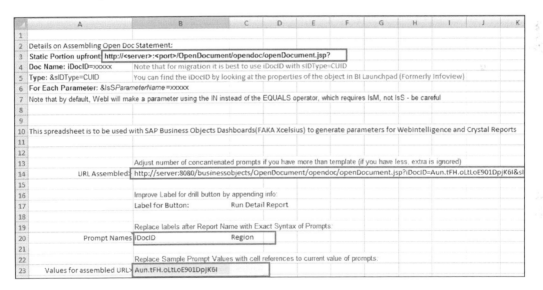

5. Drag a **URL Button** component onto the canvas from the **Web Connectivity** section of the **Components** window. In the **URL Button** properties, change the **Label** text to **Open WEBI report**, and bind the URL to the OpenDoc URL cell B14 from step 2.

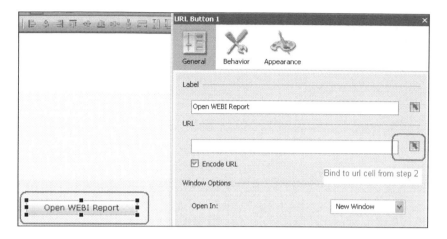

How it works...

In this example, we use what is called an OpenDoc call to open up a WEBI report with our desired input parameter from the dashboard.

The OpenDoc URL is very complex, where there are many options that you can choose from to build the URL, and is out of the scope of this cookbook, so it is best to read the OpenDoc manual in order to get a list of all the options and how to use them. You can find the URLs to retrieve the OpenDoc manual in the *See also* section next.

To open up an external link from the dashboard, the **URL Button** component is used.

An example of a fully constructed URL is as follows:

```
http://server:8080/businessobjects/OpenDocument/opendoc/openDocument.
jsp?iDocID=Aun.tFH.oLtLoE901DpjK6I&sIDType=CUID&lsSRegion=EAST
```

There's more...

The syntax for OpenDoc on SAP BusinessObjects XIR2 is different than for XI 3.1+. Thus, the way you construct the URL will be different for both versions; however, the concept is the same. In this recipe, the OpenDoc URL was generated for Business Objects Enterprise XI 3.1+.

See also

See also

Please go to `http://help.sap.com/businessobject/product_guides/boexir31/` `en/xi3-1_url_reporting_opendocument_en.pdf` to retrieve the OpenDoc manual for Business Objects XI 3.1.

For the Business Objects XI R2 OpenDoc manual, go to `http://resources.` `businessobjects.com/support/communitycs/TechnicalPapers/boe_xi_` `opendocument.pdf`.

For a template on using OpenDoc on Xcelsius please download it from here: `http://www.` `davidlai101.com/blog/media/blogs/bobj/opendoc/OpenDoc_Template.xls`.

Selecting calendar dates

Calendars are a common component found in dashboards if a user is interested in seeing values on a particular day. This is great for going back in history to see our past performance.

In this example, we will work with one month of data for September 2010 and the chart will change according to what the user selects on the calendar.

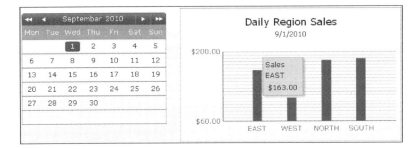

Getting ready

The spreadsheet portion containing the chart data will need to be set up in the following fashion. Each row of chart data will belong to a selectable day in the calendar. In this example, each row contains region sales data for a particular date.

	A	B	C	D	E
2	Date	EAST	WEST	NORTH	SOUTH
3	1-Sep	$163.00	$107.00	$183.00	$186.00
4	2-Sep	$182.00	$294.00	$147.00	$268.00
5	3-Sep	$260.00	$134.00	$112.00	$242.00
6	4-Sep	$109.00	$250.00	$161.00	$129.00
7	5-Sep	$298.00	$247.00	$239.00	$292.00

How to do it...

1. Drag a **Calendar** component from the **Other** section of the **Components** window onto the canvas.

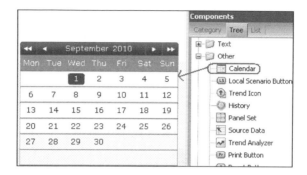

2. In the **Calendar** properties, select **Date** as the **Insertion Type** and bind the **Destination** to the cell G3 of the spreadsheet, as shown next:

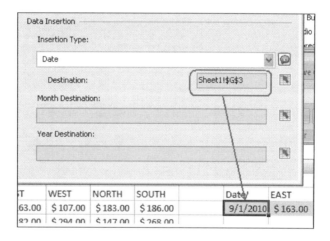

3. Now, we will need to take the value from the destination date cell G3 in step 2 to find the corresponding row data from the *Getting Ready* section. To do this, drag a **Combo Box** selector onto the canvas. In the **Combo Box** properties, select **Row** as the **Insertion Type** and bind **Source Data** to the chart data set. Then bind the **Destination** to the cells to the spreadsheet area in yellow (H3:K3). You will also need to set the **Labels** to the date values of the dataset.

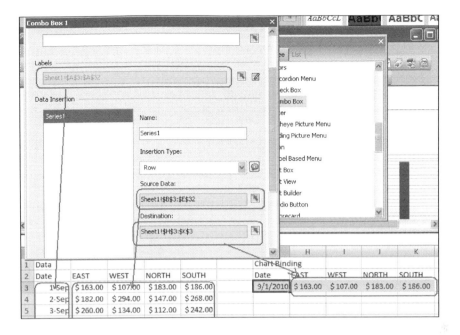

4. On the **Behavior** icon of the combo box selector, bind the **Item** from the **Selected Item** area to the **Destination** cell G3 of the Calendar set from step 2. Then drag the **Combo Box** selector to the same position as the chart, and order the **Combo Box** selector to the **back** so that the user cannot see the **Combo Box** selector during runtime.

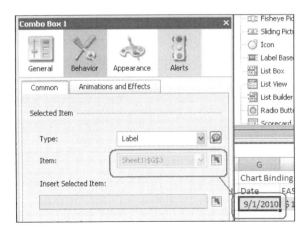

5. Bind the **Chart** data to the chart destination cells H3:K3 from step 3.

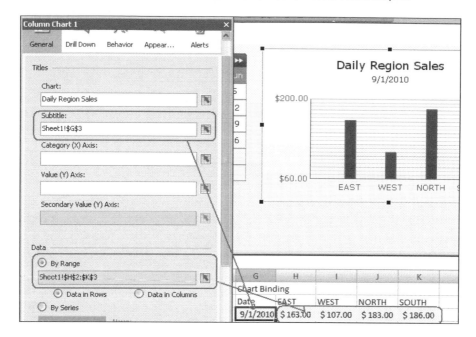

How it works...

In this example we use a combination of a calendar date component, a combo box selector, and a column chart component. The calendar date component controls the date selected in step 1. Then the combo box selector will connect the date to the appropriate data row from the chart data set in steps 3 and 4. Finally in step 5, the chart is bound to the correct data row that was selected in steps 3 and 4.

See also

You can read recipes on using a chart object to display data and how to use the combo box selector in *Chapter 2, Data Visualization*.

Using sliders to create a what-if scenario

What-if scenarios are very important as they allows users to project what future values will look like, depending on one or more variables.

In our recipe, we will reuse the simple what-if scenario from the recipe *Inputting data values*. The only difference here is that we will use a horizontal slider instead of inputting the values with text.

Getting ready

Set up the sales data, as shown circled in red in the following screenshot, and have a column chart ready on the canvas:

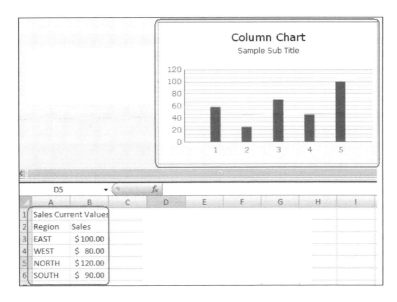

How to do it...

1. Insert a **Horizontal Slider** component from the **Single Value – Horizontal Slider** section of the **Components** window.

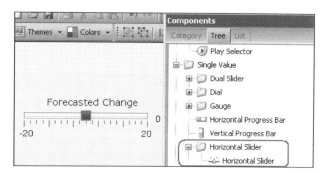

2. Set the **Title** text to **Forecasted Change**. Bind the **Data** to cell D3 highlighted in yellow. Set the **Minimum Limit** to **-20** and **Maximum Limit** to **20** on the **Scale** section.

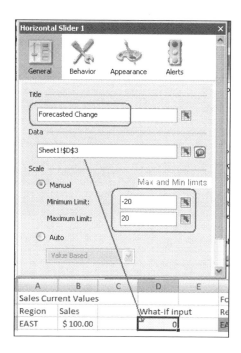

3. Go to the **Appearance** section of the slider properties and make sure that the **Limits checkbox** is checked.

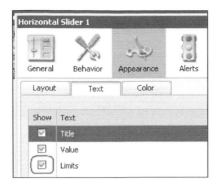

4. Now in the **blue chart data area**, each formula will be adding the what-if value D3 to the chart data values B3:B6 prepared in the *Getting ready* section.

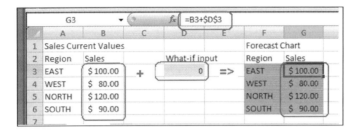

5. Bind the **Forecast Chart values in blue** to the **Chart component** and then preview.

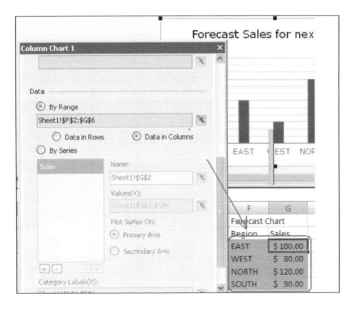

How it works...

In this example, the slider controls the what-if value on cell D3. The chart data cells G3:G6 then use the appropriate calculation—taking the user what-if rate, adding it to the current sales value, and displays the correct chart data.

See also

For a more complex 'what-if' example, read the *What-if example* in *Appendix A*.

4
Dynamic Visibility

In this chapter, we will cover:

- ▸ Switching between different charts
- ▸ Building a pop-up screen
- ▸ Creating a mouse-over help text pop up
- ▸ Password protecting your dashboard

Introduction

Dynamic visibility makes it possible to control the visibility of components. With this functionality, a component can be made visible or hidden on a running dashboard, based on a status value that is inserted in a certain spreadsheet cell.

Dynamic visibility is useful when your dashboard contains many visual components and you don't want to overload the user with information. Usually, it is used in combination with selectors that let the users choose what they want to see and when.

Switching between different charts

This recipe will show you how to create a dashboard with the possibility to switch between two charts.

Getting ready

Open a new Dashboard Design file and drag two different chart components (for example, a line chart and a pie chart component) to the empty canvas. Drag the label-based menu component to the canvas, as well.

How to do it...

1. Click on the line chart component and go to the **Behavior** tab of its properties pane. At the bottom of the pane, you will see a section called **Dynamic Visibility**.

2. Bind the **Status** field to spreadsheet cell B1.

3. Put the value **1** in the **Key** field.

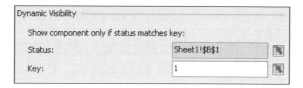

4. Click on the pie chart component and go to the **Behavior** tab.

5. Here you also bind the **Status** field to cell B1.

6. In the **Key** field, you fill in the value **2**.

7. Go to the spreadsheet and type **Status:** in cell A1 and put value **1** in cell B1.

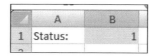

8. Now click on the label-based menu component and go to the **General** tab of its properties pane.

9. To set the labels, click on the button on the extreme right-hand side.

10. Enter two labels: **Trend** and **Division**. Make sure that **Trend** has the first position and **Division** has the second position. You can change this by using the little arrows on the bottom left-hand side of the window.

11. In the **Data Insertion** area, set the **Insertion Type** to **Position**.

12. Bind the **Destination** field to spreadsheet cell B1.

13. Click on the **Preview** button to run the dashboard. You will now only see the label component. If you click on line chart or pie chart the selected chart will appear. Now leave the preview mode.

14. To display an initial chart (shown before the first selection) you have to deselect the **Clear Destination When No Selected Item** option in the **General** tab of the properties of the label-based menu component.

15. Place both charts on top of each other. Use the options in the **Format** menu for precise alignment and sizing.

16. Try your dashboard!

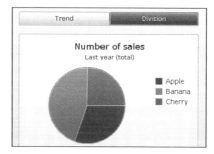

How it works...

In this recipe, we used one of the selector components in combination with dynamic visibility functionality to switch between the two charts. Each chart got a unique key assigned: value 1 for the line chart and value 2 for the pie chart. By making a selection in the label-based menu selector, either the value 1 or the value 2 was put in spreadsheet cell B1. The **Dynamic Visibility** setup in this recipe implies that if cell B1 has value 1, the line chart will be shown. If cell B1 has value 2, the pie chart will be shown.

Thus, a component is hidden when any other value than its key is entered in the status cell.

There's more...

Other components

This recipe used two chart components with **Dynamic Visibility** settings. But, the dynamic visibility functionality is embedded in all other Dashboard Design components too, except for the source data component. You can even use **Dynamic Visibility** with grouped components to dynamically show or hide a group of components!

Status values

Besides numerical values, you can use any value you want as a dynamic visibility key for a component. If you do this, make sure you also change the Insertion Type of your selector component into label. Of course the labels should be exactly the same as the values used for the keys.

Building a pop-up screen

This recipe will show how a pop-up screen can be created within a dashboard. Such a pop-up screen can, for example, be used to provide additional information to the contents of the dashboard. In this recipe, the pop-up screen can be activated and deactivated by clicking on buttons.

Getting ready

No specific preparation is needed for this recipe. You can use any dashboard you already created or just start with an empty one. In this example, we will use the dashboard from the previous recipe.

How to do it...

1. Drag a background component into the canvas.

2. Drag the label component on top of the background component and enter some text.

3. Now drag a push button component into the canvas and position it in the upper right-hand side corner of the background component. Rename its label into **Close**. We will use this button to close the pop-up screen.

    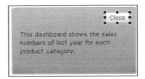

4. Set up the spreadsheet: Enter value **1** in cell E1 and value **0** in cell E2.

5. Bind the **Source Data** field of the push button component properties to spreadsheet cell E2 and bind the **Destination** field to cell E3.

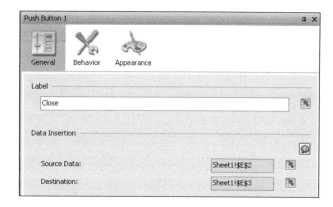

6. Group the three components (see the recipe *Grouping the canvas components* in *Chapter 1, Staying in Control*).

7. Add another push button component to the canvas and rename its label as **Info**. This button will be used to activate the pop-up screen.

Bind the **Source Data** field of this second push button component to spreadsheet cell E1 and bind the **Destination** field to cell E3.

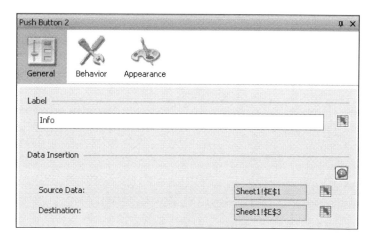

8. Now we are a ready to set up the dynamic visibility functionality. Select the grouped components and go to the properties pane. You will see only one **Common** tab now. Bind the **Status** field to spreadsheet cell E3. Also, put the value **1** in the **Key** field.

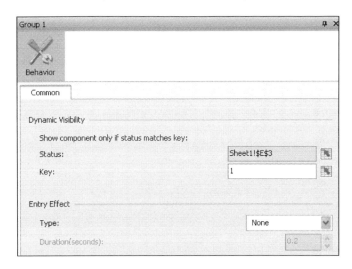

9. Preview the dashboard to test the functionality!

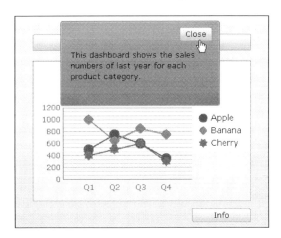

How it works...

In this recipe, we combined the push button functionality with dynamic visibility. The three grouped components are only visible when the **Dynamic Visibility** status is **1** (spreadsheet cell E3). When clicking on the push button **Info**, the value 1 is put into spreadsheet cell E3. Now the grouped components appear. After clicking on the **Close** push button, the value 0 is put into this cell and the grouped components will disappear as the status cell does not match value 1 anymore.

There's more...

After clicking on the **Info** push button, the pop-up screen appears. Now this button does not have any useful functionality: Nothing happens if you click it as the pop-up screen is already active. To make this button disappear, you can easily use the dynamic visibility functionality you already set up!

1. Go to the **Behavior** tab of the **Info** push button properties pane.
2. Bind the **Status** field to spreadsheet cell E3 and enter value 0 into the **Key** field.
3. Now preview the dashboard to see the effect.

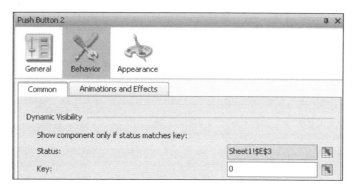

Creating a mouse-over help text pop-up

This recipe shows how you can create a pop-up screen that is activated by moving the mouse over a certain area of the dashboard. This can be handy if you want to add some minor additional information on a specific part or functionality of the dashboard.

Getting ready

No specific preparation is needed for this recipe. You can use any dashboard you already created or just start with an empty one. In this example we are reusing the dashboard we created in the previous two recipes.

How to do it...

1. Drag a chart component (for example a pie chart component) into the canvas. If you are using an existing dashboard you can use one of the components of your dashboard instead.
2. Drag a label component into the canvas and enter the text you want to show.
3. Go to the properties pane of this label component. Select the **Appearance** tab and select the **Show Fill** option.

4. After this, select the **Show Border** option and set the **Border Thickness** to **2**.

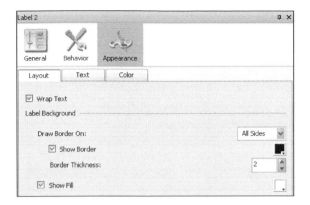

5. Move the label component over the chart.

6. Now drag a toggle button component into the canvas and position it on top of the title of the chart you added to the canvas in step 1. Resize it so that it covers the total area above the chart, as shown in the following screenshot:

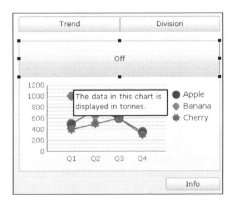

7. In the **Toggle Button** properties pane, go to the **General** tab. Bind the **Destination** option to spreadsheet cell H1.

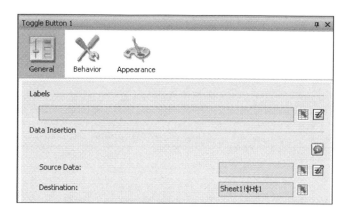

8. Put value **0** in cell H1:

9. Now go to the **Behavior** tab. Under **Interaction Options** in the **Common** menu, change **Mouse Click** to **Mouse Over**.

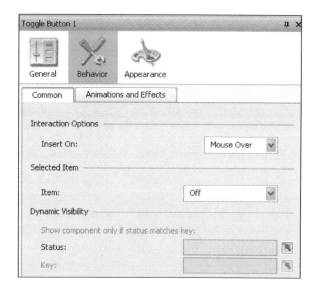

10. Now go to the **Appearance** tab and set the **Transparency** to **100%** under the **Layout** menu.

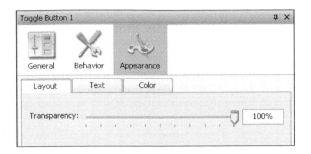

11. Also, under the **Text** menu within the **Appearance** tab, deselect the **Show Labels** option. Now the component won't be visible anymore on the canvas.

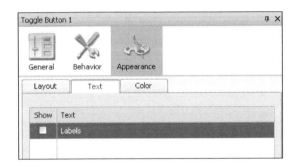

12. To finish this recipe, we have to set up the dynamic visibility functionality for the label component. First, select the label component. Go to the **Behavior** tab in the properties pane. Within the **Dynamic Visibility** section, bind the **Status** field to spreadsheet cell H1. Also put value **1** into the **Key** field.

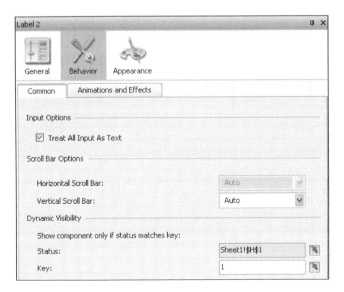

13. Now your dashboard is ready to be tested. Hit the **Preview** button and see what happens!

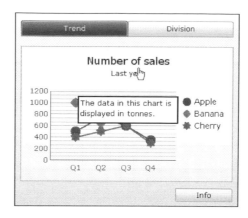

How it works

For this recipe, we used the toggle button functionality in combination with dynamic visibility. Also, instead of clicking on the toggle button to activate it, we switched the insertion trigger from **Mouse Click** to **Mouse Over**. If you run the dashboard and hover the mouse over the upper part of the dashboard, the toggle button component will put value 1 in spreadsheet cell H1. This cell triggers the dynamic visibility of the label component that will now appear.

If you go to the properties pane of the toggle button component, you can set the **Source Data**, which is in the **General** tab. Here, you can define which values should be put into the **Destination** cell.

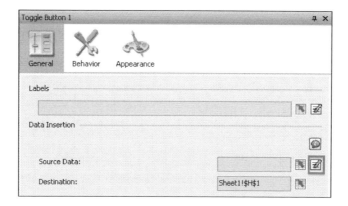

The following screenshot shows the source data table:

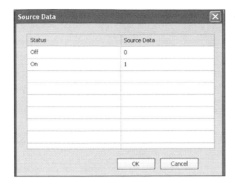

 Keep in mind that if you cover a certain section of your dashboard with a toggle button component to evoke this **Mouse Over** activation, the interactivity options of the underlying components cannot be used anymore!

Password protecting your dashboard

In this recipe, we will look at a scenario that uses some basic login functionality for an Dashboard Design dashboard. Before you can use the actual functionality of the dashboard, a password has to be entered.

Getting ready

For this recipe you can use any dashboard you created before. We will use the dashboard we created in the previous recipes.

How to do it...

1. Drag a rectangle component into the canvas and resize it so that it covers the whole dashboard.

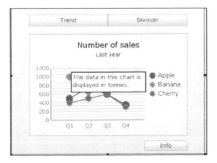

2. Go to the properties pane of the rectangle component and switch the **Type** setting from **None** to **Solid**. You can also change the color and the level of transparency here.

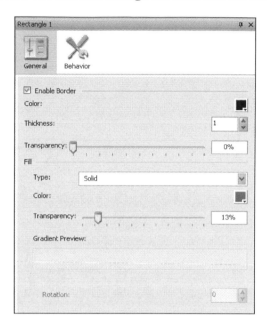

3. The result should look like the following screenshot:

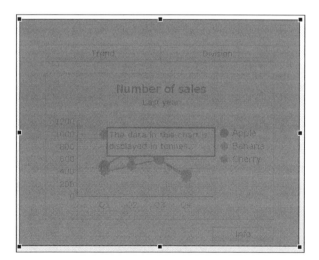

4. Add a label component to the canvas and place it in the middle of the dashboard.

5. Enter the following text: **Please enter your password:**. In the **Layout** menu of the **Appearance** tab, you can check the **Show Fill** option to show a background color for this component.

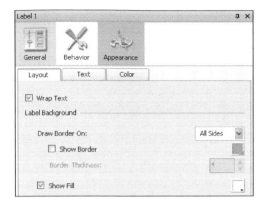

The canvas should look like the following screenshot:

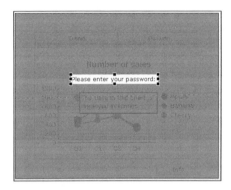

6. Now add an input text component and place it below the label component. In the **General** tab of the properties pane, you should bind the **Destination** field to spreadsheet cell K2. In the **Behavior** tab, check the option to **Enable Password Protection**. This ensures that only asterisks (*) are displayed when the user enters the password.

7. Select the three components you just added and group them.

8. Go to the properties pane for the grouped components. It is time to set up **Dynamic Visibility**. Bind the **Status** option to spreadsheet cell K1. Enter value **1** in the **Key** field.

9. Now we have to set up some Excel logic to make this work. In spreadsheet cell K1, enter the following formula: **=IF(K2="YourPassword",0,1)**, where 'YourPassword' should be replaced with a password of your choice.

10. Your spreadsheet should now look like this:

11. Hit the **Preview** button and try to log in to this dashboard by entering your password.

How it works...

In this recipe, the dynamic visibility functionality is now used to make some parts of the dashboard disappear instead of showing them. The dynamic visibility status is now set by an Excel formula. This if then' formula checks whether the value in the input text component matches **YourPassword** or not. If it does match, the result of the formula will be a 0 and the layer we put on top of the dashboard will disappear. Now you can use the dashboard.

This is a method that can be used to protect your dashboard for unauthorized access. However, in an enterprise environment, when the Dashboard Design dashboard is published in SAP BusinessObjects Enterprise, the security is managed by the BusinessObjects Enterprise platform.

5
Using Alerts

In this chapter, we will cover:

- ▶ Adding alerts to a column chart
- ▶ Using alerts in a gauge
- ▶ Making alert ranges dynamic
- ▶ Displaying alerts on a map
- ▶ Displaying alerts of different thresholds on a map
- ▶ Using bindable colors to control alert coloring from a central location
- ▶ Using alerts in a scorecard

Introduction

Dashboard Design provides a flexible way of alerting a user when something special has occurred. This can be a variety of events, be they positive or negative. For example, if certain offices have hit a target threshold for sales, we may want to show these to highlight the positives. If offices fall below a certain threshold for sales, we may also want to highlight these so that we can compare the offices and figure out how to improve the lagging offices.

Adding alerts to a column chart

When looking at a bar chart, we may want to see which items are below or above a particular threshold. In this recipe, we will learn how to add alerts to a bar chart. Our example will consist of a column chart with a list of regions and their sales. Each region column will be colored appropriately, depending on their sales value vs. threshold.

Getting ready

Make sure you set up the sales data and threshold values, as shown in the following screenshot. You'll also need to insert a **Column Chart** component onto the canvas.

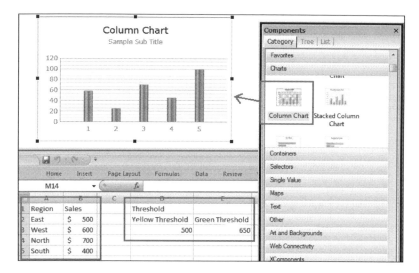

How to do it...

1. First we'll need to bind the sales data to the chart, as shown next:

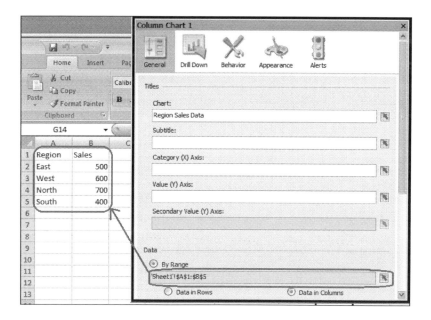

2. Go to the **Alerts** section of the chart properties and ensure that **Enable Alerts** is checked.

3. Select alerts **By Value** as we will be comparing our sales data to the threshold values.

4. In the **Alert Threshold s**ection, click on the **Use a Range** checkbox. Bind the data to the threshold data that was set up in the *Getting ready* section.

5. In the **Color Order** section, select the radio button **High values are good**.

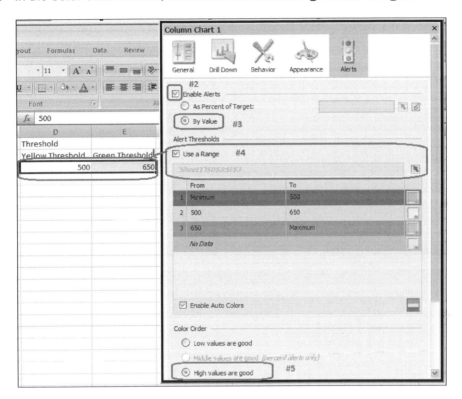

6. In the following screenshot, you will then see that the bars on the chart are now colored according to the sales thresholds:

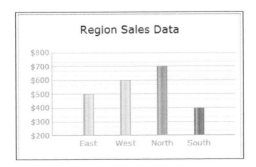

How it works...

In this recipe, binding the initial data is straightforward but the part you'll want to take note of is setting up the alerts.

 Note that there will always be N-1 (N minus one) number of threshold values if you are binding the range to your data. For example, if I had two colors (red and green), I would only have one threshold value. If I had four colors, then I would have three threshold values set up on my spreadsheet.

In step 4, we bind the threshold range to cells D3 and E3 prepared in the *Getting ready* section. Anything that is equal to or greater than the yellow threshold value but less than the green threshold value will be colored as yellow. Anything that is equal to or greater than the green threshold value will be green.

See also

For recipes on different charts you can create, please read the recipes in *Chapter 2, Data Visualization*.

There's more...

Let's say you wanted to display a critical alert that would stand out even if one region was below a threshold. You can accomplish this by following the recipe, *Using bindable colors*.

Using alerts in a gauge

A **gauge** is a commonly used dashboard component because it allows users to easily visualize how a particular value is doing. Using a gauge with alert thresholds provides great value. We are able to visually perceive how a value is doing compared to a set of thresholds. The following image shows a gauge with colors representing how well we are doing in terms of **# of Errors**:

In this recipe, we will show how to set up alerts on a gauge component.

Getting ready

Have your gauge component inserted onto the canvas.

The gauge only has one value, so we will only require a single cell to hold that value.

Also, we will need to have the threshold values set up in cells C3 and D3.

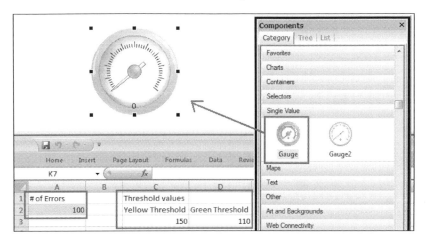

How to do it...

1. In the **Gauge** properties, bind the gauge data to cell A3 from the *Getting ready* section marked in yellow. In the **Scale** section, select the **Auto** radio button.

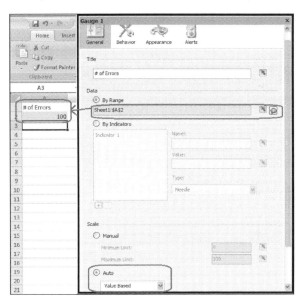

2. Go to the **Alerts** section of the gauge properties and ensure that **Enable Alerts** is checked.

3. Select alerts **By Value**, as we will be comparing our gauge value to the threshold values.

4. In the **Alert Threshold** section, click on the **Use a Range** checkbox. Bind the data to the threshold cells C3:D3 prepared in the *Getting ready* section.

5. At the bottom of the **Alerts** properties, there is a section called **Alert Location**. Make sure that **Background** and **Marker** are checked. You will now see that the sections of the gauge and gauge needle are colored appropriately, as seen in the next screenshot:

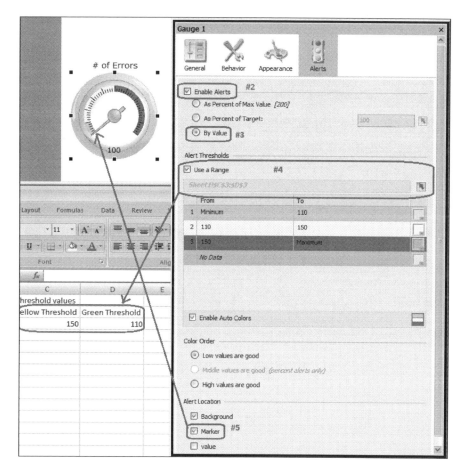

How it works...

In this recipe, binding the initial data is straightforward but the part you'll want to take note of is setting up the alerts.

Note that there will always be N-1 (N minus one) number of threshold values, if you are binding the range to your data. For example, if I had two colors (red and green), then I would only have one threshold value. If I had four colors, then I would have three threshold values set up on my spreadsheet.

In step 4, we bind the threshold range to cells C3 and D3. Anything that is equal to or greater than the yellow threshold value but less than the green threshold value will be colored as yellow. Anything that is equal to or greater than the green threshold value will be green.

Making alert ranges dynamic

It is common that different dimensions contain different thresholds for alert metrics. For example, sales threshold targets may be different for each region of a company, as shown in the following screenshot:

	A	B	C	D	E	F	G	H
1	Region	Yellow Threshold	Green Threshold		Selected Threshold			
2	East	20	50			Yellow Threshold	Green Threshold	
3	West	30	60					
4	North	25	55					
5	South	28	66					
6								

Thresholds / Chart Data / Selection

In our example, we have four regions and different thresholds for each region. So anything below the yellow threshold value will be red, anything that is equal to or greater than the yellow threshold but less than the green threshold will be yellow, and anything equal to or greater than the green threshold value will be green.

The following recipe will contain a column chart that contains monthly values for a selected region. As the user changes their region selection, the alert threshold will also change. The appropriate alert coloring for each bar will be displayed on the chart.

Getting ready

We will have one worksheet that contains the threshold values as well as a spot that will house the thresholds for the selected region. Please refer to the first screenshot from the introduction of this recipe. This is how the threshold data layout will look. There will be another worksheet **Chart Data** that contains the chart data.

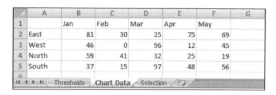

How to do it...

1. Insert a **Column chart** and a **Combo Box selector** onto the canvas.

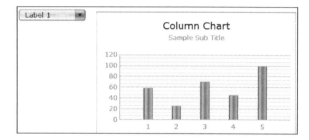

2. Open the **Combo Box** selector properties and bind the **Title** and **Labels** to the cells shown in the following image:

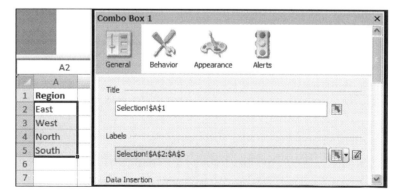

3. First, we will set up the threshold value by linking to the appropriate label. In the **Data Insertion** section of the **Combo Box** properties, rename the text to **Threshold.** Then set the **Insertion Type:** as **Row**. Bind the **Source Data** to cells A2:C5. Bind the **Destination** to the section highlighted in yellow E3:G3.

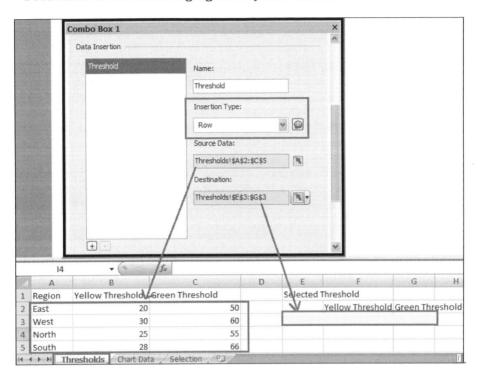

4. Next, you will need to press the **+** button on the **Data Insertion** section to add another row selection. Name the next insertion type as **Chart Data.** Set the **Insertion Type** to **Row**. Go to the **Chart Data** worksheet, bind the **Source Data** to cells A2:F5, and then bind the **Destination Data** to cells H3:M3.

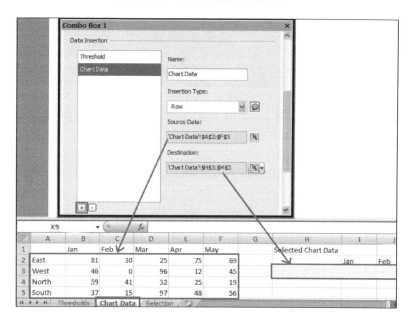

5. Bind the chart data to the **Chart Data** worksheet cells that we populated from step 4. Set the **Subtitle** of the chart to cell H3, which contains the selected region name.

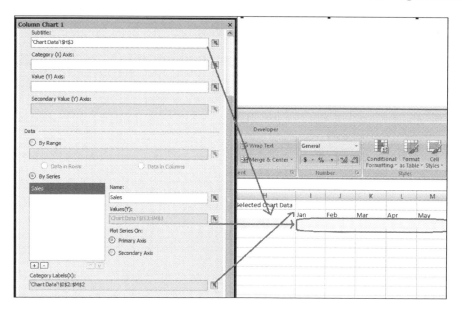

6. Go to the **Alerts** section of the **Chart Properties** and check the **Enable Alerts** checkbox.

7. Select the radio button that says **By Value**.

8. In the **Alert Thresholds** section, check the **Use a Range** checkbox and bind to the cells F3:G3 on the **Thresholds worksheet**.

9. In the **Color Order** section, select the radio that says **High values are good**.

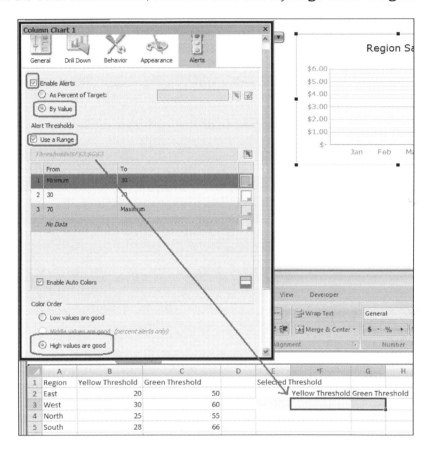

How it works...

In our example, we bind the alert thresholds in steps 6 through 9 to the cells that dynamically change according to the user selected dropdown. The first threshold, which is red, is anything that is less than the yellow threshold value on cell F3. The yellow threshold is anything greater or equal to the yellow threshold value on cell F3 but less than the green threshold value on cell G3. The green threshold is anything that is greater or equal to the green threshold value on cell G3. Using the bindable range in the **Alert Thresholds** section, we are able to dynamically change our threshold settings.

There's more...

In this example, we hardcode all the threshold and chart data values. But in reality, we can populate the values in the yellow destination cells of steps 3 and 4, using any of the available Dashboard Design data connectivity options.

See Also

For using different data connectivity options, please read the recipes in *Chapter 8, Dashboard Connectivity*.

Displaying alerts on a map

A map on a dashboard allows us to visually identify how different regions are doing using a picture instead of a table or chart. With alerts on the map, we can provide even more value. For example, look at the following image. We can see that different regions of the map can be colored differently depending on their value. This allows users to identify at a glance, whether a region is doing well or poorly.

Provincial Sales

Getting ready

Insert a Canadian map object onto the canvas and bind data to the map. We will use the same example from the recipe *Using maps to select data of an area or country*.

 You may also refer to the data prepared in the source file Displaying alerts on a `map.xlf`.

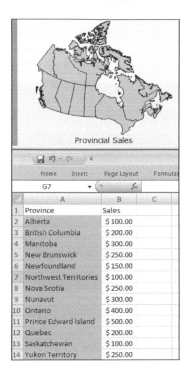

How to do it...

1. In a separate area of the spreadsheet (highlighted in yellow), we will set up the threshold values. Assume that all provinces have the same threshold.

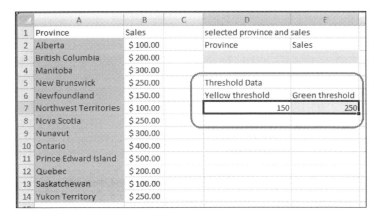

2. Go to the **Alerts** section of the **Map** properties and check **Enable Alerts**.
3. Select the radio button **By Value**.

4. In the **Alert Thresholds** section, check **User a Range**. Then bind the range to the Threshold data set in step 1.

5. In the **Color Order** section, select the radio **High values are good**.

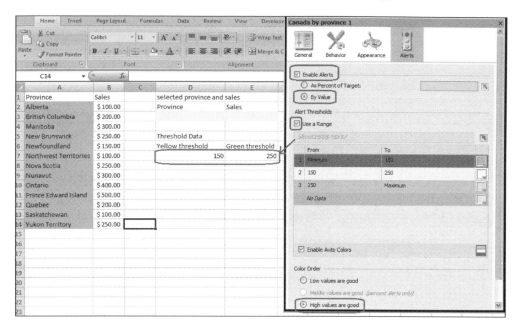

How it works...

In this recipe, we show how to set up alerting for a map component. The way we set it up is pretty standard from steps 2 through 5. Once the alerting mechanism is set up, each province in the map will have its value associated with the alert threshold that we have set up in step 1. The province will be colored red if the sales value is less than the yellow threshold. The province will be colored yellow, if the sales value is greater or equal to the yellow threshold but less than the green threshold. The province will be colored green if the sales value is greater or equal to the green threshold.

There's more...

In our example, we assumed that all the provinces have the same threshold. There is also a way to set up alerts so that each province can have their own threshold. The following recipe, *Displaying alerts of different thresholds on a map,* will explain how to accomplish this. We can also use the GMaps plugin found in the recipe *Integrating Google Maps with the GMaps plugin* to accomplish the same task but in a more flexible fashion.

In this recipe, we reused the data setup from *Using maps to select data of an area or country*. Please read that recipe to learn how to bind data to a map. In addition, if you are interested in how to set different thresholds for each province, please read the next recipe, *Displaying alerts of different thresholds on a map*. Finally, read *Integrating Google Maps with the GMaps Plugin* for more advanced mapping capabilities.

Displaying alerts of different thresholds on a map

The previous recipe was really useful in showing how we can incorporate alerts onto a map. However, the threshold values for all provinces were the same. In reality, this may not be the case for metrics, such as sales. For example, a province such as Nunavut is much smaller than Ontario, thus should not have the same sales threshold as Ontario.

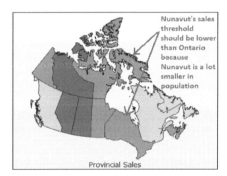

Getting ready

Insert a Canadian map component onto the canvas and bind data to the map. We will use the data setup from the recipe, *Integrating Google Maps with the GMaps plugin* to select data of an area or country.

Please refer to the first screenshot in the introductory section of the recipe *Making alert ranges dynamic*, to understand how the data should look.

You may also refer to the data setup in the source file Displaying alerts of different `thresholds.xlf`.

How to do it...

1. To the right-hand side of the **Sales** (column B), we will add the target thresholds for each province. The larger provinces will have a target threshold of **250**, whereas the smaller provinces will have a target threshold of **150**. It is important that you use key/value relationship for the thresholds, as shown next, for the map component:

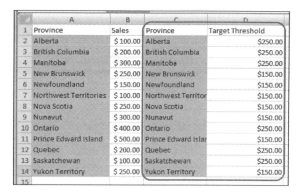

	A	B	C	D
1	Province	Sales	Province	Target Threshold
2	Alberta	$ 100.00	Alberta	$250.00
3	British Columbia	$ 200.00	British Columbia	$250.00
4	Manitoba	$ 300.00	Manitoba	$250.00
5	New Brunswick	$ 250.00	New Brunswick	$150.00
6	Newfoundland	$ 150.00	Newfoundland	$150.00
7	Northwest Territories	$ 100.00	Northwest Territor	$150.00
8	Nova Scotia	$ 250.00	Nova Scotia	$150.00
9	Nunavut	$ 300.00	Nunavut	$150.00
10	Ontario	$ 400.00	Ontario	$250.00
11	Prince Edward Island	$ 500.00	Prince Edward Islar	$150.00
12	Quebec	$ 200.00	Quebec	$250.00
13	Saskatchewan	$ 100.00	Saskatchewan	$250.00
14	Yukon Territory	$ 250.00	Yukon Territory	$150.00
15				

2. Go to the **Alerts** section of the map properties and check **Enable Alerts**.

3. Select the radio button **As Percent of Target:** and bind to the key/value pair cells C2:D14.

4. For the target percentage, we will have anything on target or above as **green**. Color anything between 70% of target and the target as **yellow**. And color anything less than **70%** of the target as **red**.

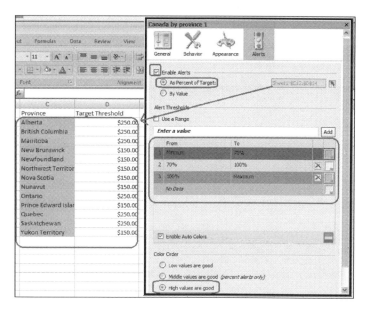

How it works...

As you can see, using the **As Percent of Target** option on the **Enable Alerts**, allows us to have a different threshold for each province, which would give a more realistic alerting mechanism.

> It is important to note that you must use a key/value pair relationship when using the **As Percent of Target** alerting mechanism on a **Map component**. For alerting on the **Chart components**, you don't have to worry about the key/value pair relationship.

See also

In this recipe, we reused the data set up from the recipe *Using maps to select data of an area or country*.

Using bindable colors to control alert coloring from a central location

With the advent of being able to dynamically bind colors to different parts of a component, we can push alerting to another level. For example, we may have a sales chart for a set of regions and want to signal if something is critically bad. Instead of having a bunch of green and red bars that may look like a Christmas tree, we can set the chart background color to red if one of the values has reached a critical point. In this scenario, a user will be drawn to the chart right away, as it will be screaming alarm bells.

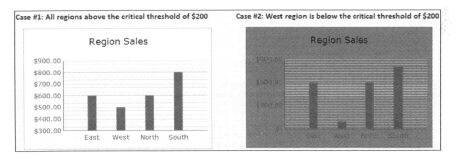

Getting ready

Be sure to have your chart data ready, shown as follows. In this recipe, we will have a set of sales data for each region.

	A	B
1	Region	Sales
2	East	$ 600.00
3	West	$ 500.00
4	North	$ 600.00
5	South	$ 800.00

How to do it...

1. Drag a **Column Chart** from the **Charts** section of the **Components** window onto the canvas.

2. Bind the chart data to the data set up in the *Getting Ready* section.

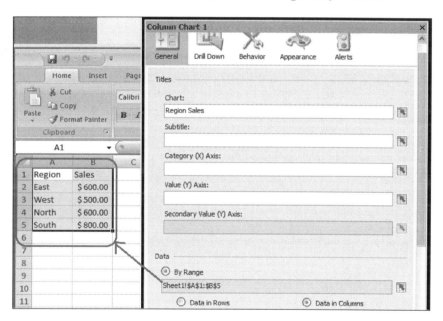

3. Create a section in the worksheet that will contain the critical threshold value. If any region sales go below that value, we want a major alert to show up.

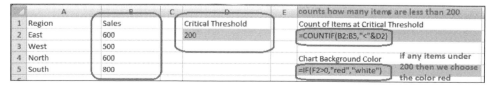

	A	B	C	D	E
					counts how many items are less than 200
1	Region	Sales		Critical Threshold	Count of Items at Critical Threshold
2	East	600		200	=COUNTIF(B2:B5,"<"&D2)
3	West	500			
4	North	600			Chart Background Color if any items under
5	South	800			=IF(F2>0,"red","white") 200 then we choose the color red

4. Bind cell F5, which determines the background color, to the background color property of the chart.

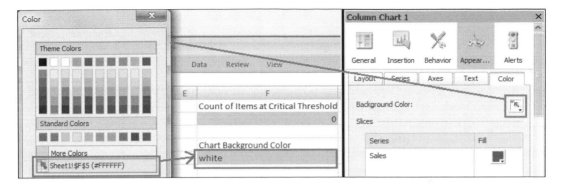

How it works...

Using bindable colors, we are able to dynamically set color properties for almost any component. In our example, we use a simple **COUNTIF** statement to determine if any of the region sales are below the critical threshold. From there we have another **IF** statement that determines the coloring of the chart background. The first case (left-hand side graph in the next image) shows that all our sales are above **$200**, thus the chart background is normally white. The second case (the right-hand side graph of the next image) shows that the West region is below **$200**, thus a major alert is shown and the chart background becomes red.

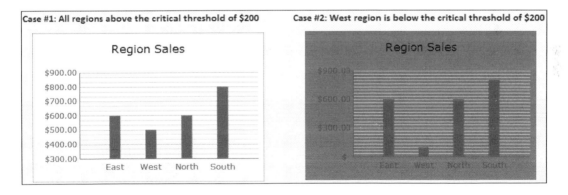

See also

There are many ways to customize alerting for different components. Our example only shows one way to do so. The easiest way can be found in the recipe _Adding alerts to a bar chart_. To learn more on customizing alerts to your desired look and feel, read the recipes in _Chapter 7, Dashboard Look and Feel_.

Using alerts in a scorecard

One of the most useful features that came out in Xcelsius 2008 SP3 was the scorecard component. With the scorecard component, we are able to easily create scorecard KPIs with the ability to insert a user desired alert/trending icon in any column of the scorecard.

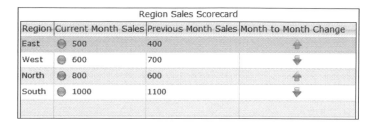

Before the advent of the scorecard component, developers would have to use either a **Listview** selector or **Spreadsheet Table** selector, and then overlay a **Label Based Menu** selector or individual alert/trend icons in each column that required alerting/trending.

This was a huge hassle, as developers had to use a major workaround in order to implement the commonly used scorecard feature.

In this recipe, we will go through an example of using the scorecard component to show a table of values, a threshold indicator that will determine if the current months sales meets the threshold or not, and a trend indicator that shows if the current month sales has risen/fallen compared to the previous month sales.

Getting ready

Set up your data as shown as follows. We have a list of **regions, current month sales, previous month sales**, and **sales threshold**. Note that I highlighted the **Month to Month Change** column because it can either come from the external data source or it could be calculated on the Excel spreadsheet.

	A	B	C	D	E
1	Region	Current Month Sales	Previous Month Sales	Month to Month Change	Sales Threshold
2	East	500	400	100	550
3	West	600	700	-100	550
4	North	800	600	200	850
5	South	1000	1100	-100	800

How to do it...

1. Select the **Scorecard** selector from the **Selectors** category of the **Components** window and drag it onto the canvas.

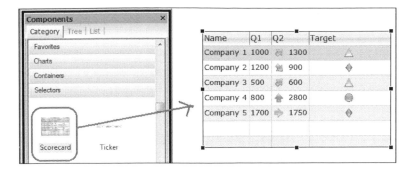

2. Bind the scorecard component to the spreadsheet data prepared in the *Getting ready* section.

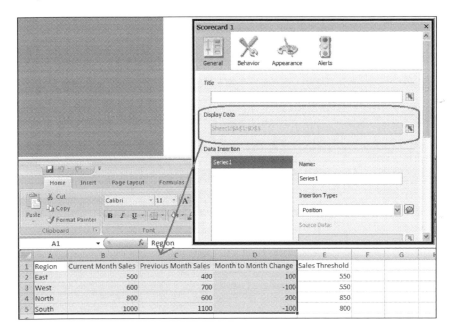

3. We will now set up the alert components. First, we will set up a calculation on column F of the spreadsheet, which will determine whether the threshold indicator for the current month will be green or red. Use the incremental formula =**IF(B2 >= E2, 1, -1)**, with each row on column F.

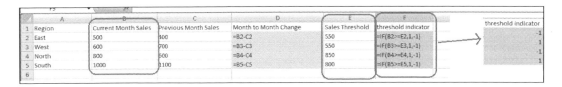

4. Go to the **Alerts** section of the **Scorecard** properties and check the **Current Month Sales** checkbox.

5. Bind the **Alert Values** to cells F2:F5.

6. Select the **By Value,** right below the **Alert Values:** section.

7. On the **Alert Thresholds** section, delete the yellow color by clicking on the **X** button in the second last column.

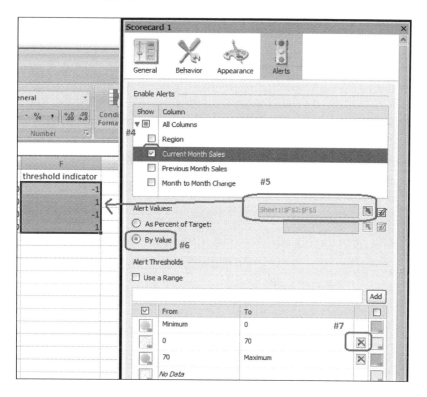

8. In the **Alert Thresholds** section, go to the **To** value of the first row and change it to **0**.

9. In the **Color Order** section, select the **High values are good** radio button.

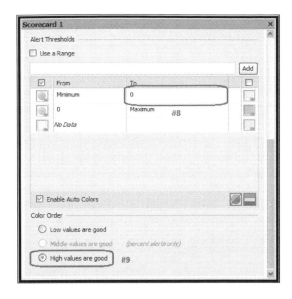

10. In the **Alerts** section of the **Scorecard** properties, check the **Month to Month Change** checkbox.

11. Bind the **Alert Values** to cells D2:D5.

12. Select the **By Value**, right below the **Alert Values:** section.

13. Set the **Alert Threshold values** to what is shown in the following image. The numbers will be explained in the *How it works...* section.

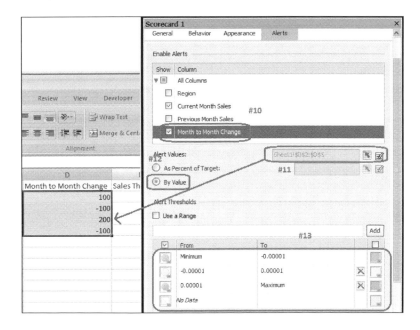

14. Click on the highlighted icon in the **Enable Auto Colors** section and select the arrow icons that we've circled in red.

15. On the **Color Order** section, select the **High values are good** radio button.

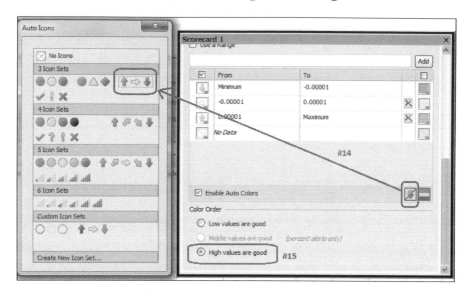

16. Go to the **Appearance** section of the **Scorecard** component. Select the **Text** tab. Uncheck **the Month to Month Change** checkbox because we only want to see the trending icon here and not the text.

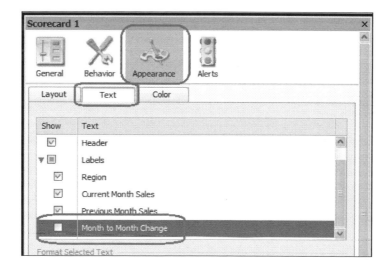

How it works...

Basically, in the scorecard component, we are able to combine different types of alerts together with our table data, as shown in the following image. Now let's explain some important points from the steps in the *How to do it* section.

Region Sales Scorecard			
Region	Current Month Sales	Previous Month Sales	Month to Month Change
East	● 500	400	⬆
West	● 600	700	⬇
North	● 800	600	⬆
South	● 1000	1100	⬇

In step 2, you will notice that we do not bind to the **Sales Threshold** column because that column is used to calculate whether the **Current Month Sales** are above or below the **Sales Threshold**. As you can see in step 3, we have column F that houses the calculation. The calculated values in column F are then bound as the alert values in step 5. From there, we are able to determine if the threshold indicator on the **Current Month Sales** column should be green or red.

The Trend icons shown in the **Month to Month Change** column are determined from the values on the **Month to Month Change** column. In step 13, you will notice the funny **0.00001** values. This is to take into account **Month to Month change** values that are **0**. Unfortunately we are not able to set **(if value = 0, then show no change arrow)**, so **0.00001** is the next closest alternative. On the column **Month to Month Change** we want to show the arrows, so in step 16, we hide the text values.

See also

You can customize the scorecard look by modifying the appearance settings. Please read the recipes in *Chapter 7, Dashboard Look and Feel*, to learn how to change appearance settings for a component.

6
Advanced Components

In this chapter, we will cover:

- ▶ Printing your dashboard

- ▶ Grouping and organizing components with the canvas container

- ▶ Using dashboard scenarios

- ▶ Using the grid component

- ▶ Creating a slide show

- ▶ Using the panel set component

- ▶ Using the history component

- ▶ Data insertion with the source data component

- ▶ Analyzing trends

Introduction

In the previous chapters, we already discussed the functionality and applicability of a lot of Dashboard Design components. In this chapter, we will be looking at a number of components that have a somewhat unique, non-standard functionality, but that may deliver great added value for your dashboards.

Printing your dashboard

The **Print** button has a single and pretty straightforward functionality—it will print your dashboard.

Getting ready

You can use any dashboard you created before or just open a blank new Dashboard Design file.

How to do it...

1. Drag a **Print** button component onto the canvas.

2. Go to the **Behavior** tab and select **Scale to**.

3. Set the scale to **70%**.

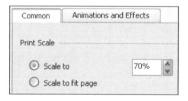

4. Try the **Print** button by previewing the dashboard.

How it works...

After clicking on the **Print** button you will see a standard Windows print window, where you can select and configure a printer, and set the number of copies to be printed.

As we saw in the previous, short recipe, the only specific settings for this component were the **Print Scale** options. The default **Scale to fit page** option makes sure that the dashboard fits on a single page. If you select the other option and scale the dashboard to a certain percentage, it might be using more than one page to be printed on.

Although the **Print** button will appear in the dashboard, it will not be shown on the printed result!

Grouping and organizing components with the canvas container

In the *Grouping canvas components* recipe in *Chapter 1, Staying in Control*, we discussed how grouping multiple components works. This solution is a good option when a limited number of components are involved. But if you are building a dashboard with a lot of overlapping layers, maybe even in combination with the dynamic visibility functionality, it is recommended to use the canvas container component.

Getting ready

No preparation required. Just open a new Dashboard Design file.

How to do it...

1. Drag a **canvas container** component into the canvas.

2. Resize the **canvas container** component to almost half the same size of the canvas.

3. Drag a **line chart** component directly into the canvas container.

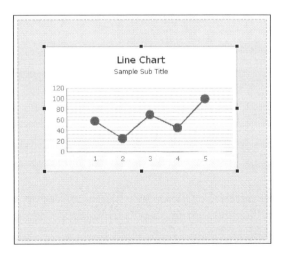

4. Have a look at the **Object Browser**. You will notice that the **Line Chart** component is placed one level below the **Canvas Container** component. This indicates that the **Line Chart** component is now part of the **Canvas Container**.

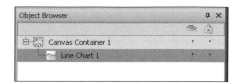

5. Select the **Canvas Container** and drag it to the far right of the canvas. As you will see, the **Line Chart** component also moves along with the **Canvas Container**.

6. Now drag a **Pie Chart** component directly into the **Canvas Container**.

7. Resize the **Canvas Container** so that only one chart remains fully visible. A scroll bar will show up on the right side of the **Canvas Container** component.

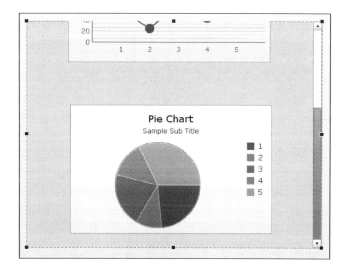

8. Preview the dashboard and check out how this looks in runtime!

How it works...

The canvas container component looks a lot like the grouping of multiple components as we have seen before in a recipe in *Chapter 1, Staying in Control*, called *Grouping canvas components*. But with this component, we also have the option to include horizontal or vertical scroll bars. In the properties pane, you can determine whether dashboard design has to show these scroll bars or not. By default, the **Auto** option is picked, which means that scroll bars are only shown if a component that is part of the canvas container component lies (partly) outside the canvas container. This happened in step 7 of this recipe.

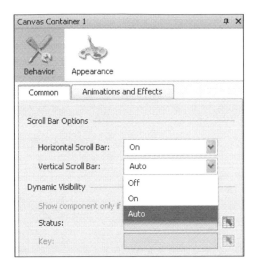

The gray background of the canvas container is only shown in the design mode. If you run the dashboard, only the possible scroll bars are visible.

Using dashboard scenarios

If your dashboard has a typical 'what-if' scenario set up with a number of variables, it would be a nice option for the dashboard user to save a scenario with some particular settings to be reviewed or compared later. The local scenario button component delivers this functionality.

Getting ready

Open a new Dashboard Design file.

How to do it...

1. Drag a vertical slider component into the canvas.
2. Drag a local scenario button component into the canvas.
3. Hit the **Preview** button.
4. Set the slider to value **50**.

5. Now click on the **Scenario** button. A menu with four new buttons will appear. Click on the **Save** button and name it **Scenario 1**.

6. Set the slider to value **75** and click on the **Scenario** button again.

7. Click on the **Load** button and select the scenario you just saved. The value of the slider will now be set to value **50**.

How it works...

The local scenario button enables the user of a dashboard to save the exact state a dashboard is in at that moment, including all the variables the user has set. These scenarios are saved locally, on the user's computer. This means that if you open the dashboard on another computer these saved scenarios cannot be loaded!

With the **Delete** button, the user can delete previously saved scenarios and with the **Set Default** button, a default scenario can be chosen, which will be loaded when the dashboard is opened.

There is more...

If the dashboard user wants to return to the initial state of the dashboard, he/she of course can close the dashboard and reopen it. Using the reset button component for this task is a way better option. The **Reset** button does exactly what its name says—it resets the entire dashboard to its initial state after clicking on it.

Using the grid component

The grid component can display a table with data in your dashboard. Therefore it looks a bit like the list view and spreadsheet table components. There are a number of differences between these two sets of components, stated as follows:

▶ The list view and spreadsheet table components allow us to make data selections; the grid component does not

▶ The grid component not only displays data, but its values can also be changed by the dashboard user

▶ The grid component doesn't have a header row

▶ The grid component has the option to make use of alerts

Getting ready

Open a new dashboard design file and enter the values in the spreadsheet as shown in the following screenshot:

	A	B	C
1			
2			
3			
4			
5	50	40	35
6	25	25	25
7	90	80	70

How to do it...

1. Drag a grid component into the canvas.
2. Bind the **Data** field to spreadsheet cells A5 until C7.
3. Go to the **Behavior** tab and set the **Increment** to 5.
4. Click on the **Appearance** tab. Set the **Vertical Margin** as well as the **Horizontal Margin** to **5**.
5. Resize the canvas container component to almost half the same size of the canvas.
6. Preview the dashboard to see how this works. Move your mouse over one of the cells and click on it as soon the cursor changes into a small vertical spike with arrows on both ends. Now drag your cursor up or down to change the value of the cell.

50	40	50
25	25	25
90	80	70

How it works...

As you have seen in the recipe the grid component works quite straightforward. It displays a simple table with the values in the spreadsheet cells we bound to the component and the value of each cell can be adjusted if we run the dashboard. As with all the insertion-like components, the actual value in the spreadsheet cell will change as well and can be used in Excel functions or other components that refer to this cell.

There is more...

In the **General** tab, we are able to set the **Minimum Limit** and **Maximum Limit** that we can change a value to. This means that if the initial value of a cell lies outside this range and you want to change the value, you can only change it to a value within the range.

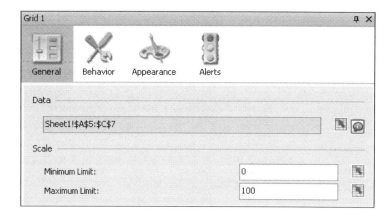

Under the **Common** tab, these limits can be set to be **Fixed** or **Open**. If you choose the **Open** option, the **Scale** fields on the **General** tab are grayed out.

Furthermore, you can set the **Mouse Sensitivity** level. This will set the speed in which the values will increase or decrease when changing them. If you set the **Scroll Behavior** to **Auto**, the values keep changing if you click the cell and drag the cursor a bit above or below the cell. If you use the **Manual** option instead, you have to keep moving your cursor up or down to change the value.

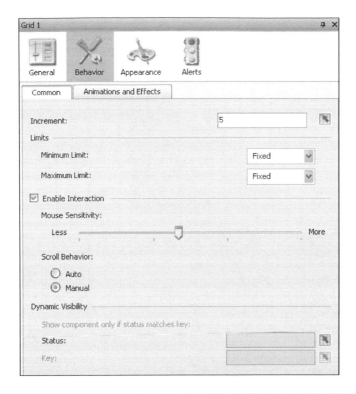

Creating a slide show

As we already discussed in *Chapter 3* recipe *Making selections from a custom image,* you can use the image component to show pictures or Flash (.swf) files in your dashboard. This recipe will show how you can create slide shows of multiple images and/or SWF files with the slide show component.

Getting ready

For this recipe, we need some images and/or SWF files. Make sure that these are all files are of the following types—.jpeg, .png, .gif, .bmp, or .swf. The files can be on your local computer or on the Web.

How to do it...

1. Enter the URLs of the images or SWF files you want to show in the spreadsheet.

2. Drag a play selector component into the canvas. Set this component up to insert rows to destination cell A4, where the cells containing the URLs are the source data cells. For more information on this component, see recipe *Using the Play Selector/Play Control* in *Chapter 3*.

3. Now drag a slide show component into the canvas.

4. Bind the **URL** field to cell A4.

5. Switch to the **Behavior** tab and set the **Transition Type** to **Wedge**.

6. Preview the dashboard to see how the slide show looks.

How it works...

The play selector does most of the work here actually. We need it to change the image that should be displayed by using data insertion. The slide show component only displays the images and provides a nice transition between two images.

There is more...

In the **Appearance** tab, there are some options that are specific for this component. First the **Sizing Method**, where you can set how the image or the SWF file should be displayed: In its original size, keeping its scale, or being stretched to the sizing of the component. Next there are settings for **Horizontal** and **Vertical Alignment**. Besides these options, the more standard **Transparency** option is also available.

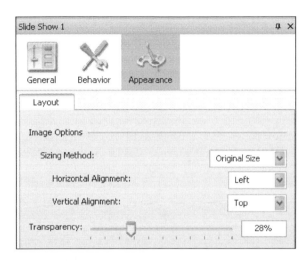

Using the panel set component

The panel set component is one of the few features of dashboard design that looks really cool at first, but which you probably won't use for your dashboard eventually. The purpose of this component is to create a showcase of images and/or Flash (.swf) files in one window. The user is able to zoom in on each panel. Unfortunately, the SWF files that are created with dashboard design are not supported and cannot be displayed, which instantly decreases the value of the component.

Getting ready

For this recipe, we need some images and/or SWF files. Make sure these are all files are of the following types—.jpeg, .png, .gif, .bmp, or .swf.

How to do it...

1. Drag a panel set component into the canvas.

2. In the **General** tab of the **Properties pane**, select **Layout2**.

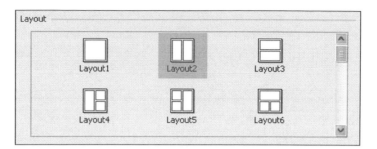

3. Click on the **Import** button in the **Content** area and click on the **Click to Add Images** button in the upcoming window. Browse to your image or SWF file and click on **Open**. The file is now added to Panel 1. Repeat this step to add another file and close this window by clicking on **OK**.

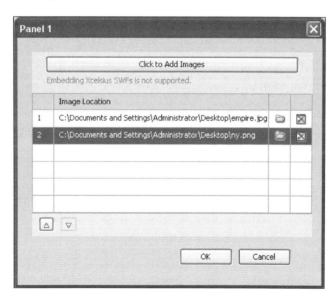

4. Click on the button on the far right-hand side of the **Drop-Down Menu Labels** field. Enter a label for each file you just added.

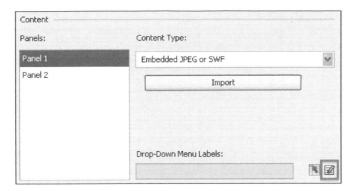

5. Select **Panel 2** and repeat the steps 3 and 4 to add some images and or SWF files to this second panel.

6. Now switch to the **Behavior** tab. In the **Selected Item** area, select **Panel 1** and set the **Item** field to **Image 1**. Do the same for **Panel 2**.

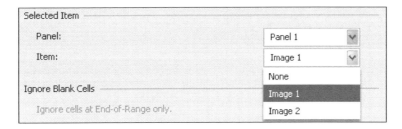

7. Preview the dashboard.

8. Click on the maximize buttons.

9. Now click on the little arrow next to the maximize button to show the menu labels. Select a label to switch to another image or SWF file.

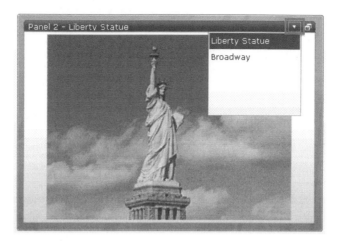

How it works...

As we saw in this recipe, the panel set component lets us display a set of panels to show multiple images and/or SWF files. There are even 27 different layouts to choose from with up to ten panels each.

The lack of support for dashboard design SWF files has already been mentioned but there are more problems with this component. First, it has no selector abilities. So even if you wanted to use this component to build a dashboard that functions as a product catalog, it is very hard to make it interactive and pass data through to other components.

Another problem is performance-related. The more (high resolution) images you embed in this component, the bigger your final Dashboard Design dashboard SWF file will get. Big SWF files take longer to load and therefore decrease your dashboard's performance. So if you are using this component, make sure you test your final dashboard on different computer setups to check if the dashboard's performance is acceptable for the users.

There is more...

Linking to files instead of embedding

In the recipe, we embedded the images/SWFs in the panel set component. Another way to show these files is by using the **By URL** option for **Content Type** and linking to them using **URLs**. You can enter these URLs by putting them in the spreadsheet and binding to these cells. Or, add them as labels by clicking on the button on the far right-hand side. The **Drop-Down Menu Labels** can be entered in the same way.

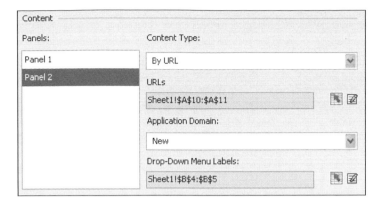

Panel behavior

A nice option for this component is the **Zoom Speed** setting. Play around a bit with this slider to make the panel transition as smooth as you want it to be. Also, here you can enable/disable the maximize button.

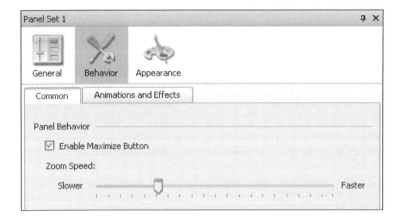

Using the history component

The history component makes it possible to plot a value in a chart that changes in real time, while conserving its historical data. Okay, that may be a bit of a cryptic description of what this component does, but you should think about those stock charts that track the fluctuation of a stock price. At the start of the day, the line in such a chart is short, while at the end of the day the complete trend of the stock prize for that day is shown. This recipe will show you how to set up this kind of functionality in your dashboard.

Getting ready

Just open a new Dashboard Design file.

How to do it...

1. Drag a line chart component, a history component, and a horizontal slider component into the canvas.

2. Select the horizontal slider component and bind the **Data** field to spreadsheet cell B1.

3. Now select the history component and bind its **Data** field also to spreadsheet cell B1.

4. Bind the **Data Destination** field to the spreadsheet range B3 to J3.

5. Go to the line chart component. Bind the **Data By Range** field to spreadsheet range B3 to J3.

6. Your setup should now look like the following screenshot:

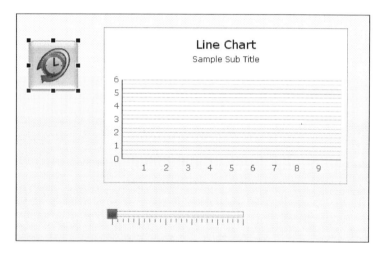

7. Hit the **Preview** button and test the dashboard. Each time you move the slider, a new value should be plotted in the chart.

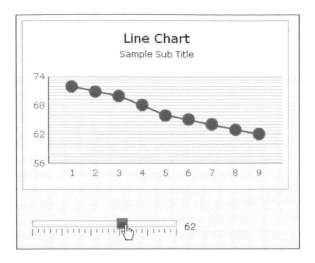

How it works...

The history component picks up a value from a certain source cell (cell B1 in this recipe) and pastes it in a horizontal or vertical range of cells that in fact stores the history of the value. These cells are bound to a chart and so a real-time changing graph is created.

The history component has, besides the bindings to the source and destination cells, only one other setting. You can determine when a value should be pasted to the destination cells. This can be either when the data changes or on an interval of a certain number of seconds.

This component works in the background and will therefore not be shown during runtime.

There's more...

If you need more series of real time changing values in your chart, just use more history components to accomplish this!

Data insertion with the Source data component

The **Source Data** component enables us to insert data into spreadsheet cells by changing the selected index value of the component. This is a different approach to inserting data than we saw in *Chapter 3* when we were discussing selectors and drill downs.

Getting ready

Open a new dashboard design file and enter the data into the spreadsheet as shown in the following screenshot:

	A	B	C	D	E
1	Value:				
2					
3	Inserted data:				
4					
5			Product A	Product B	Product C
6		2007	15%	60%	25%
7		2008	30%	40%	30%
8		2009	25%	25%	50%
9		2010	20%	30%	50%
10					

How to do it...

1. Drag a pie chart component to the canvas.

2. Bind the **Chart** field to cell B3 and leave the **Subtitle** field empty.

3. Bind the **Data Values** field to the spreadsheet range from C3 to E3. Select the **Data in Rows** options.

4. Bind the **Labels** field to cells C5 to E5.

5. Drag a horizontal slider component to the canvas.

6. Bind the **Data** field to cell B1.

7. Set the **Minimum Limit** to **0** and the **Maximum Limit** to **3**.

8. Now drag the source data component to the canvas.

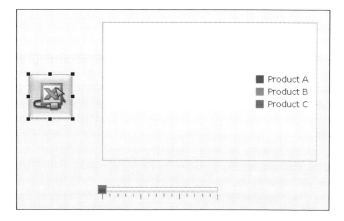

9. Select **Insertion Type Row**.

10. Bind the **Source Data** field to cell range B6 to E9.

11. Bind the **Destination** field to cells B3 to E3.

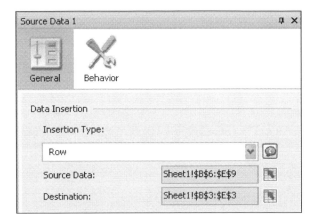

12. Go to the **Behavior** tab. Bind the **Selected Item Index** field to cell B1.

13. Preview the dashboard!

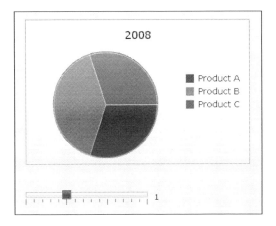

How it works...

As already mentioned in the introduction of this recipe, the source data component has the same data insertion functionality as selector components and drilling down from charts. But, the data insertion of the source data component is triggered by a changing value in a spreadsheet cell and not directly by a user interacting with a component.

In this recipe, we used a horizontal slider component to change a cell value (cell B1) to trigger the data insertion. But, you can of course also use this component in combination with Excel formulas, dynamic visibility, or the inserted data by other components.

Analyzing trends

With the trend analyzer component dashboard design is able to calculate trends in a series of data. You can display these trends in a chart so you can view them next to the actual data and make your analysis. This component is also able to forecast future trends based on the actual data.

Getting ready

For this recipe we need some data, so open a new Dashboard Design file and enter the values in the spreadsheet as shown in the following screenshot:

	A	B	C	D	E	F	G	H	I	J	K	L	M	N	O
1															
2															
3															
4															
5	jan	feb	mar	apr	may	jun	jul	aug	sep	oct	nov	dec	jan	feb	mar
6	50	150	80	120	105	135	155	180	165	175	205	240			
7															
8															

How to do it...

1. Drag a combination chart component into the canvas.
2. Bind the data **By Range** to spreadsheet cells A5 through O7.
3. Drag a trend analyzer component into the canvas.
4. Bind the **Data** field to cells A6 through L6.
5. Select **Trend/Regression Type Linear**.
6. Bind the **Analyzed Data Destination** field to cells A7 through O7.
7. Set the **Number of Forecast Periods** to **3**.

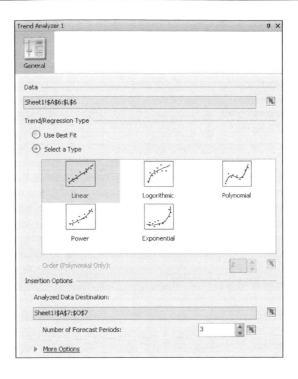

8.   Now preview the dashboard.

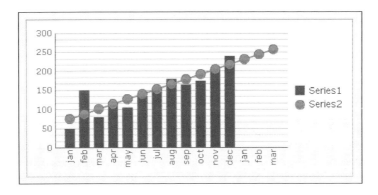

How it works...

In the previous example, we created a chart that shows a data series over a 12-month period. We selected the **Linear** trend type so the trend analyzer component calculates a linear trend based on the 12 values. Also, a forecast is calculated for the three months we don't have data on. The combination chart visualizes both the actual and the calculated trend data series, where the latter is a straight line. As the trend analyzer component is a background component, it won't be shown during runtime.

Besides the option **Linear** for **Trend/Regression Type**, we can choose **Logarithmic**, **Polynomial**, **Power**, or **Exponential**. Also you can use the **Best Fit** option and trust Dashboard Design to pick the right one for us.

There is more...

The properties pane of the trend analyzer component has a **More Options** section. Here you can bind information about the chosen trend/regression type to spreadsheet cells and display them in your dashboard. The fields you can show are the **Equation Type Destination**, the **Equation Destination** (that's the equation), the **R2 Value Destination**, and the **F Value Destination**.

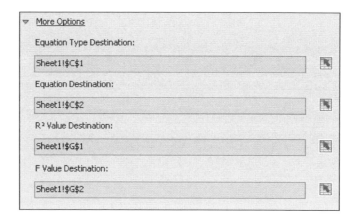

7
Dashboard Look and Feel

In this chapter, we will cover the following:

- ▶ Changing the look of a chart
- ▶ Adding a background to your dashboard
- ▶ Using color schemes
- ▶ Sharing a color scheme
- ▶ Working with themes
- ▶ Making component colors dynamic
- ▶ Using the panel container
- ▶ Using the tab set container
- ▶ Making tables look pretty
- ▶ Smart use of quadrants

Introduction

In this chapter, we will go through certain techniques on how you can utilize the different cosmetic features Dashboard Design provides, in order to improve the look of your dashboard. Dashboard Design provides a powerful way to capture the audience versus other dashboard tools. It allows developers to build dashboards with the important 'wow' factor that other tools lack. Let's take, for example, two dashboards that have the exact same functionality, placement of charts, and others. However, one dashboard looks much more attractive than the other. In general, people looking at the nicer looking dashboard will be more interested and thus get more value of the data that comes out of it.

Thus, not only does Dashboard Design provide a powerful and flexible way of presenting data, but it also provides the 'wow' factor to capture a user's interest.

Changing the look of a chart

This recipe will run through changing the look of a chart. Particularly, it will go through each tab in the appearance icon of the chart properties. We will then make modifications and see the resulting changes.

Getting ready

Insert a chart object onto the canvas. Prepare some data and bind it to the chart.

How to do it...

1. Double-click/right-click on the chart object on the canvas/object properties window to go into **Chart Properties**.

2. In the **Layout** tab, uncheck **Show Chart Background.**

3. In the **Series** tab, click on the colored square box circled in the next screenshot to change the color of the bar to your desired color.

4. Then change the width of each bar; click on the **Marker Size** area and change it to **35**.

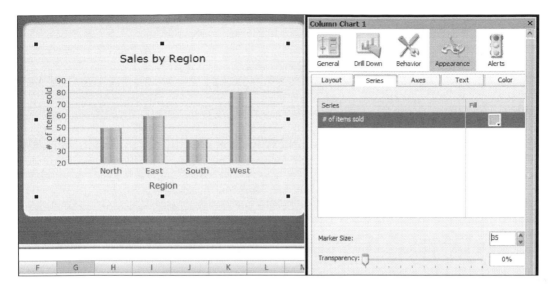

5. Click on the colored boxes circled in red in the **Axes** tab and choose dark blue to modify the horizontal and vertical axes separately.

6. Uncheck **Show Minor Gridlines** at the bottom so that we remove all the horizontal lines in between each of the major gridlines.

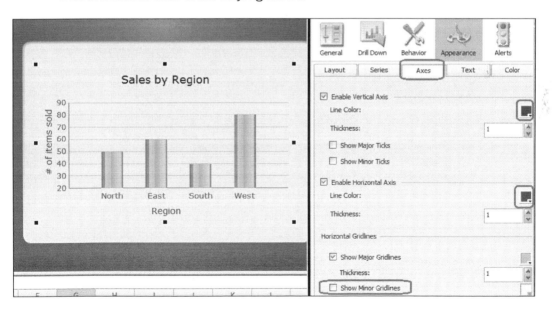

7. Next, go to the **Text and Color** tabs, where you can make changes to all the different text areas of the chart.

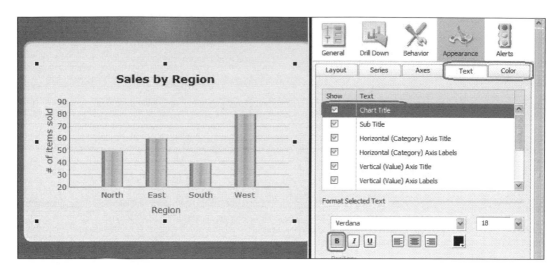

How it works...

As you can see, the default chart looks plain and the bars are skinny so it's harder to visualize things. It is a good idea to remove the chart background if there is an underlying background so that the chart blends in better. In addition, the changes to the chart colors and text provide additional aesthetics that help improve the look of the chart.

See also

Adding a background to your dashboard.

Adding a background to your dashboard

This recipe shows the usefulness of backgrounds in the dashboard. It will show how backgrounds can help provide additional depth to objects and help to group certain areas together for better visualization.

Getting ready

Make sure you have all your objects such as charts and selectors ready on the canvas. Here's an example of the two charts before the makeover. Bind some data to the charts if you want to change the coloring of the series.

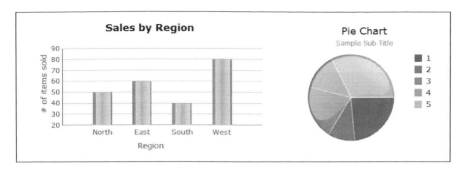

How to do it...

1. Choose **Background4** from the **Art and Backgrounds** tab of the **Components** window.

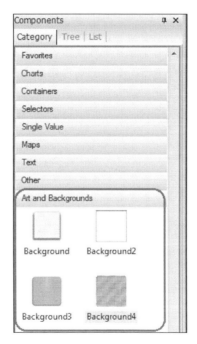

2. Stretch the background so that it fills the size of the canvas.

3. Make sure that ordering of the backgrounds is before the charts. To change the ordering of the background, go to the object browser, select the background object and then press the "-" key until the background object is behind the chart.

4. Select **Background1** from the **Art and Backgrounds** tab and put two of them under the charts, as shown in the following screenshot:

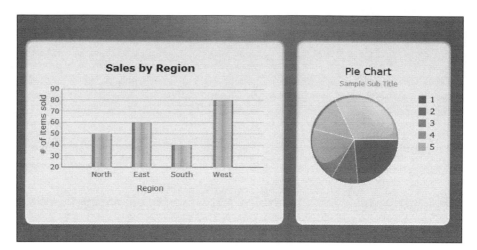

5. When the backgrounds are in the proper place, open the properties window for the backgrounds and set the background color to your desired color. In this example we picked turquoise blue for each background.

How it works...

As you can see with the before and after pictures, having backgrounds can make a huge difference in terms of aesthetics. The objects are much more pleasant to look at now and there is certainly a lot of depth with the charts.

The best way to choose the right backgrounds that fit your dashboard is to play around with the different background objects and their colors. If you are not very artistic, you can come up with a bunch of examples and demonstrate it to the business user to see which one they prefer the most.

There's more...

It is important to use backgrounds carefully and not to use them in the wrong places. A good reference that we recommend is *Information Dashboard Design* by *Stephen Few*. *Information Dashboard Design* is a great book that will guide you on the best dashboard design practices and when to use backgrounds.

Using color schemes

Dashboard Design conveniently has a set of built-in color themes that developers can use to instantly change the look of their dashboard. Using color themes helps provide consistent coloring among your objects and allows you to change the colors for multiple objects at a time without having to go into the properties of each object to make the necessary changes.

Getting ready

Have your set of objects that you want to change the colors for ready on the canvas. In this example we have the sales by region chart, a pie chart, and a set of underlying backgrounds that we want colors modified.

How to do it...

1. Click on the **colors** icon and make sure that **Current Theme Colors** is selected. The backgrounds will be grey and the charts bluish.

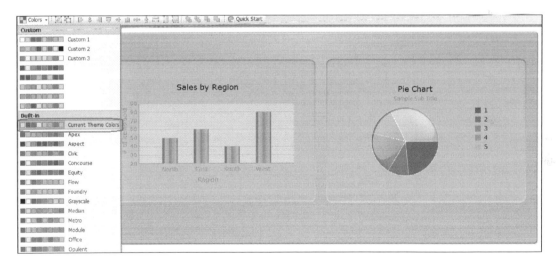

2. Click on the **colors** icon and select the **Concourse** color scheme.

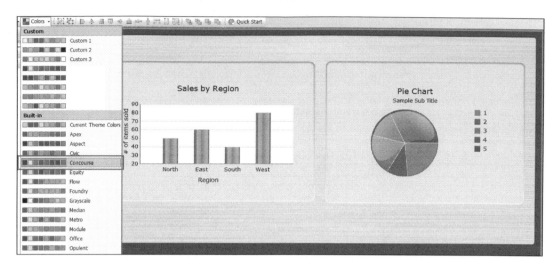

How it works...

As you can see, the default color scheme initially looked kind of bland and the coloring for each series in the pie chart is very similar, making it tough to decipher between each of the series. Changing it to the **Concourse** color scheme lightens up the background considerably with a light bluish background which is easy on the eyes. In addition, the series on the pie chart are more easily distinguishable; however the blues in our opinion are still too similar. We can fix that by modifying the color scheme, which will be explained in the next recipe.

There's more...

Using a good coloring scheme requires a lot of trial and error and there are many best practices that need to be accounted for. For example, different series on a chart should be colored differently so that users don't have to spend a lot of time figuring out which bar belongs to which series.

We also want colors that are soothing for the eyes. Colors that are too bright or too dark may cause strain to the eyes, thus making it more difficult to find information.

When going through color schemes, it is best to demo to the end users who will be using the dashboard and go with a coloring scheme that is most comfortable to their eyes, as it will allow them to find information more easily.

Sharing a color scheme

Developers may want to customize a dashboard's charts and objects to follow a company's coloring guidelines. Most likely, the company's coloring guidelines will not match any of the built-in coloring schemes, so we'll need a way to create a coloring scheme that we can re-use every time a new dashboard is built for the same company.

Getting ready

You must be able to view hidden files and folders in the `c:\Documents and Settings\` `your_user_id` folder. If you are a Windows Vista or Windows 7 user, you will need to be able to view hidden files and folders in `c:\Users\your_user_id`.

How to do it...

1. Click on the colors icon and select the **Create New Color Scheme** at the bottom of the list.

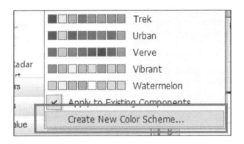

2. Change the background color to whatever color you want by clicking on the colored square.

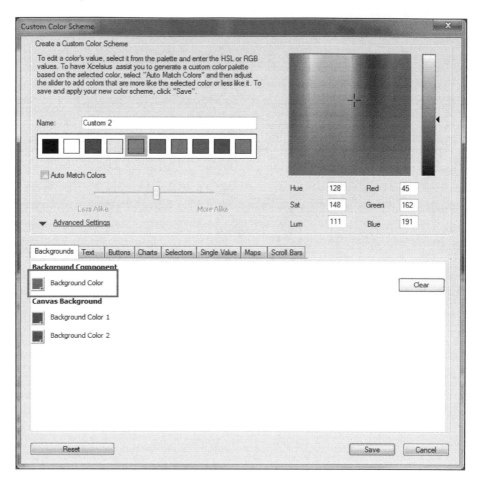

3. Click on the **Charts** tab and change the **Series** color to something other than the default color.

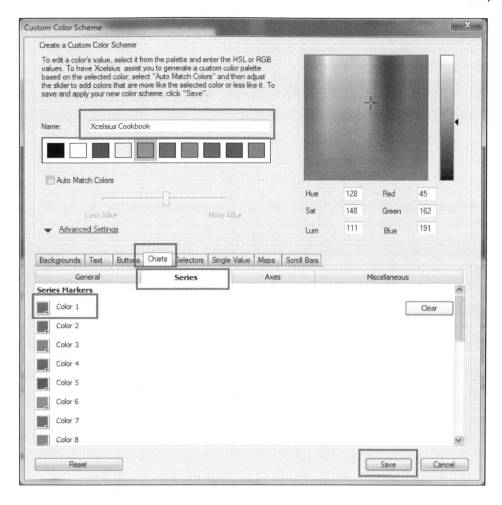

4. Click the **Save** button when you are finished.

5. Your color scheme has now been saved and you can now transfer it to other computers. Copy the XML files of the theme that you want to share from the following two folders to the exact same directory in the destination computer. The XML filenames will have the same names as the files that you saved at the following location: `c:\Documents and Settings\your_user_id\Application Data\ XcelsiuscustomThemes` and `c:\Documents and Settings\your_user_id\ Application Data\XcelsiuscustomThemesAutoInfo`.

6. For Windows Vista and Windows 7, the directory path before Xcelsius will be: `c:\Users\your_user_id\AppData\Roaming\`.

How it works...

Every time you save a custom coloring scheme, it will create two XML files in the directories mentioned earlier. From there, you can easily share the coloring scheme with other developers or other machines that have Dashboard Design installed.

As you can see, once you have the coloring scheme XML files in place, you will be able to select them from the **Color Scheme Toolbar**.

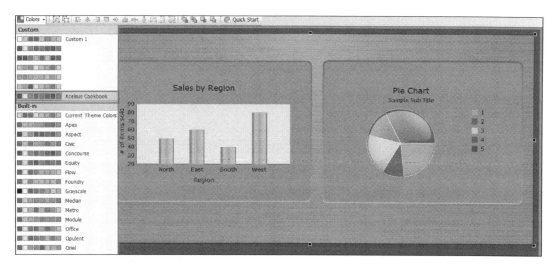

Working with themes

Dashboard Design 2008 has a library of themes that developers can use to change the chart and object styles to the look that suits them most. The ability to select different themes is important because it gives developers more options on customizing the look of their dashboards to what fits best. There are eight themes that developers may choose from. In this recipe, we will be showcasing the default theme and two other themes.

How to do it...

1. Click on the **Themes** icon and by default, you will see that **Aqua** is selected.

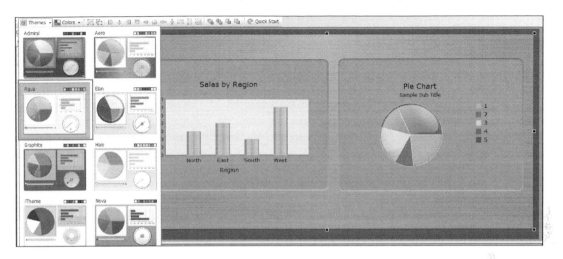

2. Change the theme to **Aero**.

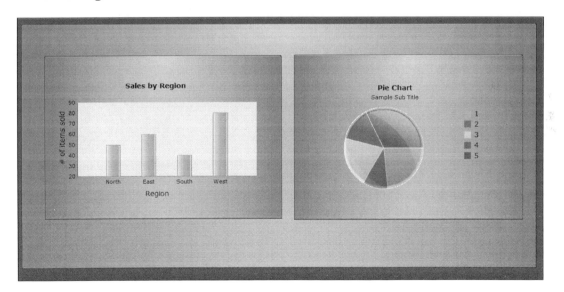

3. Change the theme to **Halo**.

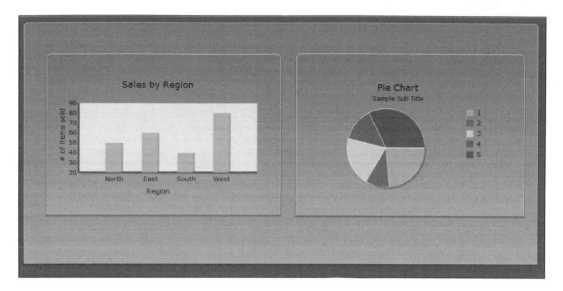

How it works...

As you can see, Dashboard Design provides a large library of themes allowing you to customize the style of your backgrounds, objects, and charts. For example, some themes may have more gradient backgrounds and charts such as the Aero theme, whereas the Halo theme has a flat but bold look.

Making component colors dynamic

Dashboard Design 2008 allows users to fully control the coloring of their components based on whatever event they desire. For example, if a major alert were to happen I could dynamically change my background to red in order to signal an emergency. This is extremely useful because developers can not only dynamically control the color of bars on a chart but also the rest of the chart components such as the background and text as well.

How to do it...

1. On the cell highlighted in yellow E2, we have a **COUNTIF** statement that will set the bar color to red, if any of the regions has their number of items sold below 40. Otherwise the bar color will be set to blue as shown in the following screenshot:

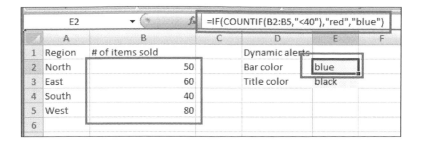

2. On the chart properties go to the **Color** tab and click on the square colored box in the fill column. On the bottom of the color palette, choose the **Bind to Color** option and bind to the cell with the color control (E2, in our case).

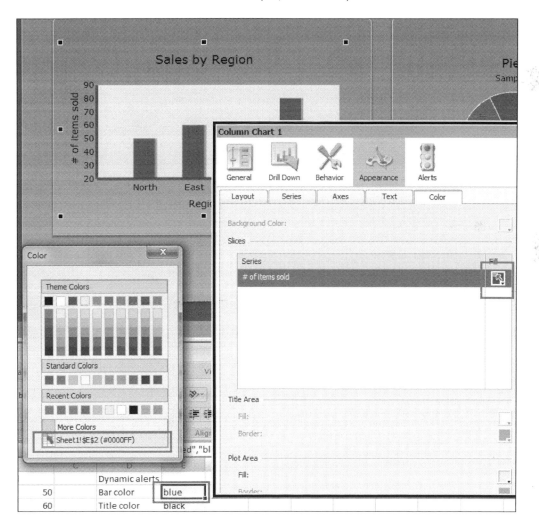

3. Go to the **Text** tab of the chart properties and click on the color square of the **Chart Title**. Bind the color to the cell that controls the title text color (in our case, E3).

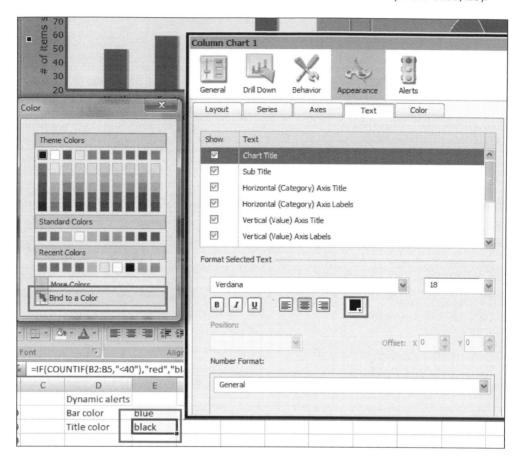

4. Change the cell from B2 to B5 to a value below 40 and verify that the **Bar color** and **Title color** are functioning correctly.

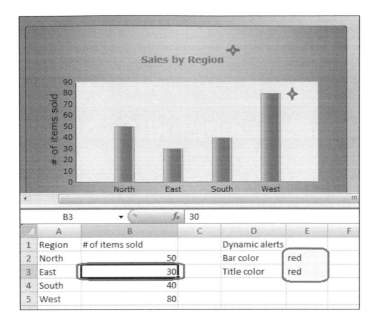

How it works...

In our example, we can easily control the coloring of our chart components with the help of some Excel formulas. Using this method, we are able to clearly alert users if something significant has occurred. For example, if it was critical that all of the regions surpass a particular threshold (40), we can send out a clear alert signal (title and bars red), if one of the regions fails.

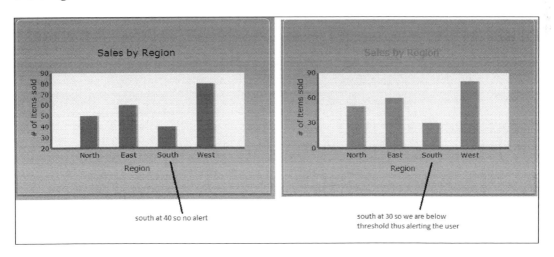

There's more...

Because the dynamic coloring depends on Boolean logic, you'll need the aid of Excel formulas to determine which color is displayed. We recommend that you become familiar with Excel Boolean logic to fully utilize the functionality of dynamic coloring.

Using the panel container

The panel container component is useful if a designer thinks that a set of item(s) is too large for the canvas and wants to be able to scroll the inside of the canvas. A good example would be a scrolling set of charts. Let's say real estate on the dashboard was an issue and we had many charts that needed to be shown but it was not mandatory to show all charts on one view. If we put it in a panel container, we can scroll through each chart kind of like a slide show.

How to do it...

1. Select the **Panel Container** from the **Containers** tab.

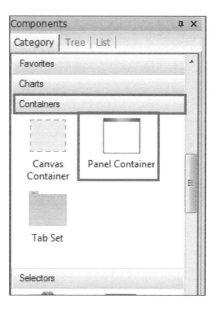

2. Insert a set of charts (these can be any type of charts that you wish to insert) inside the panel container.

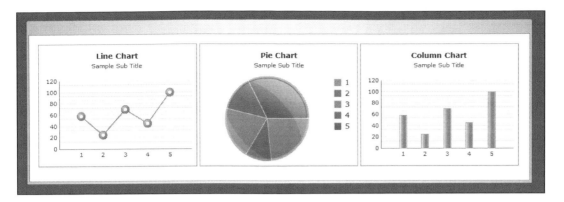

3. Shrink the panel container so that it doesn't take up too much real estate on the dashboard. You can do this by hovering your mouse to the edge of the panel and resizing from there.

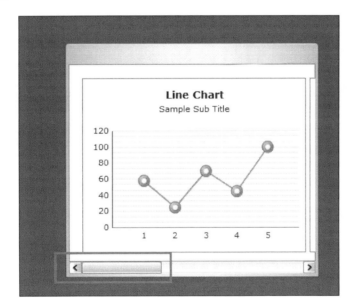

How it works...

In our example, we were able to emulate a slideshow of charts. This is useful if the charts do not need to be visible in one screen all together and will allow designers to save on real estate.

There's more...

If you are putting multiple objects in a panel container you must make sure that the business is okay with the scrolling. In the majority of cases, it is best practice to have everything show up on the same screen without having to scroll. However in some cases such as a large table that may contain large report type information, we may have to resort to using the panel container in order to facilitate the best use of real estate.

Using the tab set container

The best analogy to a **tab set** would be the tabs that you see in Internet Explorer and Firefox. Before the advent of tabs, we would have multiple windows of Internet Explorers open, which was very cumbersome. With tabs we are able to flip through the different pages that you have opened very easily. Before Xcelsius 2008, developers who wanted to work with multiple pages on one dashboard needed to do a lot of work with dynamic visibility. With the tab set container, we are able to separate different pages within the dashboard very easily. This allows us to flip through pages that are independent of each other but related to the same topic without having to reload separate dashboards or set dynamic visibility for each page.

How to do it...

1. Select the **Tab Set Container** from the **Containers** tab.

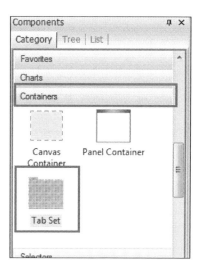

2. In the **Properties** window of the canvas, you can rename the tab. In our example we named the first tab as **Sales**.

3. To add a new tab, press the **+** button on the top left-hand side of the canvas. It will then pop up a window that lets you name your tab. In our example, we named the second tab **Trend Analysis**, as seen in the following screenshot:

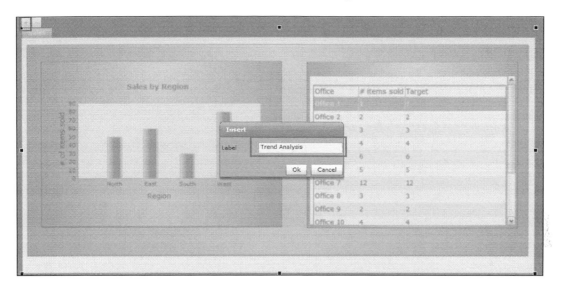

4. The different tabs will be separated as different canvases on the object browser window. All components residing in each canvas will be as a child of the canvas on the object browser window.

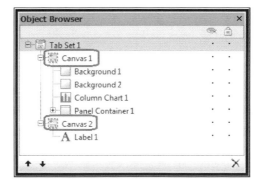

How it works...

The tab set container is basically a set of canvas containers that hold your objects. The set of canvas containers are distinguished by the tab at the top of the main container. Users are able to switch through tabs at run time very easily. This emulates the tabs found on popular browsers such as Internet Explorer and Firefox.

There's more...

When building tab containers, designers should be careful of having too many tabs or too many levels of tab hierarchies. It is recommended to keep the number of tabs in each level to a maximum of five.

For example, look at the following screenshot. If we have nine tabs, we can see that the dashboard starts becoming overwhelming and complex. It is also good to keep the number of hierarchies to a maximum of two. Again, we can see once we get past two hierarchies, it starts to become messy and users will have too many paths to choose from.

Finally, each additional tab means an additional page. With each additional page comes a set of components and charts which equate to a larger footprint. Dashboards with a larger footprint will take longer to load due to the size of the SWF file and performance will take a hit due to the number of objects.

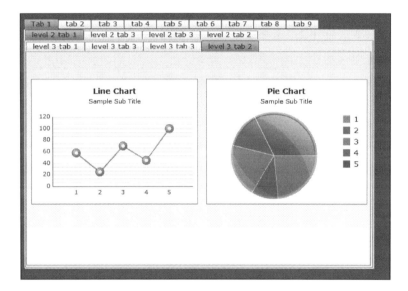

Making tables look pretty

With Dashboard Design 2008, we are able to create tables that look just like a table in an Excel spreadsheet. Unfortunately, our everyday tables look quite bland. If we start off with a default spreadsheet table, it will look kind of like this:

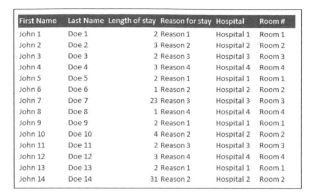

First Name	Last Name	Length of stay	Reason for stay	Hospital	Room #
John 1	Doe 1	2	Reason 1	Hospital 1	Room 1
John 2	Doe 2	3	Reason 2	Hospital 2	Room 2
John 3	Doe 3	2	Reason 3	Hospital 3	Room 3
John 4	Doe 4	3	Reason 4	Hospital 4	Room 4
John 5	Doe 5	2	Reason 1	Hospital 1	Room 1
John 6	Doe 6	1	Reason 2	Hospital 2	Room 2
John 7	Doe 7	23	Reason 3	Hospital 3	Room 3
John 8	Doe 8	1	Reason 4	Hospital 4	Room 4
John 9	Doe 9	2	Reason 1	Hospital 1	Room 1
John 10	Doe 10	4	Reason 2	Hospital 2	Room 2
John 11	Doe 11	2	Reason 3	Hospital 3	Room 3
John 12	Doe 12	3	Reason 4	Hospital 4	Room 4
John 13	Doe 13	2	Reason 1	Hospital 1	Room 1
John 14	Doe 14	31	Reason 2	Hospital 2	Room 2

It looks okay, but with the help of some Dashboard Design objects, we can spice it up to look much more attractive.

Getting ready

Prepare the data on your Excel spreadsheet and set up a table like in the previous image.

How to do it...

1. Change the theme to **Aero**.

2. Select the first Background object from the **Art and Backgrounds** tab from the **Category** window.

3. Place the background so that it is under the table.

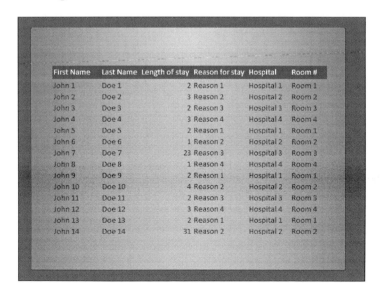

4. Select the **Rectangle** object from the **Art and Backgrounds** tab and place it under the body of the table to give it a background color.

5. Select the **Rectangle** object from the **Art and Backgrounds** tab and place it on top of the header and give it a linearly gradient background color. This will be the background for the table title.

6. Select **Label** from the **Text** tab of the **Category** window. Center it on the title background to give the table a title.

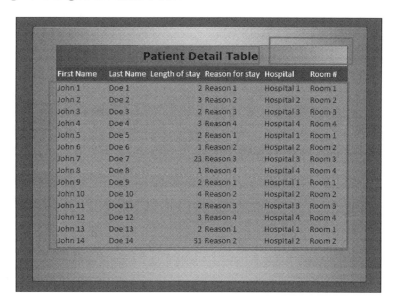

How it works...

As you can see, with the help of a few Dashboard Design components such as backgrounds, rectangles, and labels, we are able to spice up the look of a table and make it much more pleasing to the eye.

See Also

Adding a background to your dashboard.

Smart use of quadrants

It is very important when designing a dashboard to make it as easy to read as possible. In addition, we want to make a dashboard conform to how humans analyze a picture. A common concept is to move from the top left-hand side to the top right-hand side and then to the bottom. This is a flow that the majority of users are comfortable with.

Now we bring in the concept of quadrants. It allows us to create groupings so that a user is not so overwhelmed when looking at the dashboard. Creating proper quadrants is very important and this recipe will give an example of the proper use of quadrants.

Getting ready

Gather the desired charts and selectors on your dashboard.

How to do it...

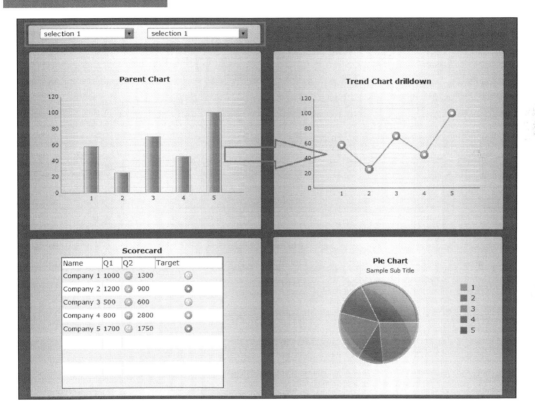

1. Set up your charts in a way where it is like four quadrants.
2. Selectors should be on the top left-hand side, if they control the whole chart.
3. Use backgrounds to help separate your quadrants.
4. Parent charts should be on the left-hand side or on top of the drill-down chart
5. Charts that we want users to look at first should be at the top.
6. If possible, size all the quadrants equally.
7. Align the components neatly so that it is easier on the eyes when looking for different items.

How it works...

As you can see, when we group things into four quadrants, it is very easy to read the dashboard. In addition, we are comfortable with navigation, as we start at the top left-hand side. The drilldown is easy to understand and navigate as we have the parent chart on the left-hand side of the drilldown chart. Secondary information such as extra details should be on the bottom of the chart and not at the top, as users are interested in the highest level data first, when coming into a dashboard. Finally, it is very important to align everything neatly and size everything as equally as possible. This makes the dashboard much easier to read.

Now let's take an example—seen in the next screenshot—of a dashboard that is not set in quadrants and aligned neatly:

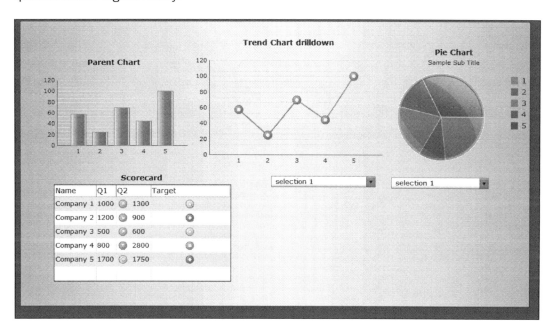

This dashboard is harder to read and navigate now, as things are not in quadrants. The drop-down selectors are on the bottom right-hand side, so we have to shift our eyes to the main parent chart diagonally whenever we make a change which is not very user friendly.

See Also

Adding a background to your dashboard.

In addition, for good dashboard layout designs you can read *Information Dashboard Design, Stephen Few*.

8
Dashboard Connectivity

In this chapter, we will cover:

- ▶ Creating a news ticker with Excel XML Maps
- ▶ Using Query as a Web Service (QaaWS)
- ▶ Using Live Office Connection
- ▶ Connecting to SAP BW
- ▶ Using Universe queries
- ▶ Passing values from dashboard to dashboard with Flash Variables
- ▶ Accessing dashboards with live data outside of InfoView using CELoginToken

Introduction

Dashboards get really powerful when they are able to display recent or even real-time data. Of course, you can manually enter the updated data in the Dashboard Design spreadsheet and publish a new dashboard every time the data changes. If your dashboard uses a lot of data that changes regularly, you will quickly find out that this is going to be a very time consuming task.

A good solution is to set up up one or more data connections between the dashboard and an external data source. If the data in the source changes, the dashboard will show this updated information.

Creating a news ticker with Excel XML Maps

In this recipe, we will show you how to integrate a real-time news ticker into your dashboard. To set up this connection to an online news website, we will use the **Excel XML Maps** connection.

Getting ready

Make sure the spreadsheet area has a **Developer** tab, if you are using MS Excel 2007. If you do not see this tab, skip to the *There is more...* section of this recipe to set this up. Furthermore, you need a connection to the Internet.

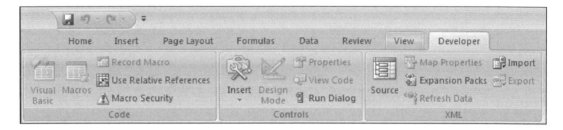

How to do it...

1. Go to `http://www.cnn.com/`. At the bottom of this site, you will see an RSS link. You can also go directly to `http://www.cnn.com/services/rss/`.

2. Copy the URL of the **Top Stories** RSS feed `http://rss.cnn.com/rss/cnn_topstories.rss`.

> RSS is an XML-based method by which the web content can be easily and quickly distributed, when it is changed or newly entered into a website.

3. Open a new Dashboard Design file, go to the **Developer** tab, and click on **Source**. The **XML Source** pane now appears.

> If you are using MS Excel 2003, you can find the **XML Source** pane in the **Data menu | XML | XML Source**.

4. Click on the **XML Maps...** button.

5. In the upcoming **XML Maps** window, click on the **Add...** button.

6. Paste the URL into the **File name** field and click **Open**. There might appear a message stating that this XML source does not refer to a schema and Excel will create one. Click on **OK**.

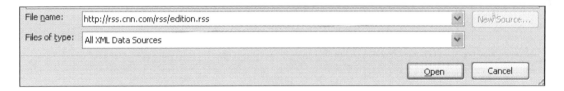

7. Click on **OK** once more in the **XML Maps** window to close it. The **XML Source** window now shows all the fields that are available in this RSS stream.

8. To create a news ticker we only need two of these fields—the title of the article and the URL to the article on the CNN website. Both the fields are located in the `item` folder—**title** and **link**. Click and drag the title field to cell A6 and drag the link field to cell B6.

9. Hit the **Refresh Data** button in the **Developer** tab. The cells below A6 and B6 will now be filled with data from the RSS feed.

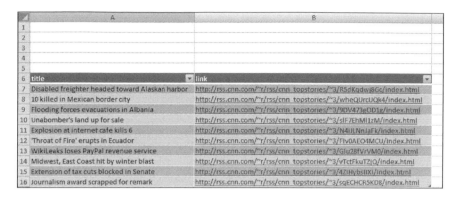

10. Open the **Data Manager**.

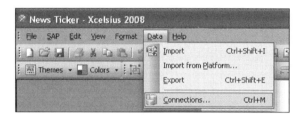

11. Click on the **Add** button and select **Excel XML Maps**. You can find this connection type in the **Existing Connections** area.

12. As you can see in the following screenshot, the **Data Manager** already picked up the RSS feed we added to the spreadsheet:

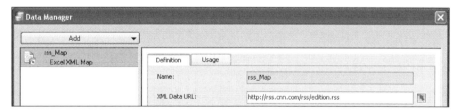

13. Go to the **Usage** tab. Select **Refresh Before Components Are Loaded**. Also, set **Refresh Every** to **1 Minutes**. Close the **Data Manager**.

14. Add a **Ticker** component to the canvas.

15. Bind its **Labels** to cells A7 through A16.

16. Select **Insertion Type Row**. Bind the **Source Data** field to cells B7 through B16. Bind the **Destination** field to cell B4.

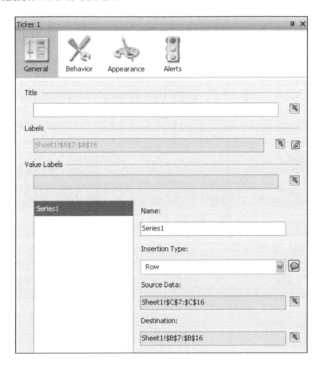

17. Now add an **URL Button** component to the canvas.

18. Bind the **URL** field to cell B4.

19. Empty the **Label** field.

20. Go to the **Behavior** tab and bind the **Trigger Cell** field to cell B4.

21. Finally, go to the **Appearance** tab and deselect the **Show Button Background** option. The **URL** button component should now be invisible.

22. Try your dashboard!

> Large spike in radiation detected at Japan nuke plant   -   Radiation from plant d

How it works...

Let's recap what we just did. First we added a RSS feed from CNN.com to our spreadsheet. We used the standard Excel XML Maps functionality to do this. A big advantage of this method is that we can preview the data directly in the spreadsheet, which makes setting up components and data bindings easy.

Next, we created a data connection in the **Data Manager**. This step is necessary to let Dashboard Design know where to get the data from and under what conditions (refresh rate). If we do not do this, the dashboard will not get fresh data from the RSS feed and will only use the data that is already stored in the spreadsheet cells.

We bound a Ticker component to the cells containing the titles of the news stories. If the user clicks on one of the titles a webpage should open with the right story. We set up row insertion to fetch the right URL for the URL Button. Finally, we configured the URL Button component so it would be triggered without clicking on it.

There is more...

Adding the Developer tab

To create a XML Maps connection in MS Excel 2007, you need the **Developer** tab. Unfortunately, this tab is not activated by default. Follow the next steps to add it:

1. Close Dashboard Design.

2. Open MS Excel.

3. Click on the Office button in the upper left-hand side of the window and click on the **Excel Options** button.

4. Now select **Show Developer tab in the Ribbon** in the **Popular** section and click on **OK**.

5. Close MS Excel and open Dashboard Design again. The **Developer** tab is now available in the spreadsheet area.

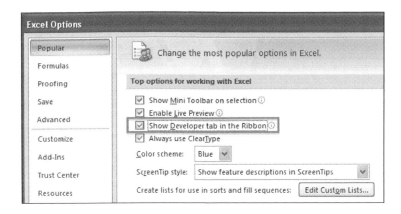

Usage tab

Most connection types in the **Data Manager** have a **Usage** tab, as we saw in step 14 of the recipe. There are two sections in this tab—**Refresh Options** and **Load Status**.

With **Refresh Before Components Are Loaded** the data connection will be used to get data as soon the dashboard starts. The **Refresh Every** option sets the refresh rate in seconds, minutes or hours. You can also choose to refresh the data when a value in a spreadsheet cell changes or a certain value is matched.

During the loading of fresh data it is possible to inform the dashboard user what is happening at the moment (loading data or idle). You can insert these messages in a spreadsheet cell and display them for example with a Label component. Also, a nice idea is to display a loading-image instead of text. You can use Dynamic Visibility to set this up (see _Chapter 4_).

If you select the **Enable Load Cursor** option, the cursor will change from the standard arrow into an hourglass. The **Disable Mouse Input on Load** option will disable user interactions (mouse clicks and mouse overs) as long as data is being loaded.

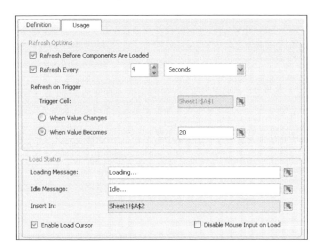

Connection Refresh button

To manually refresh data when using the dashboard, we can use the **Connection Refresh Button** component. This component can refresh one or more connections that are defined in the **Data Manager**.

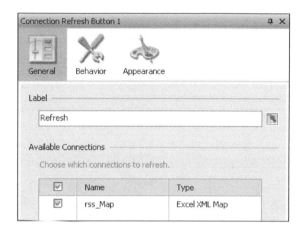

Using Query as a WebService (QaaWS)

Query as aWebService (**QaaWS**) is a small but powerful tool in the SAP BusinessObjects Enterprise portfolio that allows us to create a query on top of a SAP BusinessObjects Universe and publish its results as a Web Service. This recipe shows you how to create such a QaaWS and how to consume the data in Dashboard Design.

Getting ready

First you need a SAP BusinessObjects Enterprise installation (with server and client components installed). Also, you need a Universe that is connected to an underlying database.

How to do it...

1. Open **Query As A Web Service** and log on to your SAP BusinessObjects Enterprise server. You can find this application in the **BusinessObjects Enterprise Client Tools** folder.

2. Click the **New Query** button in the upper left. Here you can enter a name for this web service and a description (not mandatory). Enter a name for your web service and click on the **Next** button.

3. In this screen, we select the Universe we want to use. Select a **Universe name** and click on **Next**.

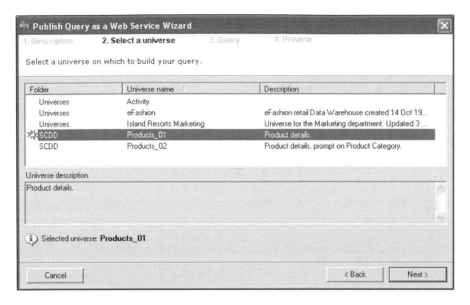

4. The next screen looks like the query panel of a web intelligence document. In the left-hand side column of this screen the available dimensions, measures, and filters from the selected Universe are displayed. Drag the ones you want to use into the **Result Objects** area and click on **Next**.

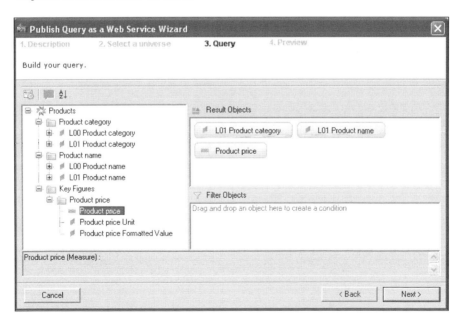

5. If the **Answer prompts** screen pops up, just click on the **OK** button. The *There is more...* section of this recipe will discuss the use of prompts.

6. The **Preview** screen is shown, which provides us with an overview of the QaaWS setup we just created. Most important here is the **Preview** part that shows how the data and its layout will look like in Dashboard Design after setting up the data connection and binding the columns to the spreadsheet. Click on **Publish**.

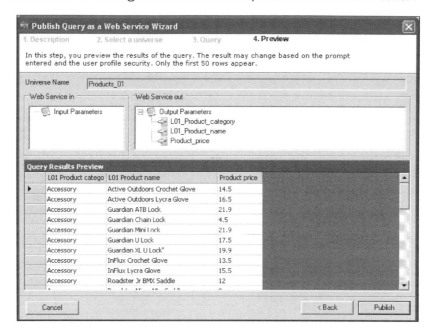

7. Now click on the **To Clipboard** button to copy the web service URL to your clipboard.

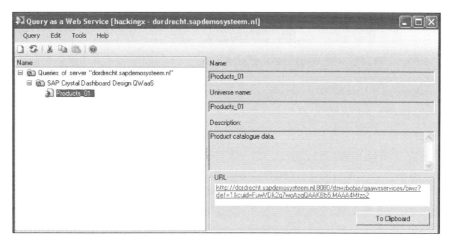

8. Open Dashboard Design and go to the **Data Manager**.
9. Add a **Query as a Web Service** connection.
10. Paste the URL into the **WSDL URL** field and click on **Import**.

11. Select the row folder in the **Output Values** section. As we have three columns of data in this Web Service, we have to bind it to a three-column area in the spreadsheet. Bind it to cells A6 until C30.

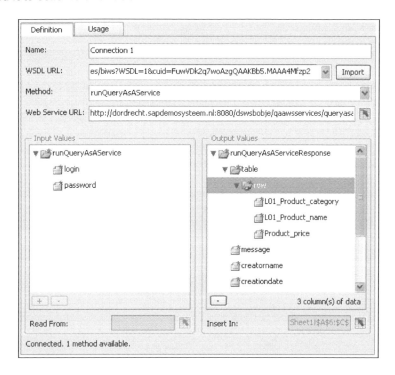

12. Go to the **Usage** tab and select **Refresh Before Components Are Loaded**. Close the **Data Manager**.

13. To see if and how the data is fetched by Dashboard Design from the web service, add a **Spreadsheet Table** component to the canvas and bind it to cells A6 until C30.

14. **Preview** the dashboard. A **User Identification** popup will appear. Enter your SAP BusinessObjects Enterprise credentials to log in. The **Spreadsheet** component will now be filled with data from the web service.

How it works...

In this recipe, we used three stages to get data into our dashboard. First was the SAP BusinessObjectsUniverse, second was the QaaWS definition on top of the Universe that created a web service, and third was the QaaWS connection set up in the Dashboard Design **Data Manager** to connect to this web service.

As we cannot preview the data in the Dashboard Design spreadsheet like we did in the *Creating a news ticker with Excel XML Maps* recipe, we used the Spreadsheet component to check how the cells are populated when running the dashboard.

There is more...

Using prompts

QaaWS prompts make it possible to load only the data that the dashboard user needs when using the dashboard.

1. Repeat steps 1 to 4 of the recipe. Before clicking on **Next** in the fourth step, add the dimension that you want to make a selection on into the **Filter Objects** area. Select the **Prompt** option by clicking on the little arrow on the right-hand side.

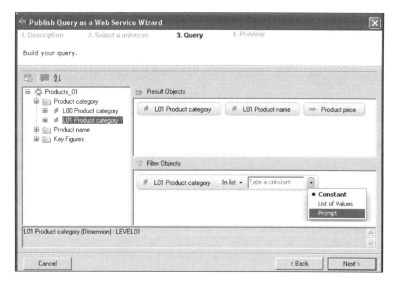

2. The **Answer prompts** window appears. Here, you have to select one of the available values to enable QaaWS to create a preview of the data in the next screen. Select a value and click on **OK**.

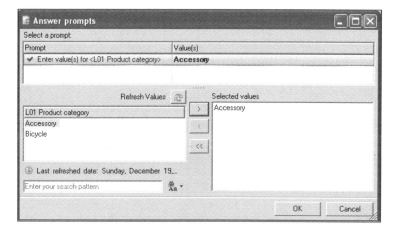

3. As you can see in the following screenshot, the prompt filter object we added is now shown as **Input Parameter**. Publish the QaaWS.

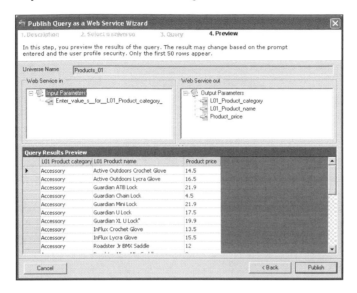

4. Repeat steps 8 through 11 of the recipe.

5. The prompt is now displayed in the **Input Values** area. Bind the prompt to cell A1.

6. Go to the **Usage** tab and bind the **Trigger Cell** field to cell A1. Now the data will only be refreshed when the value in this cell changes. Close the **Data Manager**.

7. Set up a **Spreadsheet** component, like we did in step 13 of the recipe.

8. Add a **Combo Box** component and add the **Labels** for the prompt. Use **Insertion TypeLabel** and bind the **Destination** field to cell A1.

9. Preview the dashboard and switch between the different labels to see the different data selections being loaded into the dashboard.

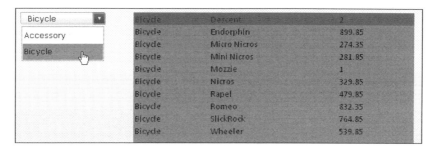

Methods

As you might have noticed while creating a QaaWS connection in Dashboard Design, there are several different **methods** you can use in the **Definition** tab. These methods can be split into two groups—to retrieve data and to list available parameter values. The methods are discussed here:

▶ `runQueryAsAService`: This is the default selected option that we used for the examples in this recipe as well. It enables us to send out parameter values and retrieve data.

▶ `runQueryAsAServiceEx`: This method gives the same output results as `runQueryAsAService`, but instead of providing an exact input parameter value, we can now also give its index.

▶ `valuesOf_parameter`: This method will return a list of values for its input parameter, which can be used to create a selector like we did in the *Using prompts* section.

Remember that each QaaWS connection can only use a single method, so you might have to set up more than one connection.

Using Live Office connection

With SAP BusinessObjects **Live Office** it is possible to insert data from Crystal Reports and Web Intelligence reports into the Microsoft Office products (Word, Excel, Outlook, PowerPoint). As the data can also be refreshed with this add-on, the Live Office Connection can be a very useful way to provide our dashboards with fresh data.

Getting ready

For this recipe, you need a SAP BusinessObjects Enterprise installation and the Live Office Connection software installed on your client computer. You need a Crystal Report, Web Intelligence report, or Universe (to connect to) as well.

How to do it...

1. Open a new Dashboard Design file and go to the **Preferences** in the **File** menu. In the **Excel Options** section, check if **Live Office Compatibility** is enabled.

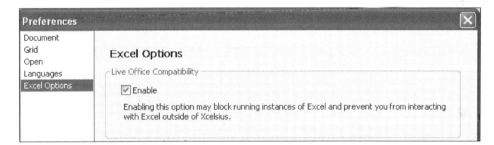

2. Go to the **Live Office** tab of the spreadsheet. Click on the **Crystal Reports** or **Web Intelligence** button to insert a report.

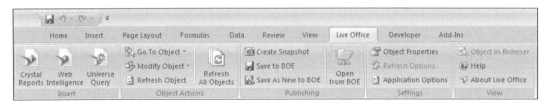

3. Log on to your SAP BusinessObjects Enterprise environment and choose a report.

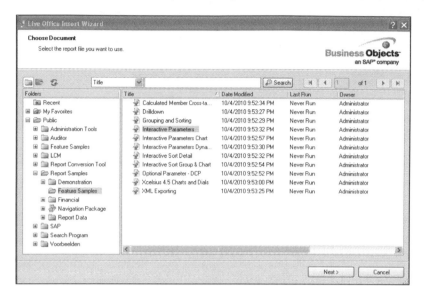

4. If your report contains any parameters, a window will appear in which you can enter the parameter values to filter the data set that should be retrieved. In the *There is more...* section of this recipe, we will discuss how to connect these prompts to the dashboard.

5. In the next window, the actual Crystal Reports or Web Intelligence report is shown. With some mouse dragging and selecting, you can select the data you want to import.

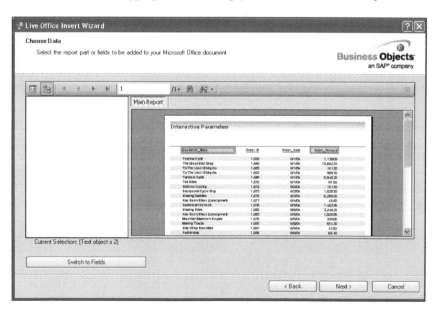

6. Click on the **Switch to Fields** button to see an overview of all available fields is shown. Here, you can also select which fields you want to use.

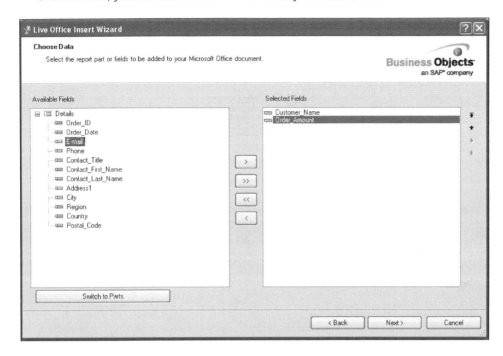

7. If you want to set some more filters on fields, you can use the window shown in the following screenshot:

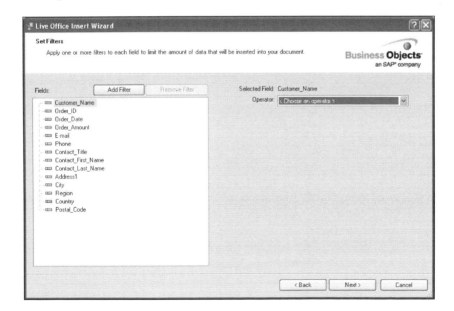

8. In the final window, you can enter a name for the Live Office Objects you just set up. Click on **Finish**.

9. As you will notice, the spreadsheet is now populated with data from the report.

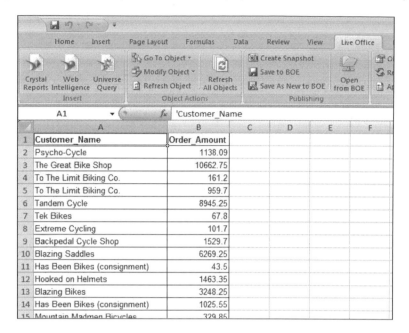

10. Go to the **Data Manager** and add a **Live Office Connections** connection. Change the **Sessions URL** in the correct URL to your SAP BusinessObjects Enterprise server. The **Ranges** are already bound to the cells in which the data has been imported. As you can see the **Headers** and **Data Grid** are separated. Do not forget to set up the **Usage** tab (see the recipe *Creating a news ticker with Excel XML Maps*).

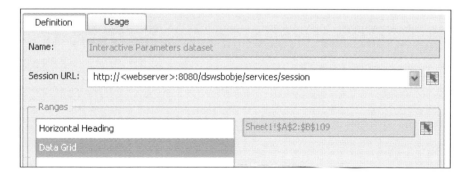

How it works...

With the Live Office Connection, we retrieve data from Crystal Reports, Web Intelligence reports, or connect directly to a Universe. The main advantage of this type of connection over QaaWS is that with Live Office we are able to use data from scheduled Crystal Reports or Web Intelligence reports, instead of querying the database every time we want to use the dashboard. In an environment with a large user base and large data sets, this can be an important factor. Another advantage of Live Office over QaaWs is that we get the benefits of Web Intelligence or Crystal Report such as using Crosstabs, formatting, and layout control. Also, just like the Excel XML Maps connection method with Live Office, we can load actual data into the spreadsheet during the design of the dashboard, which eases the development.

There is more...

Using prompts

Just like we have seen in the *Using Query as a Web Service (QaaWS)* recipe, it is possible to use prompts to select the data that we want to retrieve and use in our dashboard with the Live Office Connection. Use the following steps to set this up:

1. In the **Live Office** tab of the spreadsheet, select the **Modify Object** button and choose **Prompt Setting...**.

2. In the window that appears, you will see the available parameters. After selecting the parameter you want to use, select **Choose Excel data range**.

3. Bind the field to a spreadsheet cell.

4. Now you follow steps 6 through 9 of the *There is more...* section on *Using Prompts* of the *Using Query as a Web Service (QaaWS)* recipe to use these prompts from within your dashboard.

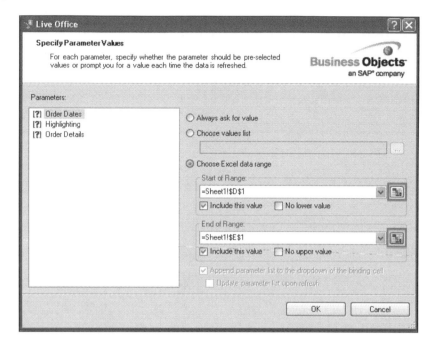

Connecting to SAP BW

The introduction of a direct connection between Dashboard Design and SAP BW over **BI Consumer Services** (**BICS**) meant a big step forward for Dashboard Design development. With this connectivity option the detour via QAAWS or Live Office is not necessary anymore to get data into dashboards from a SAP BW system.

Getting ready

To set up a connection between Dashboard Design and SAP BW you have to make sure that your installation fulfils the following technical requirements:

▶ SAP BW 7.01, service pack 05 with ABAP and Java stacks deployed

▶ SAP BusinessObjectsXcelsius Enterprise 2008 Service Pack 02

▶ SAP Frontend 7.x installed at client with BI Add-Ons

For this recipe, we are using a simple BEx Query to connect to.

How to do it...

1. Open a new Dashboard Design file and open the **Data Manager**. Add a new **SAP NetWeaver BW Connection**.

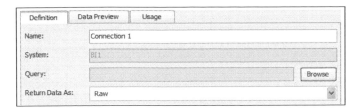

2. Click on the **Browse** button to log in to the SAP BW system. Select the correct SAP BW system, enter your login credentials, and click on **OK**.

3. Use the **Find** option to search for your query. Click on **Open** to select the query.

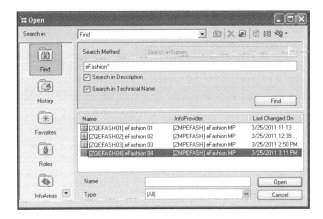

4. Go to the **Data Preview** tab and click on the **Refresh Data Preview** button. A preview of the layout of the returned data will now be shown here. In our example, there are seven columns shown—four characteristics and three key figures.

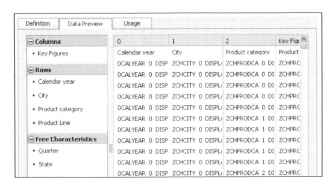

The **Data Preview** tab has the option to rearrange the layout of the output of the BEx Query and add/remove characteristics by using drag-and-drop.

5. Go back to the **Definition** tab.

6. Select **Cross-Tab Data** from the **Output Values** section and bind it to the spreadsheet. For each column in the **Data Preview** tab (step 4) you need a column in the spreadsheet.

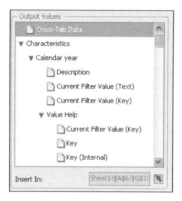

7. Go to the **Usage** tab and select the **Refresh Before Components Are Loaded** option. **Close** the **Data Manager**.

8. Add a **Spreadsheet** component to the canvas and bind it to the same cell range as you bound to in step 6.

9. If you hit the **Preview** button, a message will appear stating that it is not possible to preview this dashboard with BI Query connection data. If you hit **Yes**, the dashboard will be previewed without live data from SAP BW.

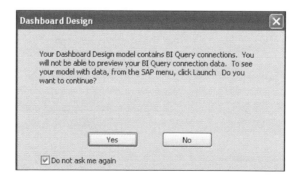

10. Click on **No**. The recipe *Publishing to SAP BW* in *Chapter 9* covers the **Launch** function to deploy the dashboard with an active connection to SAP BW.

How it works...

The **SAP NetWeaver BW Connection** enables us to retrieve data from a SAP BW system via a **BEx Query**. For this example, we used a simple BEx Query we created in the **BEx Query Designer** with four characteristics in the rows and three key figures in the columns. In the properties settings for the characteristics, we defined the **Results Rows** as **Always Suppress** so the output won't include this row.

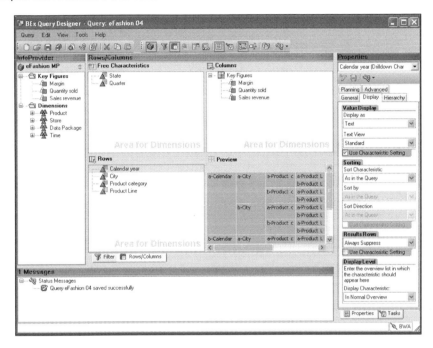

If we run this BEx Query, the result would be as in the following image. The first row shows the headers for the three key figures. In the second row, the headers for the four characteristics are shown. In this row as well, the Unit information for the key figures placed (EUR) is placed when available.

Running the original BEx Query is a great way to get an overview of how the data output will eventually look for setting up the spreadsheet. Especially, if you are using multiple characteristics and key figures this will give you a view that is much clearer than the **Data Preview** tab in the **Data Manager**.

There is more...

Using variables and filters

Just as we have seen how to use prompts in the *Using Query as a Web Service (QaaWS)* recipe, we can use BEx Query variables and filters to fetch a limited set of data.

1. Go to the **Data Manager**.

2. In the **Output Values** area search for **Variables** and select **Value Help** for the variable you want to use.

3. Bind **Current Filter Value (Key)** to a range of cells. In these cells the values you can choose from will be inserted.

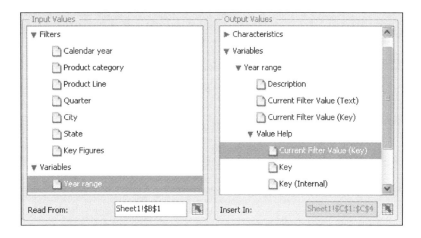

4. In the **Input Values** area, select the variable and bind it to a cell. This cell should contain the value that the BEx Query uses as input for the variable.

5. Now add a selector component to the canvas.

6. Bind its **Labels** field to the cell range you bound to in step 3.

7. Set the **Insertion Type** to **Label** and bind the **Destination** field to same cell as you bound to in step 4.

The procedure for filters is the same as for variables. The only difference is that in the **Output Values** area you need to select the **Characteristics** instead of the **Variables** elements.

If you are using a BEx Query variable that represents a data interval, the value that you use as input for this variable should have the following format: `StartValue - EndValue`, (a space before and after the minus). You can use the Excel `Concatenate` function to combine the output of two selectors in a single cell and bind this cell to the variable in the **Input Values** area.

Other Output Values

The **Output Values** area includes the following elements:

▶ **Cross-Tab Data**: Provides the complete query output

▶ **Characteristics**: Provides fields to create a list of values

▶ **Variables**: Also provides fields to create a list of values

▶ **Static Filter**: Gives information about the filters that already have been created in the BEx Query

▶ **Information**: Provides information about the BEx Query, such as the **Query Technical Name** or the **Last Data Update**

▶ **Messages**: Provides BEx Query error messages

Returned data format

The SAP NetWeaver BW connection gives us the option to let the data return as **Raw** or **Formatted**. By default, the **Raw** option is selected. If you choose **Formatted**, the BExformat will be used, which means that the data includes information such as the number of decimals and currency.

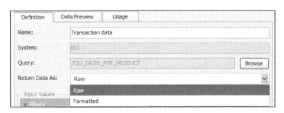

Using Universe queries

The **Universe query** feature differs from the other data connection methods in that we can create a query from a Universe without leaving Dashboard Design and that we are able to bind the result data not only to the spreadsheet, but also directly to the components on the canvas.

Getting ready

Open a new Dashboard Design file and activate the **Query Browser** pane from the **View** menu. You also need an SAP BusinessObjects Enterprise environment with a Universe you want to connect to.

 Unfortunately, only `.unx` Universes are supported. You can use the **Information Design Tool** to convert `.unv` Universes to `.unx`.

How to do it...

1. Go to the **Query Browser** and click on the **Add Query** button.

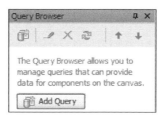

2. If you are not already connected to the SAP BusinessObjects Environment a pop up will appear asking you to log in. Enter the system and user credentials to log in.

3. A list with available Universes appears. Select the Universe you want to use and click on **Next**.

4. In the **Build Query** screen you can define the Universe query. Drag a dimension and a measure to the **Results Objects** section.

5. Drag a dimension you want to filter onto the **Filter Objects** area.

6. Set this filter to **Equal to Prompt**. The **Edit Prompt** screen pops up. Click on **OK**.

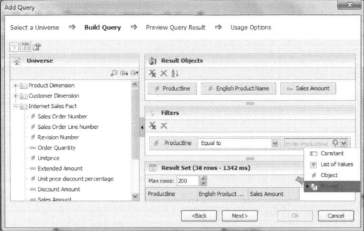

7. Click on the **Next** button to go to the **PreviewQuery Results** screen.

8. As we added a prompt, we now need to select a value to fill this prompt to retrieve some preview data. Select a value from the list and click on **Run**.

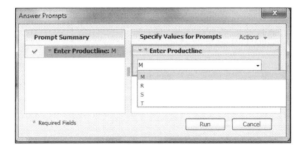

9. The result of the query will be shown now. Click on **Next**.

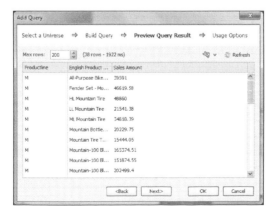

10. The final screen is the **Usage Options** screen, which looks exactly the same as the **Usage** tab in the **Data Manager**. Click on **OK**.

11. The query has been added to the **Query Browser** pane, including the **Result Objects**, **Filters**, and **Prompts** you selected.

12. Bind each dimension and measure of the **Result Objects** area to a column in the spreadsheet.

13. Add a Spreadsheet Table component to the canvas. Bind its **Display Data** field to the cells you bound the dimensions and measures to in the previous step.

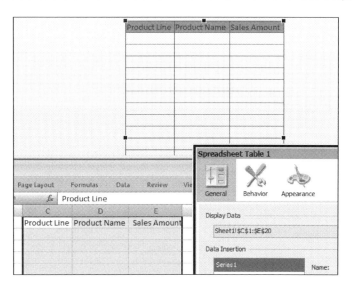

14. Now add a List Box component to the canvas. Click on the button to the right-hand side of the **Labels** field and select **Query Data**.

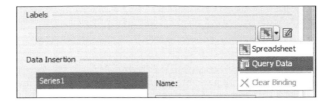

15. Select the dimension you want its values to be used as selection labels and click on **OK**.

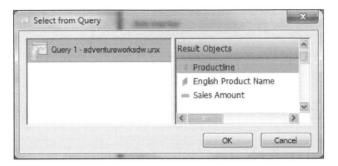

16. Set the **Insertion Type** to **Label** and click on the button to the right-hand side of the **Destination** field and again select **Query Data**. Now select the prompt we created in step 6 and click on **OK**.

17. Preview the dashboard!

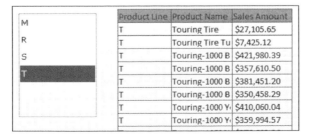

How it works...

The Universe query feature gives us the opportunity to connect a dashboard to a Universe without leaving Dashboard Design to set up QaaWS or Live Office and without using the spreadsheet in Dashboard Design, as we can bind the query results directly to the components.

In the recipe, we set up a List Box component with this Universe query feature by retrieving the Label values directly from the Universe. The selected label was used as input for the query prompt we created earlier while setting up the Universe query.

From the **Query Browser**, we inserted the output of the query into the spreadsheet, from which we used the data to be displayed in a Spreadsheet Table component. Of course you can also add for example a chart component and use the **Query Data** option to connect to the result data, just like we did with the labels for the List Box component.

There is more...

Query Prompt Selector

With the Query Prompt Selector component we are able to use prompts that we defined in the query, again, without using the spreadsheet. From the **Query Browser** you can select and drag the prompt onto the canvas to add such a Query Prompt Selector component. You can also find this component in the Components list.

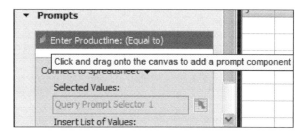

In the **General** tab of the properties pane of this component, you can define whether you want the query to be refreshed after the selection has been made or after clicking on the button. Here, you can also change the **Button Label**.

The following screenshot shows this component:

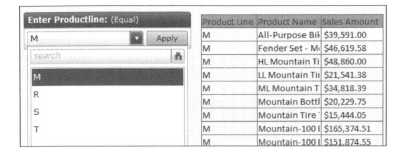

Query Refresh button

With the Query Refresh button component you are able to manually refresh the query. After adding this component to the canvas you need to select the Universe queries that should be refreshed after clicking on the button.

Passing values from dashboard to dashboard with Flash Variables

As we have seen in *Chapter 6*, recipe *Creating a slide show* we can show .swf files inside a dashboard. If you load a Dashboard Design .swf file into another Dashboard Design dashboard, a big drawback is that it seems impossible to let them have some kind of interaction. Both dashboards of course have their own separated spreadsheet logic.

In this recipe, we will show you how to workaround this problem and pass values from one dashboard to another using Flash Variables.

Getting ready

No preparations are needed for this recipe.

How to do it...

1. Drag an **Input Text** component and a **SWF Loader** component to the canvas.

2. Go to the spreadsheet and enter in cell A1: **Company A**. This is the default value that will be passed to the second dashboard.

3. Type the following in cell A2: **child.swf?Variable1=**.
   Type the following in cell A3: **=CONCATENATE(A2,A1)**.

4. Link the **Input Text** component to cell A1. Also, make sure you select the **Insert Data On Load** option and bind its **Destination** field to cell A1.

5. Bind the **Source URL** field of the **SWF Loader** component to cell C3.

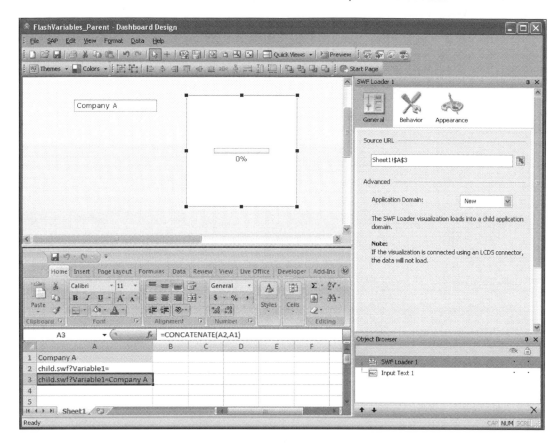

6. Save and export this dashboard to an `.swf` file. See the *Chapter 10* recipe, *Exporting a Standard SWF* for more information. Name this `.swf` file `parent.swf`.

7. Open a new Dashboard Design file and drag a **Label** component to the canvas.

8. Now bind this **Label** component to cell A1.

9. Define this cell as Named Range **Variable1**. See *Chapter 1* recipe *Using Named Ranges* for more information on how to do this.

10. Decrease the size of the canvas by clicking on the **Fit Canvas To Components** option in the **Standard Toolbar**. You can also find these options in the **View** menu.

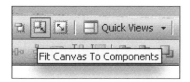

11. The following is the screenshot of canvas that is decreased in size:

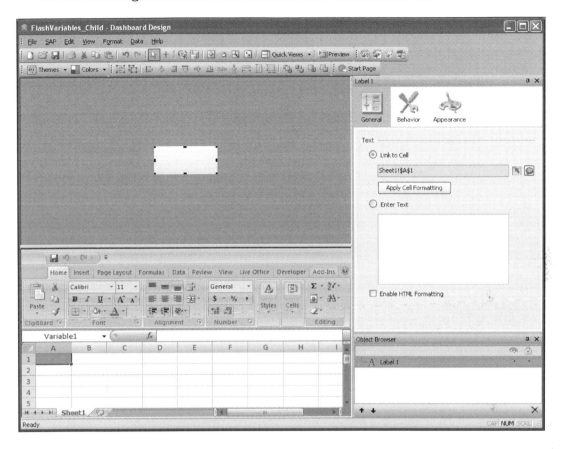

12. Now go to the **Data Manager** and add a **Flash Variables** connection.

13. Click on the **Import Named Ranges** button. The named range you just created will pop up in the **Ranges** window. You can now close the **Data Manager**.

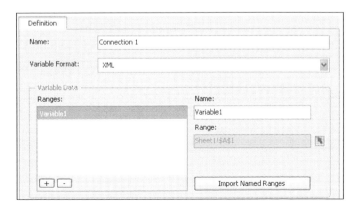

14. Save and export the dashboard to an SWF file. Make sure the name of this SWF file is `child.swf`.

15. Open `parent.swf`. Change **Company A** into another value, click outside the text input box, or hit the *Enter* key and see what happens.

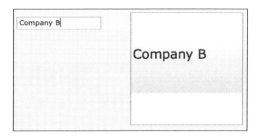

How it works...

We just created two dashboards: a parent and a child dashboard, where the child dashboard is loaded in the parent dashboard with the **SWF Loader** component. The source URL in this **SWF Loader** component not only pointed to the location of the child dashboard (`child.swf`), but also contained a variable with a value (`?Variable1=CompanyA`). With the Flash Variables data connection the child dashboard is able to read the value data for this variable and put it in a spreadsheet cell during runtime.

We used the Excel Concatenate formula so each time the variable value changes a new URL is created. The SWF Loader reloads the child dashboard after each time the Source URL changes.

There is more...

Using multiple variables

Using more than one variable is easy. Just repeat the steps of this recipe and make sure you separate the variables with an ampersand (&). An example URL with two variables would look like this: **child.swf?Variable1=Value1&Variable=Value2**.

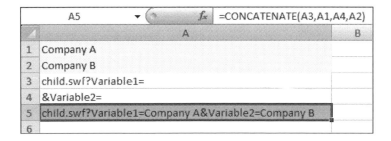

Passing multiple values

Besides using more than one variable it is also possible to pass multiple values through a single variable.

1. Reopen the child dashboard you created earlier.

2. Open the **Data Manager** and select the **Flash Variables** connection we already created.

3. Change the **Variable Format** from **XML** to **CSV**.

4. Bind the **Range** of Variable1 to cell A1 through A3. Close the **Data Manager** windows.

5. Replace the **Label** component with a **Spreadsheet** component.

6. Bind this **Spreadsheet** component to cells A1 until A3.

7. Export the dashboard to an SWF file again. Name it `child.swf`.

8. Open the `parent.swf` file.

9. Enter multiple values, separated by a comma (,) and see what happens.

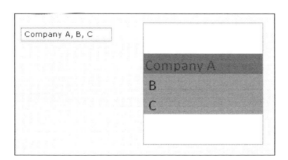

Accessing dashboards with live data outside of Infoview using CELogonToken

Not all corporations want their employees to access dashboards through BI Launch Pad (Infoview). Some may want to access dashboards through a third-party website or portal such as MS Sharepoint. Unfortunately, a logon prompt will pop up if a user tries to execute a live query when they are not logged into BI Launch Pad.

So we will need some sort of hidden login mechanism that bypasses the pop up to refresh data on the dashboard. In our example, we assume that there is one login that can view dashboards. Using that login we will then populate the CELogonToken, which then allows authentication to occur transparently.

Getting ready

Create a dashboard that has a connection to either a Query as a Web Service object or Live Office object. In this recipe, we create a QaaWS object, using the eFashion 1997 demo universe. Select the **Month** dimension and **Sales Revenue** measure as the **Result Objects**. On the **Filter** insert **Holiday Y/N** and choose **equal to** and **prompt**.

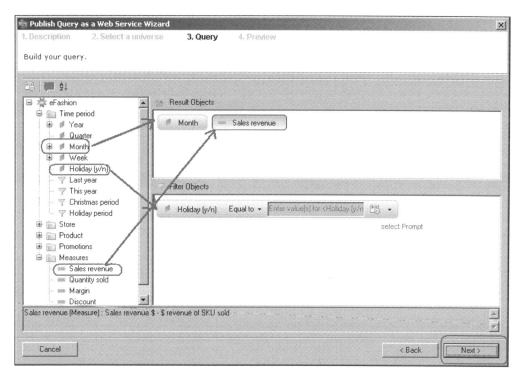

Drag a **Spreadsheet** component and a **Combo Box** selector onto the canvas. Set up the **Query as a Web Service** connection, bind the **input prompt** to the **Combo Box** selector, and the **output** to the **Spreadsheet** component. Name the dashboard as Test.swf.

> Read the recipe _Using Query as a Web Service (QaaWS)_ for a step-by-step guide to creating a QaaWS object and using it on a dashboard.

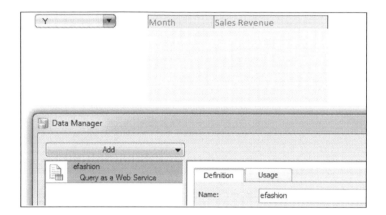

How to do it...

1. Create a folder called DashboardTest in <BO Installation>\Tomcat55\ webapps\InfoViewApp\ (In the _How it works..._ section, we will explain why).

2. Insert the Test.swf file in the directory that you created in step 1 (<BO Installation>\Tomcat55\webapps\InfoViewApp\DashboardTest).

3. Create a file called dashboardTest.jsp in <BO Installation>\Tomcat55\ webapps\InfoViewApp\DashboardTest.

4. Insert the code snippet below into the dashboardTest.jsp file. The highlighted server, username, password, port, and SWF name are the variables that you will need to change to match your configuration.

```
<%@ page import=""com.crystaldecisions.sdk.exception.SDKException,
com.crystaldecisions.sdk.framework.*,
com.crystaldecisions.sdk.occa.infostore.*,
com.crystaldecisions.sdk.occa.security.*,
java.net.*,
com.crystaldecisions.Enterprise.*,
com.crystaldecisions.sdk.plugin.admin.*,
com.businessobjects.webutil.Encoder""
%>
<%@ page import=""java.sql.*""%>
<%
```

```
//--------------------------------------------------------------
---Create BO Session and redirect to Infoview

IEnterpriseSessionenterpriseSession;
/* * Set Enterprise Logon credentials. */
final String BO_CMS_NAME = ""server"";
final String BO_AUTH_TYPE = ""secEnterprise"";
final String BO_USERNAME = ""username"";
final String BO_PASSWORD = ""password"";

ILogonTokenMgrlogonTokenMgr;
String defaultToken = """";


final String INFOVIEW_URL = ""http://server:port/InfoViewApp/
logon/start.do"";
/*
* Log onto Enterprise
*/

booleanloggedIn = true;

try {
enterpriseSession = CrystalEnterprise.getSessionMgr().logon(BO_
USERNAME,BO_PASSWORD, BO_CMS_NAME,
BO_AUTH_TYPE);

logonTokenMgr = enterpriseSession.getLogonTokenMgr();

defaultToken = logonTokenMgr.createWCAToken("""", 20, 1);


}
catch (Exception error)
{
loggedIn = false;
}

//--------------------------------------------------------------
---If login successful

if(loggedIn) {

String Flashvars=""""&CELogonToken="" + Encoder.encodeURL(defaultTok
en);
Flashvars += ""&CEWebServiceURL="" + Encoder.encodeURL(""http://
server:port/dswsbobje/services/session"");

String output = """";
```

```
output = output + ""<OBJECT classid=''clsid:D27CDB6E-AE6D-
11cf-96B8-444553540000 codebase=''http://download.macromedia.
com/pub/shockwave/cabs/flash/swflash.cab#version=7,0,19,0''
id=''myMovieName'' style=''width: 355px; height: 237px''> \r\r"";

output = output + ""<PARAM NAME=movie VALUE=''Test.swf''> \r\r"";
//( \r = carriage return to make output more legible )

output = output + ""<PARAM NAME=quality VALUE=high> \r\r"";

output = output + ""<PARAM NAME=FlashVars value=\"""" + Flashvars
+ ""\"">\r\r"";

output = output + ""<EMBED src=''Test.swf'' flashvars=\""
"" + Flashvars + ""\"" quality=high bgcolor=#FFFFFF
WIDTH=''1000'' HEIGHT=''600'' NAME=''myMovieName'' ALIGN=\""\""
TYPE=''application/x-shockwave-flash'' PLUGINSPAGE=''http://www.
macromedia.com/go/getflashplayer''></EMBED></OBJECT>\r\r"";

out.println(output);

}

//------------------------------------------------------------
---If login failed
else {

out.println(""Login to Business Objects Failed."");

}

In your Internet browser, go to the URL http://server:port/
InfoViewApp/DashboardTest/dashboardTest.jsp.
```

How it works...

Let's first go through how a dashboard SWF is normally consumed inside InfoviewInfoView. The most important part here is that there is a CELogonToken flash variable that gets assigned a session token that BOE creates when you successfully log in to InfoviewInfoView.

How does Dashboard Design consume CELogonToken?

If you look inside the <OBJECT> tag in the code below, you will see that there is a flash variable called **CELogonToken**, which is highlighted. When SAP BusinessObjects renders the HTML page, it dynamically inserts the current logon token into the CELogonToken variable. Any dashboard that uses a QaaWS or Live Office connection will automatically consume the CELogonToken flash variable.

```
<OBJECT classid=""clsid:D27CDB6E-AE6D-11cf-96B8-444553540000""
codebase=""http://download.macromedia.com/pub/shockwave/cabs/flash/
swflash.cab#version=6,0,40,0"" WIDTH=""100%"" HEIGHT=""100%""
id=""myMovieName"" VIEWASTEXT>
<PARAM NAME=movie VALUE=""../../../../opendoc/documentDownload?iDocID=
10000&sKind=Flash"">
<PARAM NAME=quality VALUE=high>
<PARAM NAME=bgcolor VALUE=#FFFFFF>
<PARAM NAME=FlashVarsVALUE=""CELogonToken=servername.domain%4066270JJ4
5M1Ox2XibIf2B66268JUPcDiNQd2vGZEBe&CEWebServiceURL=http%3A%2F%2Fserver
name %3Aportnumber%2Fdswsbobje%2Fservices%2Fsession"">
<EMBED src=""../../../../opendoc/documentDownload?iDocID=10000&s
Kind=Flash"" flashVars=""CELogonToken=servername.domain%4066270
JJ45M1Ox2XibIf2B66268JUPcDiNQd2vGZEBe&CEWebServiceURL=http%3A%2
F%2Fservername%3Aportnumber8443%2Fdswsbobje%2Fservices%2Fsessio
n"" quality=high bgcolor=#FFFFFF WIDTH=""100%"" HEIGHT=""100%""
NAME=""myMovieName"" ALIGN="""" TYPE=""application/x-shockwave-flash""
PLUGINSPAGE=""http://www.macromedia.com/go/getflashplayer"">
</EMBED>
</OBJECT>
```

CELogonToken at runtime

Dashboards that have a QaaWS or Live Office connection will search for the CELogonToken when the connection is triggered. With each transaction to SAP BusinessObjects, the token is passed back to SAP BusinessObjects for authentication. If CELogonToken does not exist, the login pop up will show up. This happens if we view the dashboard outside of Infoview. Thus, our goal in this recipe is to retrieve a SAP BusinessObjects logon token and insert it into the CELogonToken flash variable. This is accomplished in the code on step 4.

Step-by-step code explanation

The first part of the code imports the required libraries from the SAP BusinessObjects SDK to retrieve the logon token. Step 1 mentions creating a directory inside tomcat55\ InfoViewApp\. The reason being that we do not have to worry about any import issues, as all the SDK JARs are inside the InfoviewApp lib folder. In reality, you can place the .jsp and .swf anywhere but you will have to make sure that the SDK libraries are loaded.

```
<%@ page import=""com.crystaldecisions.sdk.exception.SDKException,
com.crystaldecisions.sdk.framework.*,
com.crystaldecisions.sdk.occa.infostore.*,
com.crystaldecisions.sdk.occa.security.*,
java.net.*,
com.crystaldecisions.Enterprise.*,
com.crystaldecisions.sdk.plugin.admin.*,
com.businessobjects.webutil.Encoder""
%>
<%@ page import=""java.sql.*""%>
```

The second part of the code sets the server, username, and password. We can use a hard coded username/password if we want one universal dashboard user that has view access to a set of dashboards, which makes maintenance easier. If you are interested in Single Sign On, you will have to write some extra code to grab the appropriate username and password (this is out of the scope of this recipe). The code bolded in the try block retrieves the SAP BusinessObjects logon token.

```
//-----------------------------------------------------------------
Create BO Session and redirect to Infoview

IEnterpriseSessionenterpriseSession;

/* * Set Enterprise Logon credentials. */
final String BO_CMS_NAME = ""server"";
final String BO_AUTH_TYPE = ""secEnterprise"";
final String BO_USERNAME = ""username"";
final String BO_PASSWORD = ""password"";

ILogonTokenMgrlogonTokenMgr;
String defaultToken = """";


final String INFOVIEW_URL = ""http://server:port/InfoViewApp/logon/
start.do"";
/*
* Log onto Enterprise
*/

booleanloggedIn = true;

try {
enterpriseSession = CrystalEnterprise.getSessionMgr().logon(BO_
USERNAME,BO_PASSWORD, BO_CMS_NAME,
BO_AUTH_TYPE);

logonTokenMgr = enterpriseSession.getLogonTokenMgr();

defaultToken = logonTokenMgr.createWCAToken("""", 20, 1);
}
```

The third part of the code does a check to see if the token generated above was valid and generates the appropriate output which will call the dashboard with the appropriate CELogonToken variable.

```
//-------------------------------------------------------------------
If login successful

if(loggedIn) {

String Flashvars=""&CELogonToken="" + Encoder.encodeURL(defaultToken)
;
Flashvars += ""&CEWebServiceURL="" + Encoder.encodeURL(""http://
server:port/dswsbobje/services/session"");

String output = """";

output = output + ""<OBJECT classid=''clsid:D27CDB6E-AE6D-11cf-
96B8-444553540000 codebase=''http://download.macromedia.com/pub/
shockwave/cabs/flash/swflash.cab#version=7,0,19,0'' id=''myMovieName''
style=''width: 355px; height: 237px''> \r\r"";

output = output + ""<PARAM NAME=movie VALUE=''Test.swf''> \r\r""; //(
\r = carriage return to make output more legible )

output = output + ""<PARAM NAME=quality VALUE=high> \r\r"";

output = output + ""<PARAM NAME=FlashVars value=\"""" + Flashvars +
""\"">\r\r"";

output = output + ""<EMBED src=''Test.swf'' flashvars=\"" "" +
Flashvars + ""\"" quality=high bgcolor=#FFFFFF WIDTH=''1000''
HEIGHT=''600'' NAME=''myMovieName'' ALIGN=\""\"" TYPE=''application/
x-shockwave-flash'' PLUGINSPAGE=''http://www.macromedia.com/go/
getflashplayer''></EMBED></OBJECT>\r\r"";

out.println(output);

}


//-------------------------------------------------------------------
If login failed
else {

out.println(""Login to Business Objects Failed."");

}
%>
```

9
Exporting and Publishing

In this chapter, we will cover:

- ► Exporting to a standard SWF, PPT, PDF, and so on
- ► Exporting to SAP Business Objects Enterprise
- ► Publishing to SAP BW
- ► Dashboard Builder/Performance Management
- ► Building widgets (Adobe AIR)

Introduction

After building your dashboard to be the way you like it, you will need to turn it into a format that everyone is able to view on their computers. This is when the developers will export and publish their dashboard.

First, the visual model is compiled to a SWF file format. Compiling to a SWF file format ensures that the dashboard plays smoothly on different screen sizes and across different platforms. It also ensures that the users aren't given huge 10+ megabyte files.

After compilation of the visual model to a SWF file, developers can then publish it to a format of their choice. The following are the available choices—Flash (SWF), AIR, SAP BusinessObjects Platform, HTML, PDF, PPT, Outlook, and Word.

Once publishing is complete, the dashboard is ready to share!

Exporting to a standard SWF, PPT, PDF, and so on

After developing a Visual Model on Dashboard Design, we will need to somehow share it with users. We want to put it into a format that everyone can see on their machines. The simplest way is to export to a standard SWF file.

One of the great features Dashboard Design has is to be able to embed dashboards into different office file formats. For example, a presenter could have a PowerPoint deck, and in the middle of the presentation, have a working dashboard that presents an important set of data values to the audience. Another example could be an executive level user who is viewing a Word document created by an analyst. The analyst could create a written document in Word and then embed a working dashboard with the most updated data to present important data values to the executive level user.

You can choose to embed a dashboard in the following file types:

- ▶ PowerPoint
- ▶ Word
- ▶ PDF
- ▶ Outlook
- ▶ HTML

Getting ready

Make sure your visual model is complete and ready for sharing.

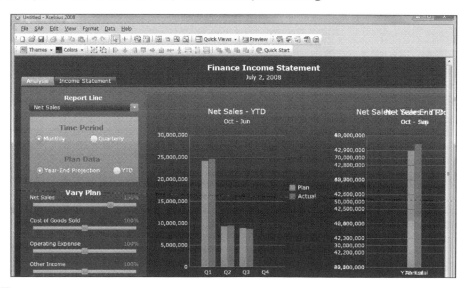

How to do it...

1. In the menu toolbar, go to **File | Export | Flash (SWF)**.

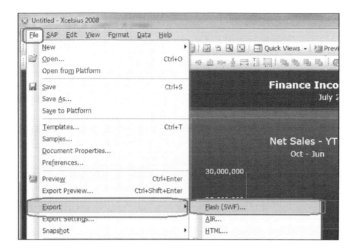

2. Select the directory in which you want the SWF to go to and the name of your SWF file.

How it works...

Xcelsius compiles the visual model into an SWF file that everyone is able to see. Once the SWF file has been compiled, the dashboard will then be ready for sharing. It is mandatory that anyone viewing the dashboard have Adobe Flash installed. If not, they can download and install it from `http://www.adobe.com/products/flashplayer/`.

If we export to PPT, we can then edit the PowerPoint file however we desire. If you have an existing PowerPoint presentation deck and want to append the dashboard to it, the easiest way is to first embed the dashboard SWF to a temporary PowerPoint file and then copy that slide to your existing PowerPoint file.

There's more...

Exporting to an SWF file makes it very easy for distribution, thus making the presentation of mockups great at a business level. Developers are able to work very closely with the business and iteratively come up with a visual model closest to the business goals. It is important though, when distributing SWF files, that everyone viewing the dashboards has the same version, otherwise confusion may occur. Thus, as a best practice, versioning every SWF that is distributed is very important.

It is important to note that when the much anticipated Adobe Flash 10.1 was released, there were problems with embedding Dashboard Design dashboards in DOC, PPT, PDF, and so on. However, with the 10.1.82.76 Adobe Flash Player update, this has been fixed. Thus, it is important that if users have Adobe Flash Player 10.1+ installed, the version is higher than or equal to 10.1.82.76.

When exporting to PDF, please take the following into account: In Dashboard Design 2008, the default format for exporting to PDF is Acrobat 9.0 (PDF 1.8). If Acrobat Reader 8.0 is installed, the default exported PDF cannot be opened. If using Acrobat Reader 8.0 or older, change the format to "Acrobat 6.0 (PDF 1.5)" before exporting to PDF.

Exporting to SAP Business Objects Enterprise

After Dashboard Design became a part of BusinessObjects, it was important to be able to export dashboards into the BusinessObjects Enterprise system. Once a dashboard is exported to BusinessObjects Enterprise, users can then easily access their dashboards through InfoView (now **BI launch pad**). On top of that, administrators are able control dashboard security.

Getting ready

Make sure your visual model is complete and ready for sharing.

How to do it...

1. From the menu toolbar, go to **File | Export | Export to SAP BusinessObjects Platform**.

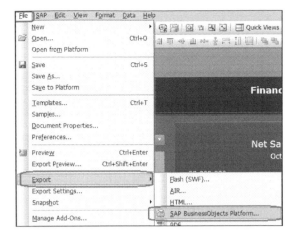

2. Enter your BusinessObjects login credentials and then select the location in the SAP BusinessObjects Enterprise system, where you want to store the SWF file, as shown in the following screenshot:

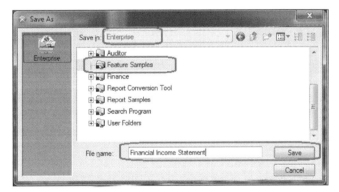

3. Log into BI launch pad (formerly known as InfoView) and verify that you can access the dashboard.

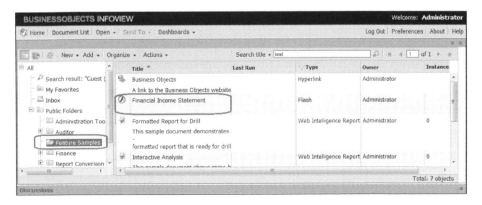

How it works...

When we export a dashboard to SAP BusinessObjects Enterprise, we basically place it in the SAP BusinessObjects Enterprise content management system. From there, we can control accessibility to the dashboard and make sure that we have one source of truth instead of sending out multiple dashboards through e-mail and possibly getting mixed up with what is the latest version. When we log into BI launch pad (formerly known as Infoview), it also passes the login token to the dashboard, so we don't have to enter our credentials again when connecting to SAP BusinessObjects Enterprise data. This is important because we don't have to manually create and pass any additional tokens once we have logged in.

There's more...

To give a true website type feel, developers can house their dashboards in a website type format using **Dashboard Builder**. This in turn provides a better experience for users, as they don't have to navigate through many folders in order to access the dashboard that they are looking for.

See Also

Please read the recipe *Housing your dashboards in Dashboard Builder* to learn how to utilize the Dashboard Builder tool in BI launch pad (formerly known as InfoView) to make the accessibility of your dashboards more user/Web friendly.

Publishing to SAP BW

This recipe shows you how to publish Dashboard Design dashboards to a SAP BW system. Once a dashboard is saved to the SAP BW system, it can be published within a SAP Enterprise Portal iView and made available for the users.

Getting ready

For this recipe, you will need an Dashboard Design dashboard model. This dashboard does not necessarily have to include a data connection to SAP BW.

How to do it...

1. Select **Publish** in the **SAP** menu. If you want to save the Xcelsius model with a different name, select the **Publish As...** option.

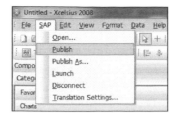

2. If you are not yet connected to the SAP BW system, a pop up will appear. Select the appropriate system and fill in your username and password in the dialog box.

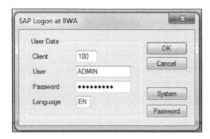

3. If you want to disconnect from the SAP BW system and connect to a different system, select the **Disconnect** option from the **SAP** menu.

4. Enter the **Description** and **Technical Name** of the dashboard. Select the location you want to save the dashboard to and click on **Save**. The dashboard is now published to the SAP BW system.

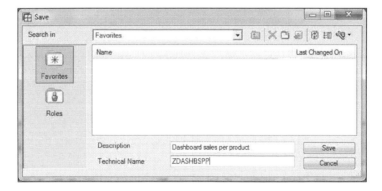

5. To launch the dashboard and view it from the SAP BW environment, select the **Launch** option from the **SAP** menu. You will be asked to log in to the SAP BW system before you are able to view the dashboard.

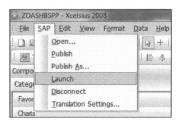

How it works...

As we have seen in this recipe, the publishing of an Dashboard Design dashboard to SAP BW is quite straightforward. As the dashboard is part of the SAP BW environment after publishing, the model can be transported between SAP BW systems like all other SAP BW objects.

There is more...

After launching step 5, the Dashboard Design dashboard will load in your browser from the SAP BW server. You can add the displayed URL to an SAP Enterprise Portal iView to make the dashboard accessible for portal users.

Housing your dashboard in Dashboard Builder

Using Dashboard Builder to organize your dashboards allows users to customize the look and feel to how the dashboards are accessed. In addition, administrators are able to control access to each navigational layout. When we house dashboards in Dashboard Builder, users don't have to navigate through numerous folders in order to get to their desired dashboard, but instead navigate through web page style type logic to access their desired dashboard. In our example, we will set up a **Corporate Dashboard** using Dashboard Builder, which will contain navigation to three dashboards.

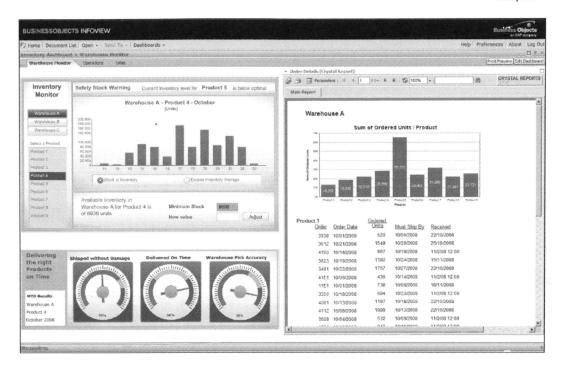

Getting ready

Make sure you have your dashboards created. In our example, we have an executive dashboard and two regional dashboards.

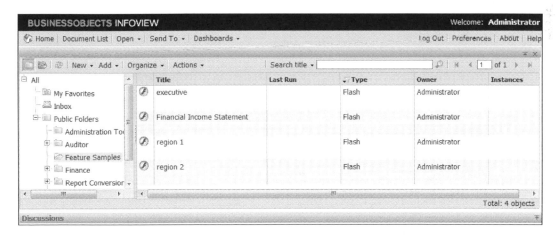

How to do it...

1. In BI launch pad (formerly known as InfoView), click on **Dashboards | Create Corporate Dashboard**.

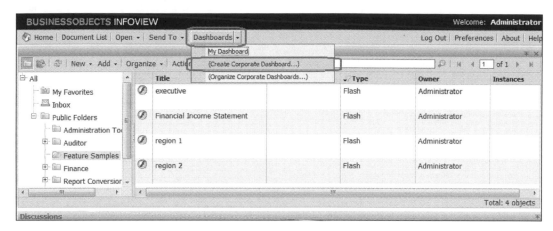

2. Type a name for the corporate dashboard.
3. Specify the folder in which you want to save the dashboard.
4. Select a category and then click on **OK**.

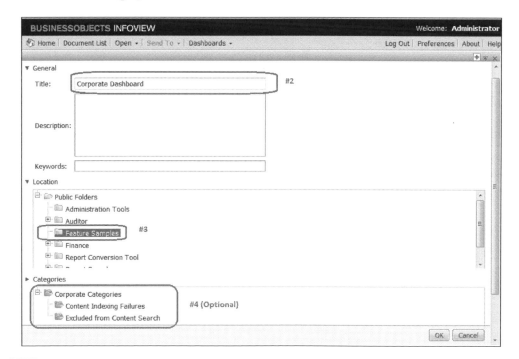

5. Next, click on **Edit dashboard**.

6. Click on the **Toolbox** link.

7. Select the **Corporate Analytic** icon.

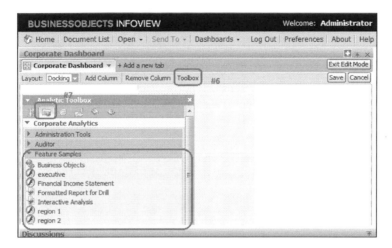

8. Drag the **executive** dashboard onto the canvas.

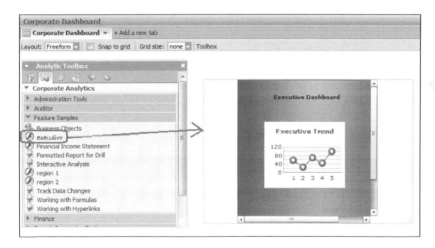

9. Click on the **Add a new tab** link and name it **Region 1 Sales**.

10. Drag the **region 1 dashboard** onto the canvas.

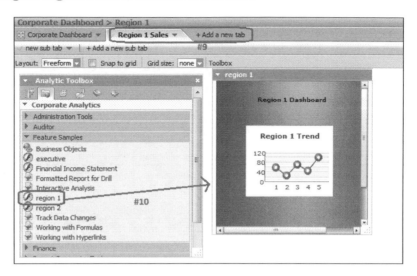

11. Click on the **Add a new tab** link and name it **Region 2 Inventory information**.

12. Drag the **region 2** dashboard onto the canvas.

How it works...

As you can see, when we set up the **Corporate Dashboard** using Dashboard Builder, it is easier to access the dashboards rather than clicking through a bunch of folders. You can think of Dashboard Builder as a container that holds all the dashboards.

There's more...

You can also customize the home page of the **Corporate Dashboard** you are creating with the Dashboard Builder as HTML. Creating an HTML homepage is out of scope of this book; however, you can go to `http://w3schools.com` to learn how. From the homepage, you can have links that go directly to whatever dashboard tab you desire, which makes navigation similar to a website.

Creating Adobe Air Applets from Dashboard Design dashboard

Why would one want to export to Adobe Air from Dashboard Design one may ask? Well, here is some background on what a widget is.

Widgets are interactive virtual tools that provide single-purpose services such as showing the user the latest news, the current weather, the time, a calendar, a dictionary, a map program, a calculator, desktop notes, photo viewers, or even a language translator—Wikipedia.

Widgets are:

► Lightweight
► Reside on desktop
► Have a simple, non-distracting interface
► Provide valuable information in real time
► Easy interface for performing common tasks

The ability to create Adobe Air Applets from a Dashboard Design dashboard is very important because it allows us to harness the power of Dashboard Design to create simple widgets that connect to live data with the same look and feel we get from our well known Dashboard Design components. An example of a three-gauge widget is shown next:

In this recipe, we will create a widget, export it to Air, and then install the widget to our system.

Getting ready

Make sure that the Visual Model is complete and ready to export.

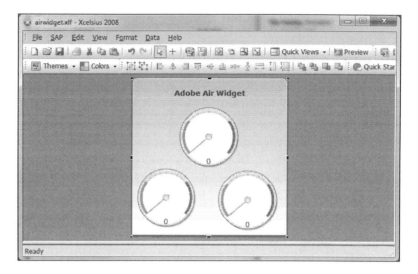

How to do it...

1. Download the Flex 3.0 SDK from the following URL:

    `http://www.adobe.com/cfusion/entitlement/index.cfm?e=flex3email`

     Note: The download will say "Download a free trial of Flash Builder 4 Premium Edition", but don't worry, the Flex 3.0 SDK is inside.

2. Unzip the SDK into the following folder:

    `C:\Program Files\Adobe\Flex Builder 3 Plug-in\sdks\3.0`

3. Update the Xcelsius `sdkPath.dat` to reflect the path above. This is usually located in the following path (you can edit the `sdkPath.dat` with Notepad):

    `C:\Program Files\Business Objects\Xcelsius\assets\air`

4. Download and install Adobe Air from:

    `http://get.adobe.com/air/`

5. On Xcelsius, click on **File | Export | Air...**

6. Choose **Gauge Air Test** for the **Name**. Choose the **air_icon.png** found in the source directory for the application icon. Finally, choose whatever destination you want the `.air` file to reside in. Name it **airwidget.air**.

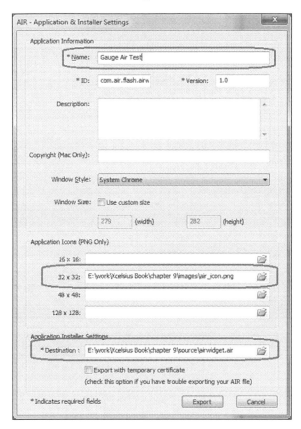

7. Install the Xcelsius widget using the `.air` file that was created from the export. Do this by double-clicking on the **airwidget.air** icon. You can choose wherever you want for the **Installation Location**.

8. Run the widget from the **desktop shortcut** or from the program directory you installed it in.

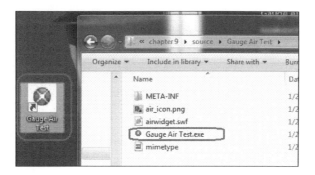

How it works...

Adobe Integrated Runtime (AIR) is a cross-platform runtime environment developed by Adobe Systems for building rich Internet applications using Adobe Flash, Adobe Flex, HTML, or Ajax, which can be deployed as a desktop application.

In steps 1 and 2, we install the **Adobe Flex SDK** to our system. Then in step 3, we link Dashboard Design to the SDK files.

 Note that by default we do not have Dashboard Design linked to the Adobe Flex SDK because if it were included in the Dashboard Design installation, the installation would be about 200 MB larger.

After linking Dashboard Design to the Adobe Flex SDK, we are able to export from Dashboard Design to an Adobe AIR file, where we can then deploy the widget to our desktop.

See also

For more samples on Adobe Air Widgets and best practices on creating Adobe Air Applets from Xcelsius, please download the presentation given by Clifford Alper on the SAP Community Network from the following URL:

```
http://ecohub.sdn.sap.com/irj/sdn/go/portal/prtroot/docs/library/
uuid/402540aa-6790-2b10-5fb3-901f52014d13
```

10
Top Third-Party Add-ons

In this chapter, we will cover:

- ▶ Managing add-ons in Dashboard Design
- ▶ Connecting to CSV-files with the CSV-Connector
- ▶ Integrating Google Maps with the GMaps plugin
- ▶ Connecting to Salesforce.com with DashConn
- ▶ Transferring data between dashboards with Data Sharer
- ▶ Presenting micro charts in a tree grid
- ▶ Integrating Web Intelligence with Antivia XWIS

Introduction

As we have seen throughout this book, Dashboard Design gives us an almost overwhelming package of tools to create the most stunning dashboards. Even this may not be enough for your specific dashboard. With Dashboard Design, SDK developers are able to create add-ons for Dashboard Design to provide that extra functionality that does not come with the Dashboard Design software.

This chapter will discuss several of the top third-party Dashboard Design add-ons that are available. Some of them can be downloaded for free while others need to be purchased. Without exception, all of these add-ons are free to tryout before you have to make the decision whether to buy or not. We will not discuss all third-party add-ons that are available at the moment, as there are simply too many of them already. We had to limit ourselves to those add-ons that stand out the most and are the most applicable for a large number of users.

The recipes in this chapter will not be as detailed as the other recipes in this book. The goal of this chapter is rather to give you a quick introduction to the basic functionality of the add-ons and how to set this up. After reading a recipe, you should have a good understanding of the possibilities of the add-on and whether it might be interesting for you to spend more time on it or not. We will also guide you to the resources for more information on each add-on.

Managing add-ons in Dashboard Design

In this recipe, we will show you where you can find third-party add-ons and how to add and remove them in Dashboard Design.

Getting ready

To install an add-on, you'll first need to download the add-on. The following recipes in this chapter will guide you to the right places to get these files.

 If you are using Windows Vista, you must turn off **User Account Control** (**UAC**), otherwise the **Add-On Manager** menu items will be disabled.

Go to **Start | Control Panel | User Accounts | Turn User Account Control on or off**

How to do it...

1. To add or remove add-ons, we need to use the **Add-On Manager.** Go to the **File** menu and select **Manage Add-Ons**.

2. The **Add-On Manager** pops up and shows which add-ons are already installed. If you already downloaded an add-on, you can click on the **Install Add-On** button. Browse to the add-on's XLX file and open it. The add-on will be installed instantly. You need to restart Dashboard Design to use the new add-on(s).

3. If you want to remove an add-on, first select the add-on and click the **Remove Add-On** button. Confirm the removal and the add-on will be deleted from your Dashboard Design installation.

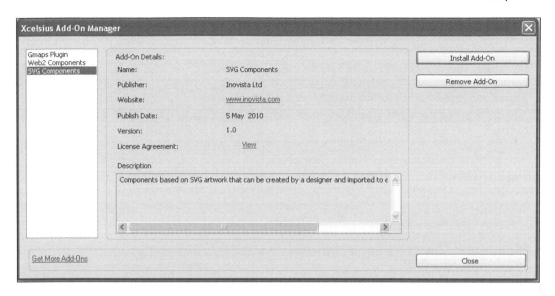

4. A good place to find add-ons is the SAP EcoHub (`http://ecohub.sdn.sap.com/`). On this website, you can find certified solutions not only for SAP BusinessObjects Dashboards, but also for other SAP enterprise applications.

5. Another place to find and download add-ons are the developer websites. In each recipe of this chapter we will guide you to these sites.

Connecting to CSV-files with the CSV-connector

In *Chapter 8, Dashboard Connectivity,* we discussed a number of data connectivity options for Dashboard Design dashboards. In addition to these standard data connections, Centigon Solutions developed an add-on that allows us to use **Comma-Separated Value** (**CSV**) files to grab data from. This recipe will give you a quick walkthrough of the features of this add-on.

Getting ready

Go to the Centigon Solutions website (`http://www.centigonsolutions.com/`) and browse for the CSV connector. Download the free trial and install it with the **Add-On Manager**. You also need a sample CSV file to use in this recipe.

How to do it...

1. Open a new Dashboard Design file and go to the spreadsheet area. Enter the location of the CSV file in cell C1.

2. Open the **Data Manager** and click on the **Add** button. Under **Add-On connection**, you will see the **CSV Connector**. Select it.

3. Give this connection a name. Bind the **CSV Data URL** field to cell C1.

4. Also, check the **Delimiter** setting. This should match the format of your CSV file.

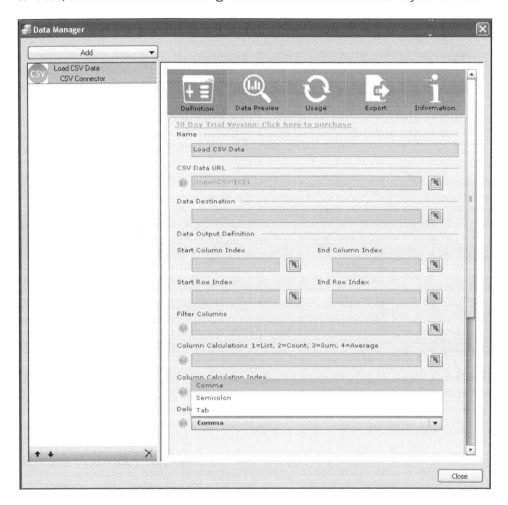

5. Go to the **Data Preview** tab and click on the **Preview Data** button. The data from the CSV file will now be shown. Note that the number of columns and rows is displayed as well.

 If nothing happens, your CSV file location might be wrong or a different delimiter is used in the CSV file.

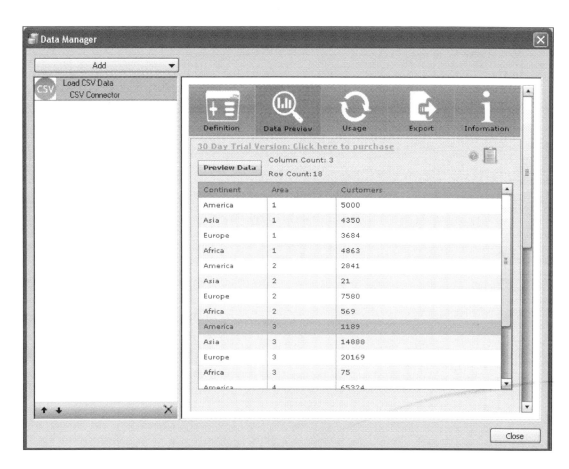

6. Go back to the **Definition** tab and bind the **Data Destination** field to a range of cells that matches at least the format, as shown in the **Data Preview** tab.

7. Now we will add a filter on the dataset in the CSV file. Bind the **Filter Columns** field to a range of cells with the same number of columns as the data destination range. Close the **Data Manager**.

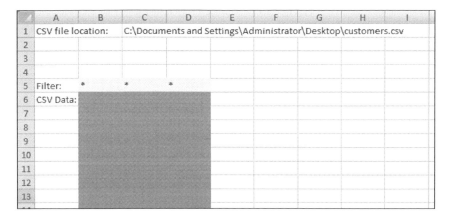

8. You can now set up a **Combo Box** component or another selector component to change the values of these cells. Use an asterisk (*) as a wildcard to show all records in a column.

9. If you want to preview your dashboard, do not forget to select the **Refresh On Load** option in the **Usage** tab of the **CSV Connector connection** in the **Data Manager**.

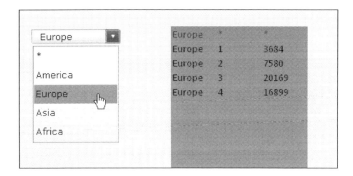

How it works...

The CSV connector add-on from Centigon Solutions is an ideal data connector, if you do not have the options to use server data providers such as QaaWS or SAP BW. Especially for the smaller enterprises, this is a very good solution to provide your dashboards with fresh data.

A nice feature of this component is the possibility to preview the data in the data manager. This will help you to set up the component without having to preview the dashboard every time to check out how the data will be loaded in the spreadsheet.

In the recipe, we showed how to filter the dataset of the CSV file. You can use this option to load only the data you will actually need, which will improve the performance of the dashboard. Furthermore, in the **Definition** tab of this add-on in the **Data Manager** you can define which columns and rows should be loaded.

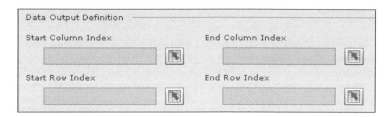

There is more...

Calculations

Besides displaying the data from a CSV file and filtering the values, the CSV connector add-on can also do some calculations.

1. Add another row above the data destination area. There are four calculation values. Enter a calculation value for each column.

    ▶ Column 1: Lists the values, separated by a comma

    ▶ Column 2: Counts the number of rows

    ▶ Column 3: Calculates the sum of values

    ▶ Column 4: Calculates the average of values

2. Next, we have to enter a single value index that indicates on which column the calculations are applied.

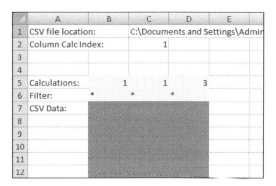

3. Open the **Data Manager** and bind the **Column Calculations** field and the **Column Calculation Index** field to the corresponding cells you just entered in the spreadsheet.

4. Preview the dashboard to try this functionality.

Exporting data to a CSV file

The CSV connector add-on is able to **export** a data range from a dashboard to a service that can generate a CSV file. To learn more about this feature visit the Centigon Solutions website at `http://www.centigonsolutions.com/`.

Integrating Google Maps with the GMaps plugin

In the recipe _Using maps to select data of an area or country_ in _Chapter 3_, we introduced the standard map options that Dashboard Design offers. Then, in the recipe _Displaying alerts on a map_ in _Chapter 5_, we discussed how to use alerts on these maps. Centigon Solutions raised the bar on this topic and introduced the **GMaps plugin** for Dashboard Design.

With this add-on, we can completely integrate Google Maps in a Dashboard Design dashboard. This means that we can use the graphics we know from Google Maps (map, satellite, hybrid, terrain, and so on) and functionalities such as zooming in or out on a map. Furthermore, the GMaps plugin integrates with other Dashboard Design components. We can make selections from a map region and display alerts, single points (such as cities or buildings), and heat maps on the map.

This recipe will introduce you to this add-on and show you how to create a map with alerts and selectable regions.

Getting ready

This recipe needs some preparation. First, go to the Centigon Solutions website (`http://www.centigonsolutions.com/`) and download the GMaps plugin add-on trial. Install it with the **Add-On Manager**.

Next we need a **Google Maps API key**. Go to the Google Maps API Family website (`http://code.google.com/apis/maps/signup.html`) and sign up to get your personal key. Without this key, the component won't be able to display any Google Maps.

We also need a so-called **shapefile**. This provides the overlay for a geographical area. There are lots of free SHP files available on the Internet; for example, on this website: `http://www.vdstech.com/map_data.htm`. In this recipe, we are using the Europe shapefile. Download the ZIP archive and extract it. The extracted folder includes at least the SHP file, a DBF file, and a SHX file.

How to do it...

1. Open MS Excel and go to **Open**.

2. Set the **Files of type** to **All Files**.

3. Browse for the DBF file and open it.

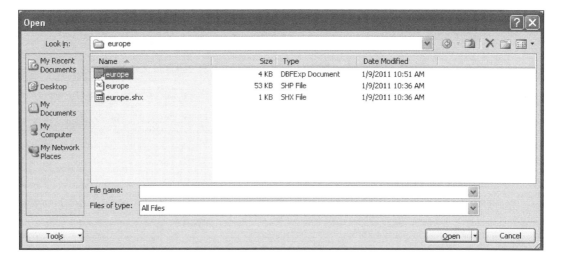

4. A spreadsheet with a list of countries will appear, including some additional, country-specific data.

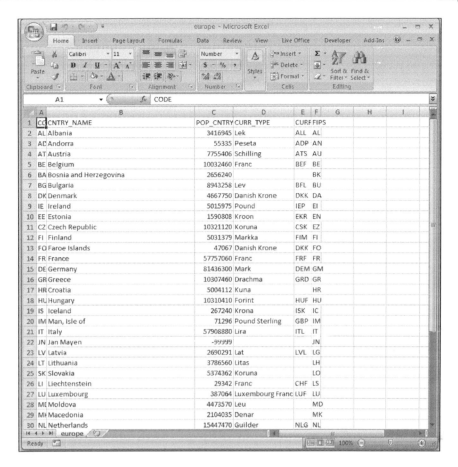

5.   Save the file as an Excel Workbook.

6.   Open Dashboard Design and import the Excel file you just created by selecting **Import** from the **Data** menu:

Or by clicking on the **Import** button:

7. A pop up is shown stating that you will lose everything in your existing spreadsheet. As we opened a blank Dashboard Design file, we can click on **Yes**.

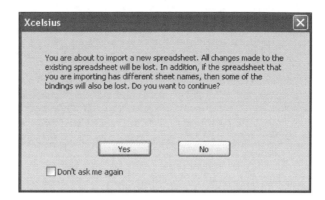

8. Insert five rows above the data from the DFB file. Right-click row 1 and select **Insert**. Repeat this four times.

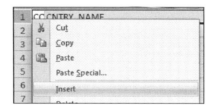

9. Enter your Google Maps API key in spreadsheet cell C1.

10. Drag the **Gmaps Plugin** component to the canvas. You will find this component at the bottom of the **Maps** components folder.

11. Bind the **Key** field of the Gmaps plugin to cell C1. The **Gmaps Plugin** component now changes into a real Google Map of the world.

12. Enter the location of the SHP file in cell C2.

	A	B	C	D	E	F	G	H	I
1	GMAPS API Key:		ABQIAAAAg1LhVivPWJy5RTpx5QZWVhT7baK43PfWUhem6_3pYhbuy5V60hS7						
2	Shapefile url:		C:\Documents and Settings\Administrator\Desktop\europe\europe.shp						
3									
4									
5									
6	AL	Albania	3416945	Lek	ALL	AL			
7	AD	Andorra	55335	Peseta	ADP	AN			
8	AT	Austria	7755406	Schilling	ATS	AU			
9	BE	Belgium	10032460	Franc	BEF	BE			
10	BA	Bosnia an	2656240			BK			
11	BG	Bulgaria	8943258	Lev	BFL	BU			
12	DK	Denmark	4667750	Danish Kr	DKK	DA			

13. Select the **Shape Data** option and bind the **Single shape file URL** field to cell C2.

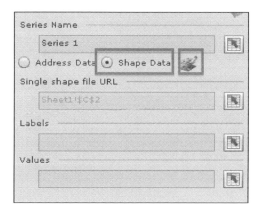

14. Click on the button on the right of **Shape Data** to enter the **Shape Data Options** screen. Here you should select **Shape File URL** and click on **OK**.

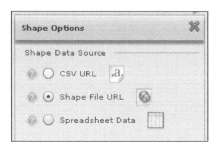

15. If you now hit the **Preview** button, the shapefile for Europe should be visible on top of the Google Map.

 The shapefile will not appear in preview mode if you are using a relative path.

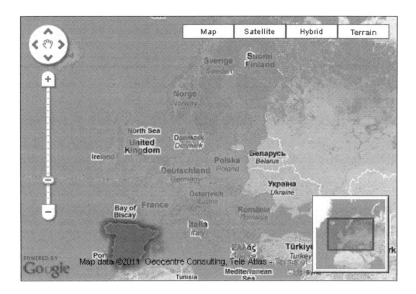

16. Now return to the properties pane of the **Gmaps Plugin** component and bind the **Labels** field and the **Values** field to the corresponding cells in the spreadsheet.

17. Set the **Insertion Type** to **Row** and bind the **Source Data** field to the cells we just bound to the **Labels** and **Values** fields. Also, bind the **Destination** field to cell range B4 until C4.

18. Add a **Gauge** component to the canvas and bind the **Title** field to cell B4 and the **Data By Range** field to cell C4.

19. Select the **Gmaps Plugin** component again and go to the **Behavior** tab.

20. Deselect **Dynamic Zoom**.

21. Bind the **Pan to Location** field to cell C3.

22. Enter **54.52596, 15.25512** in cell C3.

23. Go to the **Alerts** tab in its properties pane. Select **Enable Alerts**.

24. Select **By Value** and set the number of **Alert Levels** to **6**.

25. Now edit the limits by double-clicking on the **Limit** values. If you click on the **Refresh** button, your changes will already be shown in the component.

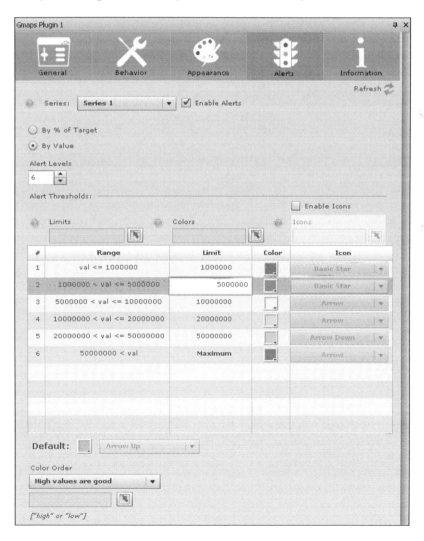

26. Preview and explore the dashboard.

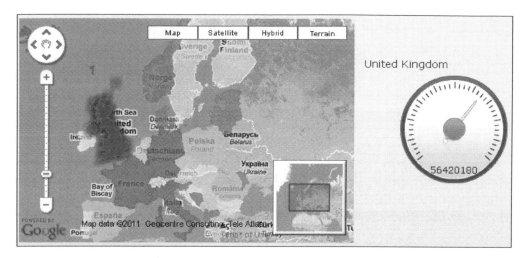

How it works...

This recipe required a lot of preparation before we could perform the actual binding of the data to the Gmaps plugin component. In this recipe, we showed you how to use SHP files. These files provide a layer on top of the Google Map. This enables us to make regions selectable or fill them with colors to show alerts.

The DBF file provided us with the meta-data on the SHP file (that is the country codes and names). After importing this information into the spreadsheet the set up of this component has a lot of similarities with the configuration of the standard Dashboard Design Map components, like we discussed in *Chapter 3* and *Chapter 5*.

The SHX file can be used to combine SHP and DBF files for GIS solutions, where this file is required to maintain the integrity between the files when used in GIS solutions. The GMaps plugin does not utilize this SHX file.

In the **Behavior** tab, we entered the coordinates for Europe, so the map will by default show Europe. You can find these coordinates for example on this site: `http://universimmedia.pagesperso-orange.fr/geo/loc.htm`.

In addition, if you want to zoom in more or less you can change the **Zoom Level**.

Setting up the alerts in the GMaps plugin works just like configuring the **Alerts** tab in the standard Dashboard Design components, with the addition that you can also use icons as alerts in the GMaps plugin component.

There is more...

More features

This recipe only covered a few of the possibilities of this add-on. Check out the Gmaps plugin website (http://www.gmapsplugin.com/) to learn more about the other features. Here you can also find a lot of tutorials, articles, videos, templates, and samples.

XGlobe and XYahooMap

Other add-ons that cover maps are **XGlobe** and **XYahooMap**, both part of the free XComponents suite. XGlobe is a component that shows an animated 3D globe with the ability to display selectable points. XYahooMap integrates Yahoo Maps in Dashboard Design dashboard and can also show selectable labels.

You can download the XComponents suite from the Antivia website: http://www.antivia.com/.

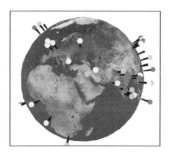

The following screenshot shows a few selected points from the globe:

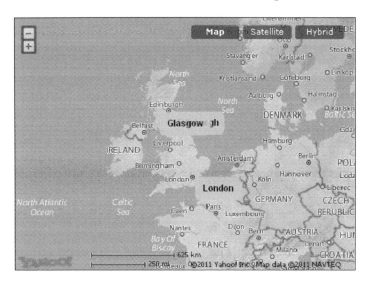

Connecting to Salesforce.com with DashConn

What about using live data from your **Salesforce.com** reports in Dashboard Design to create interactive dashboards to show, track, and analyze your sales activities? **DashConn** is a Dashboard Design add-on by IdeaCrop that delivers this integration. Let's have a look at the features of this add-on and how to set it up.

Getting ready

As we are connecting to Salesforce.com you obviously need a Salesforce.com account. You can sign up for a free trial at `http://www.salesforce.com/`.

To connect to Salesforce.com from a Dashboard Design dashboard a security token is required. You can get this security token from the **Personal Setup** menu at Salesforce.com.

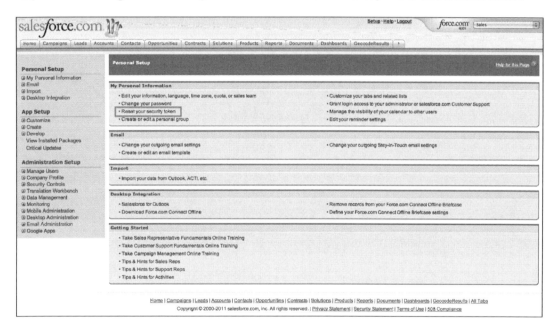

A free trial version of the DashConn add-on can be downloaded from the IdeaCrop website: `http://www.ideacrop.com/`.

How to do it...

1. Open a new Dashboard Design file and drag the **Salesforce.com DataViewer** component into the canvas.

2. Go to the **Reports** tab and enter your **Salesforce.com** credentials. A list with your Salesforce.com reports will appear.

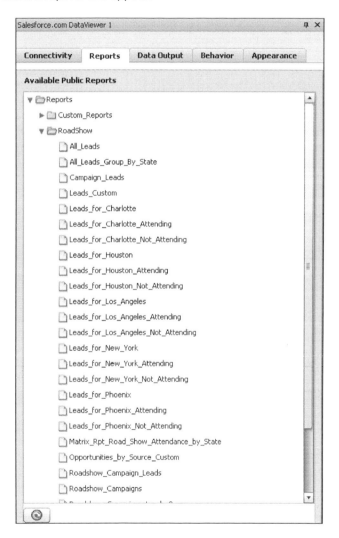

3. Select the report you want to use. A loading message will appear.

4. Now go to the **Data Output** tab and bind the **Main result destination** field to spreadsheet cell range A6 through E20.

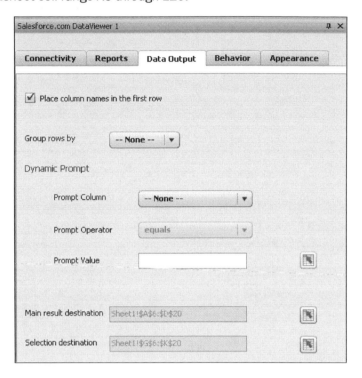

5. Bind the **Selection** destination field to cell range G6 until K20.

6. Make sure that the **Place** column names in the first row option are selected. We can use these column names later on when we add some chart components and have to bind the series names.

7. Preview the dashboard to see how the data is being returned (and filled in the spreadsheet cells that we bound in step 4). You will be asked to fill in your credentials.

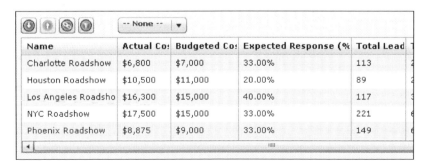

8. Leave preview mode and drag a **Column Chart** component to the canvas.

9. Bind the **Column Chart** component to the columns you want to show in the chart. Remember that the first row will show the column names. Also, do not forget to select the **Ignore Blank Cells** options in the **Behavior** tab of the chart component. In this recipe example, we are showing two series—**Actual Costs** and **Budgeted Costs**.

10. Now add another chart to the canvas and bind it to one or more columns from the **Selection destination area** (step 5). In this recipe example, we want to show the **Total Leads** in a **Bar Chart**.

11. **Preview** the dashboard. As you will see the **Column Chart** will display data right away. If you select a row in the **Salesforce.com DataViewer**, the **Bar Chart** will also be filled.

 You can use *CTRL* and click or *SHIFT* and click to select multiple rows.

12. Leave the preview mode and add a **Horizontal Slider** component to the canvas.

13. Bind the **Data** field of this component to cell C1.

14. Select the **Salesforce.com DataViewer** component again and go to the **Data Output** tab.

15. We want to filter the records based on the value in the **Total Responses** column. To do this, select the correct column from the **Prompt Column** selector and bind the **Prompt Value** field to cell C1. For the **Prompt Operator**, we select **greaterOrEqual**.

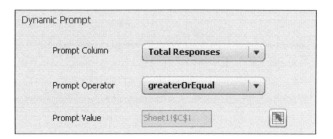

16. Preview the dashboard once more.

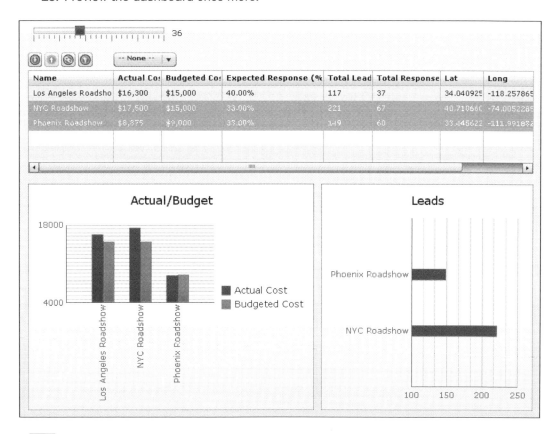

How it works...

The Salesforce.com DataViewer component does most of the work for us. As you have seen we only had to enter our Salesforce.com credentials, select a report, and preview the dashboard to see how the data will be returned. After binding the fields of the **Data Output** tab we are able to reuse the report data in other components.

The Salesforce.com DataViewer component has some nice run-time features to **drill down** or **up** in the report data, open the Salesforce.com **details page** of all selected items, **set filters**, and **aggregate data** by a certain field. With these options you can dynamically change the data being retrieved by the **Salesforce.com DataViewer**. This also means that the values in spreadsheet cells that are bound to the **Main result destination** field in the **Data Output** tab change as well.

There is more...

Salesforce.com Data Manager Connection

A very nice feature of this add-on is that it also has a **Connection** option that is available from the **Data Manager**. With this **Connection**, you can use data Salesforce.com report data in your dashboards without having to use the **Salesforce.com DataViewer** component. Another important feature of the connection option is that it offers the ability to constantly refresh data from Salesforce.com reports—just like other connection options—without being prompted for credentials. Except for the **Usage** tab, most settings are similar to those of the **Salesforce.com DataViewer** component.

Working Mode settings

In the **Behavior** tab of the component and **Data Manager** connection, you can find the **Working Mode** setting. In the default **Online** setting, an Internet connection is required to use the component to connect to Salesforce.com. In offline mode, the (first level of) report data is embedded within the dashboard. The third online/fallback to offline mode is a combination of the online and offline modes and will try to retrieve live data first; but if this fails, it uses the embedded data.

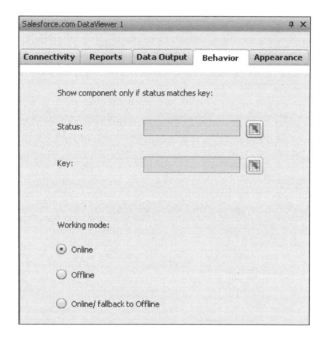

Transferring data between dashboards with Data Sharer

The **Data Sharer** add-on by Inovista is a very simple but powerful add-on that lets you share data between separate Dashboard Design dashboards.

Getting ready

You can get the Data Sharer add-on at the Inovista website: `http://www.inovista.com/`.

How to do it...

1. Open a new Dashboard Design file and add a **List Box** component to the canvas.

2. Enter some **Labels**.

3. Set the **Insertion Type** to **Label** and bind the **Destination** field to spreadsheet cell B1.

4. Drag a **Data Sharer** component to the canvas.

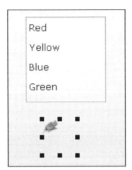

5. Select **Transmit Values** and bind the **Transmit Data Cells** field to cell B1.

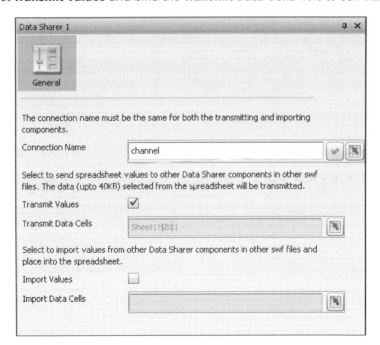

6. Export the dashboard to an SWF file.

7. Open a new Dashboard Design file and add a **Label** component to the canvas.

8. Bind this **Label** component to cell B1.

9. Add a **Data Sharer** component to the canvas.

10. Select the **Import Values** option and bind the **Import Data Cells** field to cell B1.

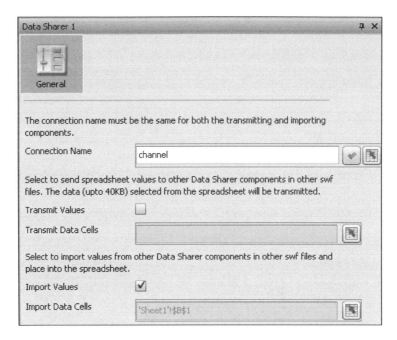

11. Export the dashboard to an SWF file.

12. Now open both the SWF files and check out what happens if you select one of the labels.

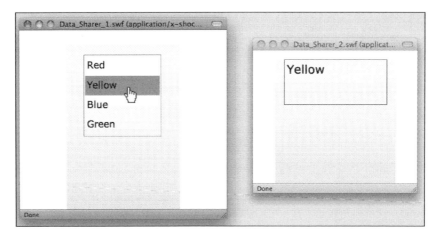

How it works...

In this recipe, we used the Data Sharer to send values from one dashboard to another. The first dashboard is the data transmitter, while the second dashboard constantly listens for incoming values. The values will be sent at startup and whenever the values change.

If you want to use more than one communication line between dashboards, you can add multiple Data Sharer components. You have to make sure that the **Connection Name** is the same for all the Data Sharer components among the different dashboards that need to communicate with each other.

 If you create a Corporate Dashboard with the Dashboard Builder in BI Launch Pad (formerly know as InfoView), you can make dashboards communicate with each other using the Data Sharer. See also the recipe *Housing your dashboard in Dashboard Builder* in *Chapter 9*.

Presenting micro charts in a tree grid

The **Micro Chart Suite** is an extensive set of small charting components by Inovista. It includes a micro version of most of the chart types that are part of the standard Dashboard Design components: A bar chart, area chart, stacked bar chart, bullet chart, column chart, line chart, and pie chart. In addition, there are components to show micro versions of a plot chart, win/lose chart, shape alerts, a traffic light, and a text/number indicator.

You can use these components separately, but another nice feature by Inovista is the tree grid component in which we can present micro charts in a hierarchical format. This recipe shows you how to set up such a tree grid component with a few of micro charts.

Getting ready

Go to the Inovista website (http://www.inovista.com/), browse for the trial downloads section, and download the Micro Chart Suite. Install the components with the **Add-On Manager**.

How to do it...

1. First, we need to add some data to the spreadsheet. Open a new Dashboard Design file and add the data, as shown in the following screenshot:

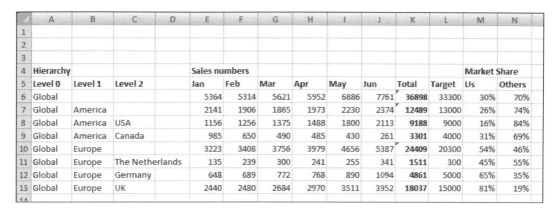

	A	B	C	D	E	F	G	H	I	J	K	L	M	N
1														
2														
3														
4	Hierarchy				Sales numbers								Market Share	
5	Level 0	Level 1	Level 2		Jan	Feb	Mar	Apr	May	Jun	Total	Target	Us	Others
6	Global				5364	5314	5621	5952	6886	7761	36898	33300	30%	70%
7	Global	America			2141	1906	1865	1973	2230	2374	12489	13000	26%	74%
8	Global	America	USA		1156	1256	1375	1488	1800	2113	9188	9000	16%	84%
9	Global	America	Canada		985	650	490	485	430	261	3301	4000	31%	69%
10	Global	Europe			3223	3408	3756	3979	4656	5387	24409	20300	54%	46%
11	Global	Europe	The Netherlands		135	239	300	241	255	341	1511	300	45%	55%
12	Global	Europe	Germany		648	689	772	768	890	1094	4861	5000	65%	35%
13	Global	Europe	UK		2440	2480	2684	2970	3511	3952	18037	15000	81%	19%
14														

2. Add a **MicroChart Tree Grid** component to the canvas.

3. Click on the **insert** button in the properties pane.

4. Select **MicroTrafficLight** as a **Chart Type**.

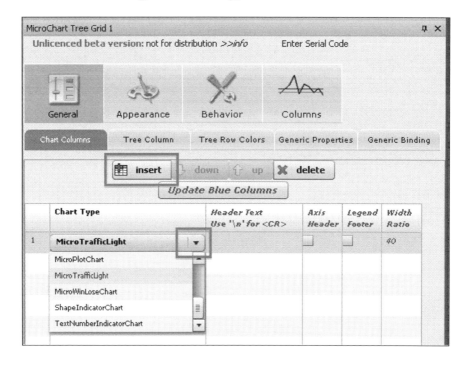

5. In the **Header Text** column, enter **Status** as a title for this chart and set the **Width Ratio** to **10**.

6. In the **Data Source for Column: 1** section, bind the **Chart Data** field to cell range K6: K13. Bind the **Target Data** field to cell range L6:L13.

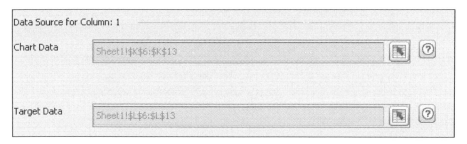

7. Insert a **MicroLineChart** into the **Tree Grid** and enter **Monthly sales trend** in the **Header Text** column.

8. Bind this chart to cell range E6 through J13.

9. Insert a **Micro100BarChart** into the **Tree Grid**. Enter **Market Share** as a title for this column.

10. Bind this chart to cell range M6 through M13.

11. Click on the **Edit Column** button. Select the **Legends** sub-tab.

12. Select **Use Chart Colors**.

13. Select a dark color for the first value and a light color for the second.

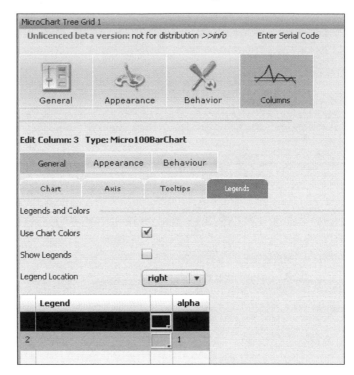

14. Now return to the **General** tab and select the **Tree Column** sub-tab.

15. Bind the **Source Data** field to cell range A6 through C13.

16. Also set the **Column With** to **250** and the **Opening Indentation** to **0**.

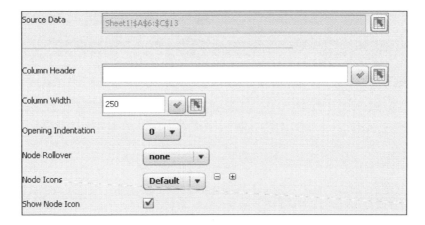

17. Preview the dashboard and try to navigate through the hierarchy tree.

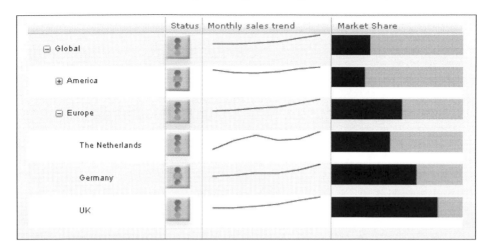

How it works...

As we have seen in this recipe, the Inovista Micro Chart Suite offers a good solution to present numerous data visualizations in a very compact way. The **MicroChart Tree Grid** component gives us a framework to display these micro charts in a structured and hierarchical way.

To use the **MicroChart Tree Grid** component, we have to define the spreadsheet in the right way. We first created a hierarchical structure with three levels—global, continents, and countries. Next, we added all the data for the graphs in the columns, where each node has its own row of data.

There is more...

Data grid

If you don't want or don't need to show a hierarchical structure in your dashboard, you can use the **MicroChart Table** component as another container to present the micro charts in. The only difference is that this component doesn't have the **Tree Column** and **Tree Row Colors** sub-tabs.

As the **MicroChart Table** component doesn't have the **Tree Column** to display the row headers, you could use a **TextNumberIndicatorChart** chart type to add these.

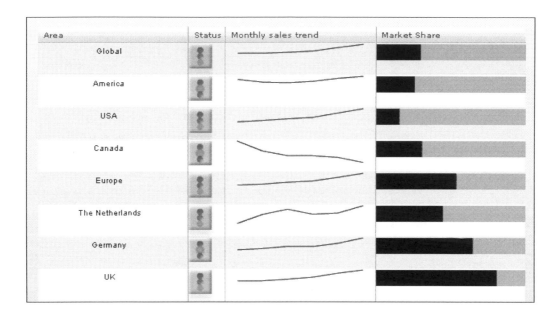

More information

Visit the Inovista website (`http://www.inovista.com/`) for more information on the tree and data grid components and the individual components in the Micro Chart Suite.

Here, you can also find the other add-ons Inovista offers.

Integrating Web Intelligence with Antivia XWIS

Antivia XWIS is an add-on by Antivia that lets us connect to Web Intelligence documents, Crystal Reports and even SQL databases and OLAP cubes. Also, it comes with a large set of components to display and analyze the retrieved data.

As we have seen in *Chapter 8*, Dashboard Design is already able to connect to a number of data sources. This recipe will show you some of the possibilities of Antivia XWIS and the advantages it has over the standard connection types.

Getting ready

Go to the Antivia website (http://www.antivia.com/) and sign up for a trial of Antivia XWIS. This recipe won't discuss the server-side installations for the Antivia Framework, which is required to run Antivia XWIS.

How to do it...

1. Open a new Dashboard Design file and add the **Antivia Connect** component to the canvas. This component controls the user authentication and generates a session token. In every Antivia XWIS data component that we are going to use, we need to bind this token.

2. Set up the spreadsheet as in the following screenshot:

	A	B	C
1	Title	XWIS Dashboard	
2	Antivia Server URL	https://xwis.yourserver.com	
3	BI System	systemname	
4	BI Username	username@yourserver.com	
5	BI Password	password	
6	Session Token		
7			

3. Bind the five fields of the **General** tab of the properties pane to the corresponding cells in the spreadsheet.

4. Fill in your **Username** and **Password** in the **Design time connection** section and click on **Connect**.

5. Add an **Antivia Table** component to the canvas.

6. First bind the **Session Token** field to cell B6.

7. Select a dataset from the **Dataset Picker**.

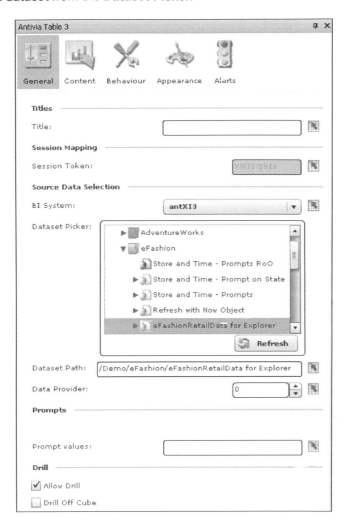

8. Now go to the **Content** tab. Here we can define the layout of the table. Drag the objects you want to show in the table from the **Available Objects** area to the **Result Objects** area. In this example, we select **Year**, **Category**, **Quantity sold**, and **Sales revenue**.

9. Preview the dashboard, click on the **Connect** button, and check out what we just configured.

10. Click on a value in the **Year** column to drill down to quarterly data. You can sort a column by clicking on its label. Now leave the **Preview** mode.

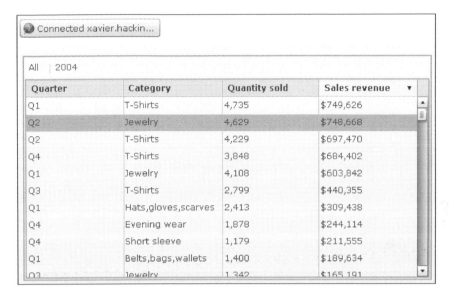

Quarter	Category	Quantity sold	Sales revenue ▼
Q1	T-Shirts	4,735	$749,626
Q2	Jewelry	4,629	$748,668
Q2	T-Shirts	4,229	$697,470
Q4	T-Shirts	3,848	$684,402
Q1	Jewelry	4,108	$603,842
Q3	T-Shirts	2,799	$440,355
Q1	Hats,gloves,scarves	2,413	$309,438
Q4	Evening wear	1,878	$244,114
Q4	Short sleeve	1,179	$211,555
Q1	Belts,bags,wallets	1,400	$189,634
Q3	Jewelry	1,342	$165,191

11. Add a **Pie Chart** component and a **Line Chart** component to the canvas.

12. Return to the **Content** tab of the **Antivia Table** component. Select the **AutoWire** sub-tab.

13. Select both the **Enable AutoWire** and **Manage layout** options.

14. Also, select **AutoWire these charts only**.

15. Select the **Bind** option for both chart components and also select the **Layout** option for the **Pie Chart** component.

16. Preview the dashboard to see what happens.

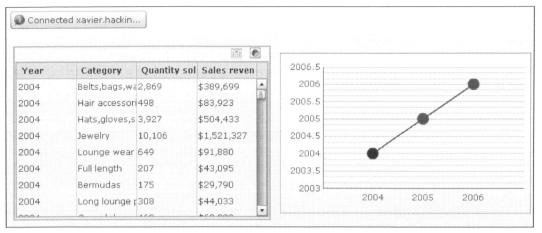

17. As you can see the **Antivia Table** component, now has two little symbols in its upper right-hand side. If you click on the pie chart symbol, the table will be replaced with the **Pie Chart** component. Click on this symbol.

18. Click on a slice of the pie chart to drill down.

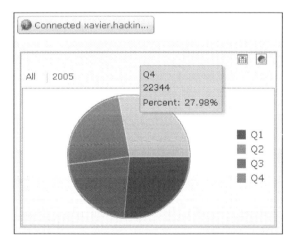

How it works...

In this recipe, we showed you only a few of the possibilities of Antivia XWIS. In the *There is more...* section, we will quickly cover most of the other features. One thing should be clear already—setting up an interactive dashboard that is capable of displaying and drilling through a large set of data is made very easy with this add-on.

The Antivia Service URL, username, password, and session token need to be bound to the spreadsheet; the BI System can be selected or bound. When connecting to a SAP BusinessObjects environment, username and password are your SAP BusinessObjects credentials.

The Antivia Table component enables us to analyze a very large set of data (30.000+ rows) from within a dashboard, without the need to configure multiple data connections with QaaWS or Live Office, setting up the spreadsheet and defining the bindings to a component. This is a huge efficiency gain!

We demonstrated the **AutoWire** feature that makes dashboard development even easier and faster because it completely takes care of the bindings of data to standard Dashboard Design chart components. If you still want to bind the data to the spreadsheet, Antivia XWIS also provides this feature.

There is more...

Antivia Slice and Dice component

The **Antivia Slice and Dice** component lets the dashboard user create his own report layout. The user can use drag-and-drop to configure the report from a set of available objects. The following screenshot shows the interface the user gets to do this:

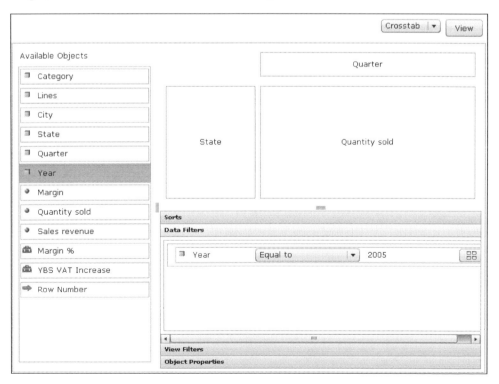

Antivia Export component

The **Antivia Export** component enables us to export data from the dashboard to MS Excel files, which is an extremely powerful option. The button gives us two options—exporting the complete dataset or exporting the data as shown in the components.

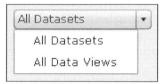

Alerts

In all data-based Antivia XWIS components, **alerts** can be used to highlight cells when a certain condition is met. A nice feature here is that these alert definitions are stored in the Antivia XWIS repository, so they can be reused in other components or even in other dashboards.

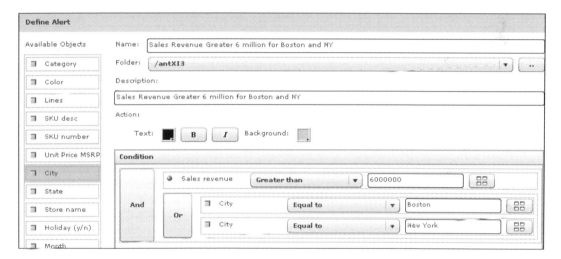

Antivia Timer component

The **Antivia Timer** component is the only component that can work standalone and does not need a session token to run. It writes the current time to a cell at a defined interval. This component can be useful to trigger components with the **Refresh on change** option or in combination with dynamic visibility.

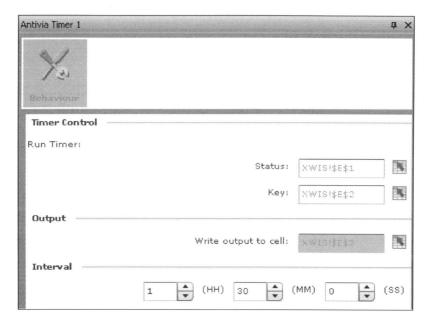

Taking the dashboard offline

With the **Antivia Disconnect** component, it is possible to take a connected dashboard offline and secure the data using 128-bit encryption within the dashboard. This allows the end users to interact with their dashboard in almost the same way as the online version. With XBroadcast, Antivia extends this feature to generate personalized dashboards that can be published and distributed beyond the enterprise via e-mail using a SAP BusinessObjects Business Intelligence platform.

Visit the Antivia website at `http://www.antivia.com/` for a complete overview of all Antivia XWIS add-on features and to check out some demo videos.

Real World Dashboard Case Studies

In order to take advantage of the full range of features and include various techniques that could be implemented while working through these chapters, we'll discuss two examples of commonly used dashboards. This rare-to-find approach will help you streamline some of the actions that you have been undertaking.

The following real world dashboard examples that we will follow are:

- ▶ What-if scenario example
- ▶ Sales/profit dashboard example

 Please find attached the respective example XLF source files.

What-if scenario: mortgage calculator

In this recipe, we will create a what-if scenario dashboard. The purpose of the dashboard is to calculate and show the monthly payments and the total costs of the mortgage, based on a set of adjustable variables.

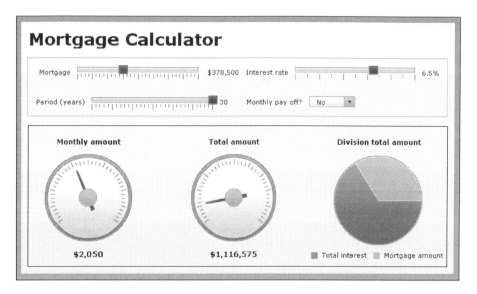

We will use techniques from the following chapters and recipes:

- ▶ *Chapter 1, Staying in Control*
- ▶ Using sliders to create a What-If scenario
- ▶ Selecting your data from a list
- ▶ Illustrating single values
- ▶ Using the pie chart
- ▶ *Chapter 7, Dashboard Look and Feel*

Getting ready

As we are starting from scratch, you only have to open a new Dashboard Design file.

How to do it...

1. The dashboard will contain four variables—**Mortgage amount**, **Mortgage term in years**, **Yearly interest rate**, and a variable that states if the mortgage will be paid off by equal monthly payments (annuity) or just at the end of the mortgage term, that is the **Monthly interest rate**.

2. First, we set up the spreadsheet. Make sure your spreadsheet looks like the following screenshot:

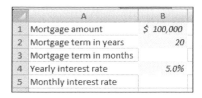

3. To calculate the monthly and total payments we need the mortgage term in months, which is the number of years multiplied by 12. Add the following Excel formula to cell B3: **=B2*12**.

4. To calculate the monthly interest rate we need the following formula: **=(1+B4)^(1/12)-1**. Enter it in cell B5.

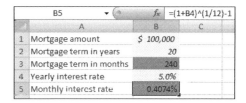

5. Now drag three **Horizontal Slider** components to the canvas.

6. Bind the **Data** field of the first **Horizontal Slider** component to cell B1. Also, set the **Maximum Limit** to **1000000**. Enter **Mortgage** as **Title**.

7. Select the second **Horizontal Slider** component and bind its **Data** field to cell B4. Set the **Maximum Limit** to **0.1**. As we are dealing with percentages, the maximum limit is now 10% due to this setting. Enter **Interest rate** as **Title**.

8. Go to the **Behavior** tab and in the **Slider Movement** section change the **Increment** to **0.001**.

9. Select the third **Horizontal Slider** component and bind the **Data** field of this one to cell B2. Set the **Maximum Limit** to **30** and enter **Period (years)** as a **Title**.

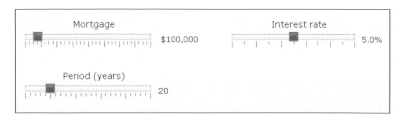

10. Now we need to add some more logic to our spreadsheet to calculate the monthly payments. Adjust your spreadsheet so it looks like the following screenshot:

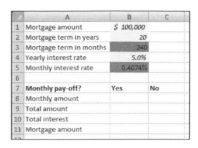

11. Enter the following formula in cell B8 to calculate the monthly annuity: **=B1*(B5/(1-(1+B5)^(-B3)))**.

12. Enter the next formula in cell B9 to calculate the total amount: **=B3*B8**.

13. Enter the formula **=B9-B1** in cell B10 to calculate the total interest amount.

14. In cell C8 enter formula **=B1*(B4^1/12)** to calculate the monthly amount, which is only the interest.

15. Enter formula **=B3*C8** in cell C10 and enter formula **=B1+C10** in cell C9.

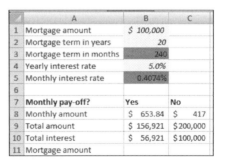

16. Add a Combo Box component to the canvas. We will use this component to determine if the mortgage will be paid off by monthly installments. Bind the Labels field to cells B7 and C7. Go to the **Behavior** tab and set **Item** to **Label 1**.

17. Return to the **General** tab and in the **Data Insertion** section set the **Insertion Type** to **Column**. Bind the **Source Data** field to cell range B8 until C10. Bind the Destination field to cells D8 until D10.

18. Finally, enter **Monthly pay off?** as a **Title**.

19. Go back to the spreadsheet and enter formula **=B1** in cell D11.

	A	B	C	D
1	Mortgage amount	$ 100,000		
2	Mortgage term in years	20		
3	Mortgage term in months	240		
4	Yearly interest rate	5.0%		
5	Monthly interest rate	0.4074%		
6				
7	Monthly pay-off?	Yes	No	
8	Monthly amount	$ 653.84	$ 417	$ 654
9	Total amount	$ 156,921	$ 200,000	$ 156,921
10	Total interest	$ 56,921	$ 100,000	$ 56,921
11	Mortgage amount			$ 100,000

20. Now our spreadsheet and all the selectors are set up, it is time to show some data in the dashboard. Add a **Gauge** component to the canvas.

21. Bind its **By Range** field to cell D8 and set the **Maximum Limit** field to 5000. Enter the **Monthly** amount as a **Title**.

22. Add another **Gauge** component to the canvas and bind its **By Range** field to cell D9. Set its **Maximum Limit** field to **10000000**. Enter **Total** amount as a **Title**.

23. Drag a Pie Chart component to the canvas. Bind its **Values** field to cells D10 and D11. Also, bind the **Labels** field to cells A10 and A11. Enter **Division** total amount as a **Title**.

24. Go to the **Appearance** tab and deselect **Show Chart Background**. Set the position of the legend to **Bottom**.

25. All right! The what-if section of the dashboard is now in place and ready to be tested. Preview the dashboard and play around with the sliders and selectors to see if everything works.

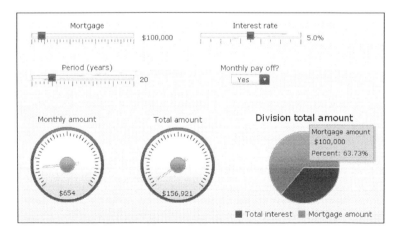

26. Leave the preview mode. We will now adjust the layout of the dashboard so it looks a bit smoother.

27. First select the **Phase** theme from the **Theme** selector in the **Format** menu.

28. Use the **Alignment** options from the **Format** menu to adjust the placement of the three sliders and the selector.

 You can also use the **Grid** to get the layout right. You can activate the **Grid** in the **Preferences** menu in the **File** menu.

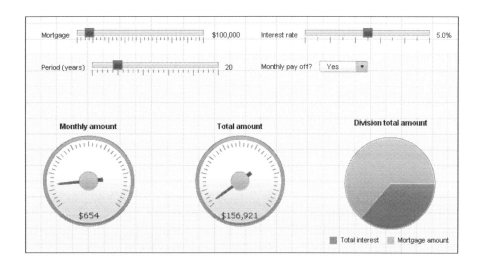

29. Add a **Rectangular** component and resize it so it will fit over the sliders and selector. Change the **Border Color** to color a bit lighter, for example gray.

30. Add a **Label** component to the canvas and enter **Mortgage Calculator** in the **Enter Text** field. Select the Appearance tab and go to the **Text** sub-tab. **Select Bold** and set the **Text Size** to 28. Make sure you resize the **Label** component if the text doesn't fit anymore.

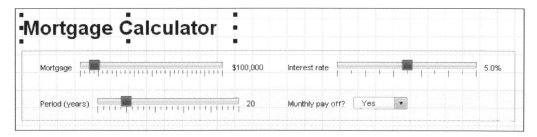

31. Select the **Pie Chart** and the **Gauge** components. Align them by **Middle** and **Space Evenly Across** .

32. As you can see the title of the Pie Chart is placed a bit higher than the titles of the **Gauges**. Select both **Gauge** components. Go to the **Appearance** tab and select the **Text** sub-tab. Now adjust the **Y Offset** so all titles will have the same height.

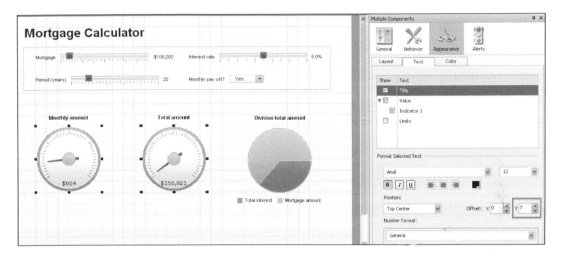

33. Select **Value**. In the **Format Selected Text** section, select **Bold** and adjust the **Y Offset** so the values of the **Gauge** components will be at the same height as the legend of the **Pie Chart** component.

34. Go to the **Behavior** tab and deselect the **Enable Interaction** option.

35. Add another **Rectangular** component to the canvas and place it over the **Gauges** and **Pie Chart**.

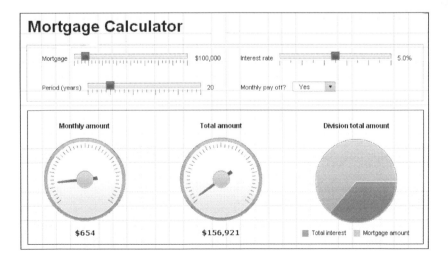

36. Select **Fit the Canvas to Components** from the **Canvas Sizing** options in the **View** menu. You can also use the buttons from the Standard Toolbar. Select the **Increase Canvas** option twice.

37. Your what-if dashboard is finished!

▶ In steps 1-4, 10-15, and 19, we utilize what we learned in the *Chapter 1* (*Staying in Control*) recipes to properly set up the spreadsheet.

▶ In steps 5-9, we set up the sliders like we did in the *Using sliders to create a What-If scenario* recipe.

▶ In steps 16-18, we use recipe *Selecting your data from a list* to define the Combo Box component to determine if the mortgage is paid off or not.

▶ Steps 20-24 use recipes illustrating single values and using the pie chart to show the data in two gauges and a pie chart.

▶ In the final steps, we used what we have learned from the *Chapter 7, Dashboard Look and Feel* recipes to implement a different dashboard theme and fine-tune the look of the dashboard.

Sales/profit dashboard example

In this example, we will utilize many techniques that we have learned in the previous recipes to create a Sales Profit dashboard.

The Sales Profit dashboard displays the sales or profit of each state on the map. From the map, a user can then select a state and then view year to date sales/profit information for products that are sold on the top right. The user can then drill down further by clicking on a product. A detailed scorecard and trend chart will then be shown for the selected state and product.

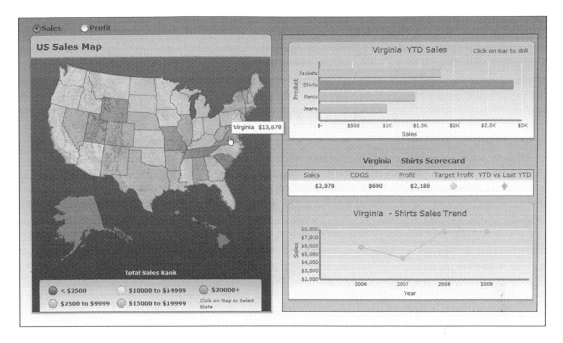

Techniques from the following chapters and recipes were used to accomplish the example:

- *Chapter 1, Staying in Control*
- Adding a line chart to your dashboard
- Using a scorecard component
- Drilling down from a chart
- Using filtered rows
- Selecting your data from a list
- Using maps to select data of an area or country
- Displaying alerts on a map

Getting ready

It is important that you have the `Sales_Profit.xlf` file as a reference. Please open it before proceeding to the next section as the spreadsheet layout is already completed for your convenience.

How to do it...

1. Drag the **Map – USA** component onto the canvas.

2. Bind the **Region Keys** to the **State** keys on the **Control Sheet** tab.

3. On the **Data Insertion** section, select **Row** as the **Insertion Type** and the **Source Data** will be the keys that we selected in step 2. The destination will be cell E1.

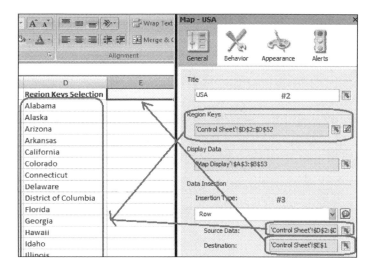

4. Bind the **Display Data** to the key value pair items in the **Map Display** worksheet.

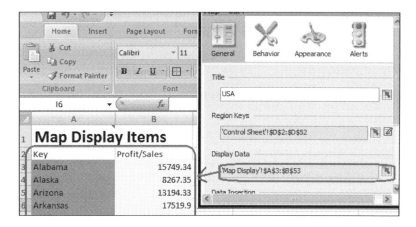

5. Go to the **Alerts** properties, check the **Enable Alerts** checkbox, select **By Value**, check the **Use a Range** checkbox, and bind to the range section in the **Map Display** worksheet. It is important that you bind starting at 2500, otherwise it will add another range starting from the minimum to 0.

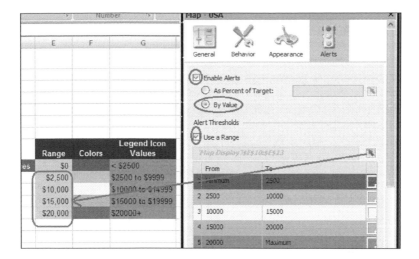

6. The next step is to complete the YTD chart on the top right-hand side. Drag a **Bar Chart** component onto the top right-hand side of the canvas.

7. Bind the **Titles** to the appropriate cells on **column T of the State and Drilldown Display Worksheet**. Then Bind the **Data** to the cells in purple. The values in the purple cells are populated depending on whether a user selects **Sales** or **Profit**. Note that the cells are pre-populated with test data.

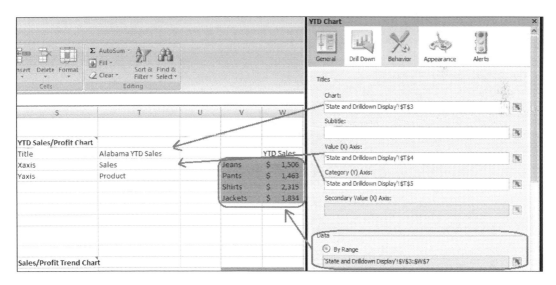

8. Go to the **Drill Down** properties of the YTD chart. Check the **Enable Drill Down** checkbox and select **Row** as the **Insertion Type**. Bind the source data to the peach section (columns A to Q) of the **State and Drilldown Display** worksheet. Bind the destination to the cells in yellow (columns A to Q). Note that the peach and yellow cells are pre-populated with test data.

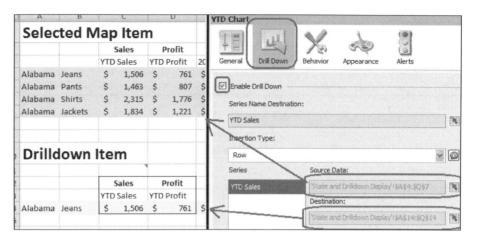

9. The next step is to complete the Scorecard on the middle right-hand side of the dashboard. Drag a **Scorecard** component onto the canvas.

10. Bind the **Display Data** to the yellow cells of the **Drilldown Scorecard** section on the **State and Drilldown Display** worksheet. These yellow cells are the drilldown values populated from the YTD chart in step 8. Note that the yellow cells are populated with test data.

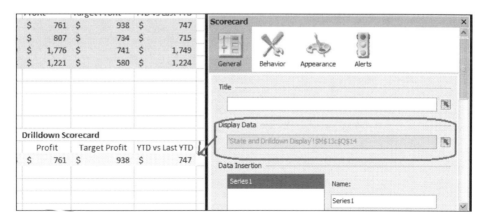

11. Go to the **Appearance** properties of the **Scorecard** and click on the **Text** tab. Unselect the **Target Profit and YTD vs Last YTD** checkboxes. The reason is that we only want to see alert shapes on these cells and not the text value.

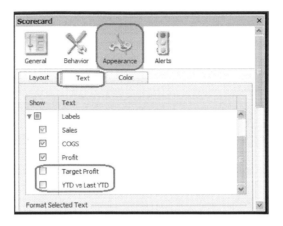

12. Go to the **Alerts** properties of the **Scorecard**. Check the **Target Profit** and **YTD vs Last YTD** checkboxes. In both cases the **Alert Values** will be bound to cell O14 of the **State and Drilldown Display** worksheet. In both the cases, make sure to have **As Percent of Target** selected. For **Target Profit**, bind it to cell P14 and for **YTD vs Last YTD** bind it to cell Q14. In the **Alert Thresholds** section, we want **Min/70%/85%/Max** for Target Profit. Set the alert threshold for the YTD vs Last YTD to **Min/99.999%/100%/Max**.

[The reason we have 99.999% is so that the yellow arrow is for anything that has YTD equal to Last YTD.]

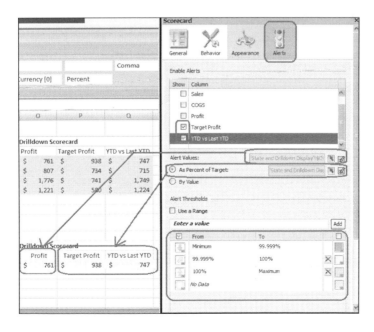

13. Next we will complete the **Trend Line Chart** on the bottom right-hand side of the dashboard. Drag a **Line Chart** component onto the bottom right-hand side of the canvas.

14. Bind the **Titles** and **Data Range** to the appropriate section in the **State and Drilldown Display** worksheet.

 Note that the purple section is populated depending on whether a user selects **Sales** or **Profit**.

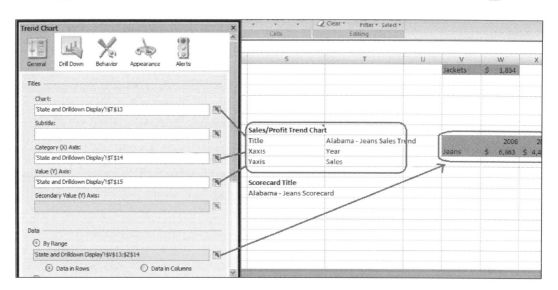

15. Now that the display elements are in place, we'll move onto the Sales/Profit Radio selector. Drag a **Radio Button** selector onto the top left-hand side section of the canvas.

16. There are two sets of data bindings here. First, we will select **Label** as **Insertion Type**, and then bind the data to the selected label (**Sales** or **Profit**) cell B1. The data is found on **columns A and B** of the **Control Sheet** worksheet.

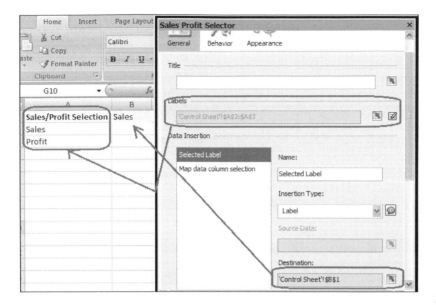

17. For the next data binding **Map data column selection**, select **Column** as the **Insertion Type**. Bind the **Source Data** to columns B and C.

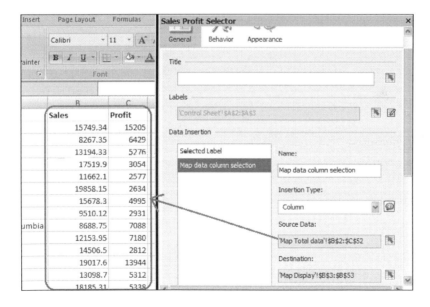

18. The final interactive component is the hidden **State** filter, which will select the appropriate data for the State and Product details. Insert a **Combo Box** selector onto the canvas and make sure it is underneath all of the backgrounds. To make sure it is underneath, right-click on the **Combo Box** selector on the **Object Browser** and select **Send To Back**.

19. Now we will bind the data from the **Product Data** worksheet. The labels will be bound to column **B**, since we are collecting all rows that belong to a state when clicking on a state from the map. Select **Filtered Rows** as the **Insertion Type** and bind the **Source Data** to cells B2:R205. The destination cells will be the peach area in the **State and Drilldown Display** worksheet.

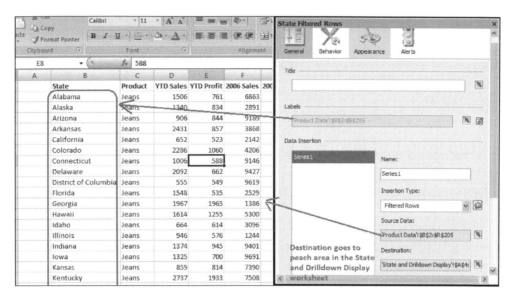

20. Go to the **Behavior** section of the hidden filter and bind the **Selected Item** to the selected **Map** item on cell E1 from the **Control Sheet** worksheet.

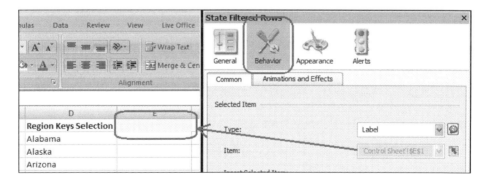

21. Now that our dashboard is complete we want to improve the look a bit. As you can see, there are several layers of background objects that add depth to the dashboard components. Drag a variety of **Background** and **Rectangle** components onto the canvas and play around with the look until it becomes something that you desire.

Please refer to the source code on the type of layering that we have accomplished with the **Background** and **Rectangle** components.

How it works...

▸ In steps 1-3, we utilize what we learned in the recipe **Using maps to select data of an area or country** to set up our map display and data on the left-hand side of the dashboard. From our map selection, we then drive the right-hand side of the dashboard.

▸ Steps 4-5 make use of the recipe **Displaying alerts on a map** to display the different colored states on the map representing the amount of sales/profit each state produced.

▸ In steps 6-8 we use what we learned in the recipes **Adding a line chart to your dashboard** and **Drilling down from a chart**, to create a YTD Sales/Profit chart that allows a user to drilldown from the data values to a particular product.

▸ In steps 9-12, the recipes **Using the scorecard component** and **Using alerts in a scorecard** are used to show a product's details and threshold for a selected state.

▸ In steps 13-14, we simply build a Line Chart that takes the trend data from a selected product and state.

▸ In steps 15-17, we use a Combo Selector component to select from two sets of data. The first set of data consists of the label **Sales/Profit**, which is important because other components in the dashboard drive off the destination of the Sales/Profit label. The second set of data contains the sales/profit data for the map object.

▸ Steps 18-20 utilize what we learned in the **Using Filtered Rows** recipe to select the appropriate data from the **Product Data** worksheet. As you can see in the **Product Data** worksheet, we need to somehow group the states together into a selection. To accomplish this, a **Filtered Rows** selection is necessary.

▸ The final steps consist of adding backgrounds and providing a uniform aligned look and feel that can be found in the *Chapter 1, Staying in Control*.

Additional Resources—Supported Excel Functions and System/Software Requirements

This appendix can be used as a great reference for developers. We have provided a list of online resources that are very useful for problem solving and additional knowledge. We have also provided the necessary Excel functions that a user can print out and keep handy on their desk. In addition, during installation and planning, users can refer to the System and Software Requirements found at the end of the appendix.

Online resources

The following is a list of online resources:

► SAP Community Network

The Official SAP Community Network provides a wealth of knowledge on SAP products, forums to help developers overcome any problems, blogs to learn new tips and tricks, and much more.

▶ Business Objects Board

http://www.forumtopics.com/busobj/index.php

Before SAP bought Business Objects, this was the largest support forum that developers would go to. Even after the acquisition of Business Objects, the forum still remains very active.

▶ EverythingXcelsius.com – Xcelsius Gurus Network

http://www.everythingxcelsius.com

Website for all your SAP BusinessObjects Dashboards (Xcelsius) news, tips, tricks, templates, consulting, and training.

▶ MyXcelsius.com

http://www.myxcelsius.com

Great blog that contains a huge amount of tips, tricks, and best practices for SAP BusinessObjects Dashboards. There are close to 10 authors who contribute to making this blog a success.

▶ HackingSAP.com

http://www.hackingsap.com/blog

Xavier Hacking's blog that provides a wealth of information on SAP related products, focusing mainly on the Business Intelligence Realm.

▶ David Lai's Business Intelligence Blog

http://www.davidlai101.com/blog

David Lai's blog that provides a great amount of tips, tricks, and best practices mainly on SAP BusinessObjects related products. He also provides insight into other Business Intelligence toolsets.

Supported Excel functions

The following is a table of supported Microsoft Excel functions taken from the latest Dashboard Design User Guide, at the time of writing:

ABS	ACOS	ACOSH	AND
ASIN	ASINH	ASSIGN	ATAN
ATAN2	ATANH	AVEDEV	AVERAGE
AVERAGEA	BETADIST	CEILING	CHOOSE
COMBIN	CONCATENATE	COS	COSH
COUNT	COUNTA	COUNTIF	DATE
DATEVALUE	DAVERAGE	DAY	DAYS360

DB	DCOUNT	DCOUNTA	DDB
DEGREES	DEVSQ	DGET	DIVIDE
DMAX	DMIN	DOLLAR	DPRODUCT
DSTDEV	DSSTDEVP	DSUM	DVAR
DVARP	EDATE	EOMONTH	EVEN
EXACT	EXP	EXPONDIST	FACT
FALSE	FIND	FISHER	FISHERINV
FIXED	FLOOR	FORECAST	FV
GE	GEOMEAN	GT	HARMEAN
HLOOKUP	HOUR	IF	INDEX
INT	INTERCEPT	IPMT	IRR
ISBLANK	ISNA	ISNUMBER	KURT
LARGE	LE	LEFT	LEN
LN	LOG	LOG10	LOOKUP
LOWER	MATCH	MAX	MEDIAN
MID	MIN	MINUS	MINUTE
MIRR	MOD	MODE	MONTH
N	NE	NETWORKDAYS	NORMDIST
NORMINV	NORMSINV	NOT	NOW
NPER	NPV	OFFSET	OR
PI	PMT	POWER	PPMT
PRODUCT	PV	QUOTIENT	RADIANS
RAND	RANGE_COLON	RANK	RATE
REPLACE	REPT	RIGHT	ROUND
ROUNDDOWN	ROUNDUP	SECOND	SIGN
SIN	SINH	SLN	SMALL
SQRT	STANDARDIZE	STDEV	SUM
SUMIF	SUMPRODUCT	SUMSQ	SUMX2MY2
SUMX2PY2	SUMXMY2	SYD	TAN
TANH	TEXT	TIME	TIMEVALUE
TODAY	TRUE	TRUNC	UPPER
VALUE	VAR	VDB	VLOOKUP
WEEKDAY	WEEKNUM	WORKDAY	YEAR
YEARFRAC			

System and software requirements

The following section will show the minimum hardware/software requirements, as well as supported software that works in conjunction with SAP BusinessObjects Dashboards.

Minimum hardware requirements for SAP BusinessObjects Dashboards and viewing SWFs are listed as follows:

- ► Minimum screen resolution
  - ❑ Screen resolution of [1024] x [768] is recommended

- ► SAP BusinessObjects Dashboards
  - ❑ 1.8 GHz processor
  - ❑ 2 GB RAM
  - ❑ 900 MB available hard drive space (installer files)
  - ❑ 350 MB available hard drive space (installed)
  - ❑ CD-ROM drive (for CD install only)

- ► Dashboard SWF
  - ❑ 1.8 GHz processor
  - ❑ 1 GB RAM

The list of supported software that work in conjunction with SAP BusinessObjects Dashboards is as follows:

- ► Supported operating systems
  - ❑ Windows Vista (32-bit and 64-bit Editions)
  - ❑ Windows Vista SP1 (32-bit and 64-bit Editions)
  - ❑ Windows Server 2003 Enterprise Edition
  - ❑ Windows Server 2003 Standard Edition
  - ❑ Windows Server 2003 SP1 Enterprise Edition
  - ❑ Windows Server 2003 SP1 Standard Edition
  - ❑ Windows Server 2003 SP2 Enterprise Edition
  - ❑ Windows Server 2003 SP2 Standard Edition
  - ❑ Windows XP SP1 Professional
  - ❑ Windows XP SP2 Professional
  - ❑ Windows XP SP3 Professional
  - ❑ Windows 7

- ▶ Supported browsers
  - ❑ Microsoft Internet Explorer 6.0+
  - ❑ Mozilla Firefox 2.0+

- ▶ Supported Flash players
  - ❑ Adobe Flash Player 9.0.151.0 and above

- ▶ Supported Microsoft Office
  - ❑ Microsoft Office 2007
  - ❑ Microsoft Office 2003
  - ❑ Microsoft Office XP SP3

- ▶ SAP BusinessObjects Enterprise connectivity

  For optimal performance, it is recommended to update all the versions of SAP BusinessObjects Enterprise, Query as a web service and Live Office to the most current Fix Pack available.

- ▶ SAP BusinessObjects Enterprise
  - ❑ SAP BusinessObjects BI 4
  - ❑ SAP BusinessObjects Enterprise XI 3.1
  - ❑ SAP BusinessObjects Enterprise XI R2 SP5

- ▶ SAP BusinessObjects Live Office
  - ❑ Live Office BI 4 connected to SAP BusinessObjects BI 4
  - ❑ Live Office XI 3.1 connected to SAP BusinessObjects Enterprise XI 3.1
  - ❑ Live Office XI R2 connected to SAP BusinessObjects Enterprise XI R2

- ▶ Query as a web service (QaaWS) for SAP BusinessObjects Enterprise
  - ❑ QaaWS BI 4 connected to SAP BusinessObjects BI 4
  - ❑ QaaWS for SAP BusinessObjects Enterprise XI 3.1
  - ❑ QaaWS for SAP BusinessObjects Enterprise XI R2

- ▶ Supported SAP NetWeaver BW
  - ❑ SAP NetWeaver BW 7.0 Enhancement Pack 1 Service Pack 5

- ▶ SAP Application Servers

  The BusinessObjects XI 3.1 Integration for SAP Solutions must be installed in order to use an SAP application server as a data source. For the latest information on SAP platforms required by BusinessObjects XI 3.1 Integration for SAP Solutions, please visit the support area of the SAP website (`http://help.sap.com`).

Other supported connectivity applications are listed as follows:

- LiveCycle Data Services
    - LiveCycle Data Services ES 2.5.1

- Reporting services
    - Reporting Services 2005
    - Reporting Services 2000 SP2
    - Reporting Services 2000 SP1

- SharePoint
    - SharePoint Server 2007
    - SharePoint Portal Server 2003 SP1
    - SharePoint Portal Server 2003
    - Windows SharePoint Services 3.0
    - Windows SharePoint Services 2.0 SP2
    - Windows SharePoint Services 2.0 SP1
    - Windows SharePoint Services 2.0

- WebSphere
    - IBM WebSphere Portal 5.1+

The following are other tools:

- Adobe Acrobat
    - Adobe Acrobat 9.0
    - Adobe Acrobat 6.0

- Adobe Reader
    - Adobe Reader 7+

- Adobe AIR
    - Adobe AIR 1.1
    - Java 2 Runtime Environment 1.4.2

- Adobe Flex SDK
    - Adobe Flex 2.0.1 Hotfix 3 (note that this is only required to create Dashboard Design 2008 add-ons with Dashboard Design 2008 Component SDK)

- Crystal Reports
    - Crystal Reports 2008

Index

G

gauge
about 128
alerts, using 128-131
General tab 120
GMaps plugin
integrating, with Google Maps 266-272
website 273
GMaps plugin-Google Maps integration
prerequisites 265
steps 266-272
working 272, 273
XGlobe add-on 273
XYahooMap add-on 273
Google Maps
integrating, with GMaps plugin 265-272
Google Maps API key 265
grid component
about 157
list view components, differentiating 157
using 157
using, steps 157
value, changing 158, 159
working 158

H

hardware requirements , SAP Business Objects Dashboards
Dashboard SWF 320
minimum screen resolution 320
SAP Business Objects Dashboards 320
history component
about 165
using, steps 166
working 167
HR Health Assessment Dashboard 85

I

Images button 162
Import Named Ranges button 231
Information Design Tool
using 224
InfoView. *See* **BI launch pad**
Inovista
website 288

K

keys
Ctrl+` 18
Ctrl + PageDown 21
Ctrl + PageUp 21
Ctrl-F3 15

L

Launch option 248
line chart
adding, to dashboard 26-29
data, binding manually 30
series, hiding 31
series, showing 31
working 30
listbox breadcrumb type approach
using 73-75
working 75
Live Office connection
about 213
prompts, using 217, 218
using 213-216
working 217
login functionality, password used
getting started 121
steps 121-124
working 124
LOOKUP function 319

M

MacOSX program loading dock
adding, to dashboard 82-85
Fisheye Picture Menu, working 86
Sliding Picture menu 86
map
about 78
alerts, displaying 136-139
different thresholds, displaying alerts on 139-141
regions, locating 80
using, for area data selection 79-81
using, for country data selection 79-81
working 82
MAX function 319

About Packt Publishing

Packt, pronounced 'packed', published its first book "*Mastering phpMyAdmin for Effective MySQL Management*" in April 2004 and subsequently continued to specialize in publishing highly focused books on specific technologies and solutions.

Our books and publications share the experiences of your fellow IT professionals in adapting and customizing today's systems, applications, and frameworks. Our solution-based books give you the knowledge and power to customize the software and technologies you're using to get the job done. Packt books are more specific and less general than the IT books you have seen in the past. Our unique business model allows us to bring you more focused information, giving you more of what you need to know, and less of what you don't.

Packt is a modern, yet unique publishing company, which focuses on producing quality, cutting-edge books for communities of developers, administrators, and newbies alike. For more information, please visit our website: www.PacktPub.com.

About Packt Enterprise

In 2010, Packt launched two new brands, Packt Enterprise and Packt Open Source, in order to continue its focus on specialization. This book is part of the Packt Enterprise brand, home to books published on enterprise software – software created by major vendors, including (but not limited to) IBM, Microsoft and Oracle, often for use in other corporations. Its titles will offer information relevant to a range of users of this software, including administrators, developers, architects, and end users.

Writing for Packt

We welcome all inquiries from people who are interested in authoring. Book proposals should be sent to author@packtpub.com. If your book idea is still at an early stage and you would like to discuss it first before writing a formal book proposal, contact us; one of our commissioning editors will get in touch with you.

We're not just looking for published authors; if you have strong technical skills but no writing experience, our experienced editors can help you develop a writing career, or simply get some additional reward for your expertise.

SAP Business ONE Implementation

ISBN: 978-1-847196-38-5   Paperback: 320 pages

Bring the power of SAP Enterprise Resource Planning to your small-midsize business

1. Get SAP B1 up and running quickly, optimize your business, inventory, and manage your warehouse

2. Understand how to run reports and take advantage of real-time information

3. Complete an express implementation from start to finish

4. Real-world examples with step-by-step explanations

Mastering SQL Queries for SAP Business One

ISBN: 978-1-849682-36-7   Paperback: 300 pages

Utilize the power of SQL queries to bring Business Intelligence to your small to medium-sized business

1. Practical SAP query examples from an SAP Business One expert

2. Detailed steps to create and troubleshoot SQL queries for Alerts, Approvals, Formatted Searches, and Crystal Reports

3. Understand the importance and benefit of keeping SQL queries simple and easy to understand

4. Benefit from special tips and tricks related directly to SQL queries within SAP Business One

Please check **www.PacktPub.com** for information on our titles

15543181R00187

Made in the USA
Lexington, KY
03 June 2012